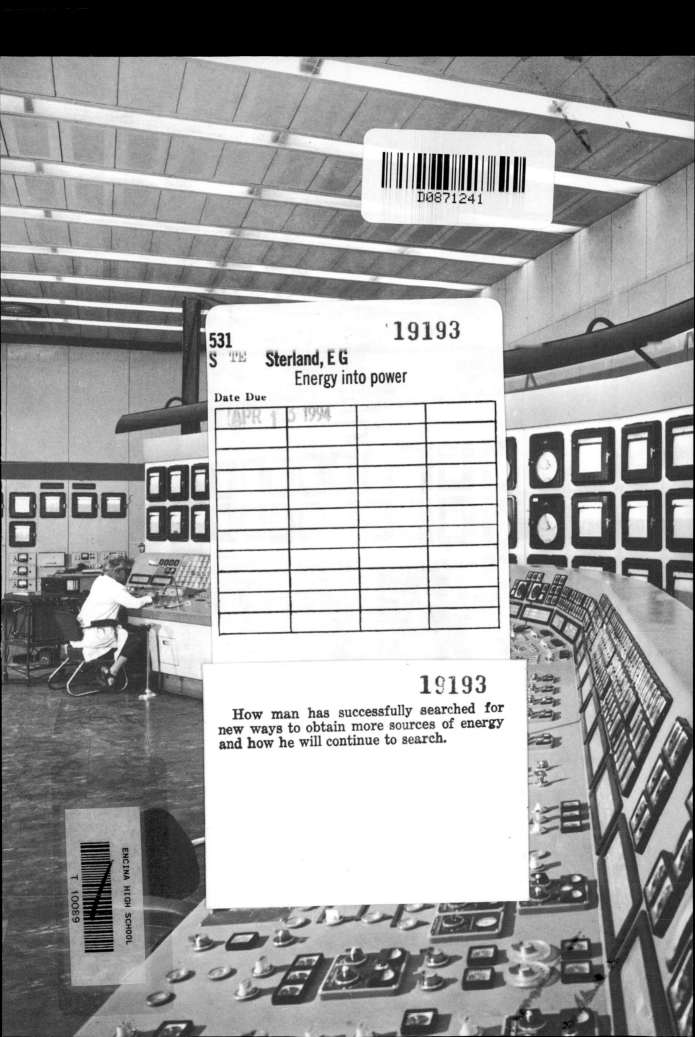

Energy into Power

E. G. STERLAND

Energy into Power

The Story of Man and Machines

Nature and Science Library
published for
The American Museum of Natural History
by The Natural History Press / Garden City, New York

The Natural History Press, publisher for The
American Museum of Natural History, is a division
of Doubleday & Company, Inc. The Press is
directed by an editorial board made up of
members of the staff of both the Museum and
Doubleday. The Natural History Press has its
editorial offices at The American Museum of
Natural History, Central Park West at 79th Street,
New York, New York 10024, and its business offices
at 501 Franklin Avenue, Garden City, New York.

First published in the United States of America in 1967 by
The Natural History Press, Garden City, New York
in association with Aldus Books Limited

Library of Congress Catalog Card Number 67-16902
© Aldus Books Limited, London, 1967

Printed in Italy by Arnoldo Mondadori, Verona

Contents

Introduction: Man and Power

Physically, man is not the most superior animal. He cannot sprint like a cheetah, nor can he uproot trees like an elephant. And yet he has at his disposal enormous amounts of power. What is it that enables man to build huge dams, to travel faster than sound, and to burrow miles deep in search of raw materials?

Man's body may not be the strongest, but his brain is certainly the most complex of all the animals. All through his long history, man has used his unique brain to work out ways of getting things done. For the characteristic that singles out man is that he has seldom been content to limit his actions to what he could do directly. It is his capacity to think and to invent that has put him outside the rest of the animal kingdom.

It may seem strange to begin a book on energy and power by talking about primitive man in search of a meal. But that is where the story begins, so we start with a Stone Age man stalking a bison. If the hunter could get close enough, he might stab his prey with a spear. But if he did get too close, he would be in danger of being kicked to death. He could, of course, try throwing a spear at short range. Even then, man might be at a disadvantage, because his muscles are made for relatively slow movements. The spear could hit the target without enough speed to penetrate the beast's thick hide and do real damage. What the hunter needed was a way of killing at a distance. Eventually he invented the bow and arrow—probably man's first machine.

There is a lot more to this simple device than you might think. What actually happens? Slowly, using his muscles to their best advantage, the hunter pulls the arrow and bowstring back. This bends the springy wood of the bow during a period of a few seconds. Then, when he is sure of his target, the hunter lets go of the arrow. All the pent-up energy in the bow is transferred through the bowstring to the arrow in a fraction of a second. The arrow flies to its target many times faster than a man could have thrown it.

What has happened in these last few seconds of such a hunt is quite complicated. It involves different kinds of energy and the conversion of one kind of energy into

Man soon learned to kill animals much stronger than himself by using a bow and arrow. This machine enables him to convert his muscular energy into pent-up energy in the bow. Lower picture: It takes the strength of many men to tow a boat against the current of the Yangtze River in China.

another. All of these concepts will be made plain as we go along. But what is worth remembering is that all through man's history there runs the same basic idea. If he cannot do a job with his own muscles, all is not lost. Imagination and techniques show the way to using muscles to the best advantage.

A man's own experience tells him that his muscles are useful. It is therefore natural for him to think soon of using other muscles in order to get jobs done. And so we find that, quite early in history, man domesticated animals and forced other men to work for him as slaves.

But the work that can be obtained from muscle-power has to come from somewhere. Like all the other devices for producing power that we shall discuss in this book, muscle-power depends on some basic source of energy. Man and animals are alike in being living machines that must convert food into energy before they can convert energy into work. It is worth mentioning that animals and men consume food whether or not they are working, just as if a car engine were kept running day and night when it was not on the road. The labor of animals and slaves is thus costly. You have to put a lot of energy in to get a little out. Moreover, all living creatures need rest; they cannot work continuously.

It was natural, therefore, that man should turn sooner or later to sources of energy that were outside the animal kingdom. The sight of a river in flood, sweeping boulders and treetrunks along, must have made him ask, "What is there in this for me?" The answer, although it came only within the last few thousand years, was some simple form of a water wheel.

In the same way, the force of the wind was a challenge. Man early learned to use wind as an occasional aid to manpower in ships, but he was much longer in developing the windmill. Perhaps this was because—unlike the fairly steady flow of water in a river bed—wind is much more variable both in strength and direction.

Of these two available forms of energy, waterpower was the one that first became the major source of power

Centuries ago, men began exploiting the power in moving water. Right: A 14th-century mill. Water fills the paddles at the top, turns the wheel, and empties below. Far right: The blades of this modern turbine rotor are adjustable to suit the rate at which the water flows.

for driving machinery. By the Middle Ages, a single water mill could produce more power than several hundred animals. The manufacturing processes of the early stages of the Industrial Revolution depended on waterpower. There was, of course, the disadvantage of a possible shortage of water, or floods might damage the machinery. Another disadvantage was that waterpower had to be used at places where water was flowing swiftly or falling from a height..That meant that mills had to be built in those places, and not where the sources of raw material and labor were most easily available.

Waterpower was the first "non-muscle-power" to be used, at least in those countries hilly enough to provide the right conditions. But waterpower was largely eclipsed in the nineteenth century by other, more convenient machines. It must have been easy for engineers a hundred years ago to conclude that the day of waterpower was finished. But in the present century, waterpower has made a big comeback. This is due to the fact that new discoveries have eliminated the original disadvantage of having to place the factory alongside running water. As we shall see in Chapters 6 and 7, there are several ingenious ways in which moving water is now made to produce more power than ever before.

We have taken a very brief look at the first two kinds of power that man used as extensions of his own muscles. And we should not become too scornful of either the toil of animals and slaves, or the centuries-old work of wind- and water mills. Much was achieved by such primitive methods. But it was nothing compared to what was to happen with the invention of the steam engine about 275 years ago. This was a real breakthrough because it emerged with a completely new discovery—heat was a form of energy that could be turned into power. At last man had let the genie out of the bottle. Fire had always seemed to be an unbeatable enemy or, at best, a means of keeping warm. Now it could be controlled and put to work. What makes the steam age, and everything that has followed it, so interesting is that there has been a kind of "snowball effect" that was unknown in the age of windpower and

Later, men learned to utilize the force of the wind. Right: A medieval windmill. Today the windmill is of only local importance as a source of power. The French wind-powered dynamo (far right), with propeller-like blades, is useful only in areas with fairly constant high winds.

waterpower. Power makes for material progress, progress produces bigger machines, some of these produce even more power. The result is that not only has man obtained more power every year but the *rate* of increase of power has been snowballing all the time. As we shall see, the situation has its risks, too. For machines, like animals, have to be fed. What happens if supplies run out?

However, the snowball effect has a hopeful side to it. Modern power-producing machines have made it possible to delve into the secrets of atomic structure. Think of the huge cyclotrons or atom-smashing machines that are used in today's research. From these may well come a fourth stage of power production, a method that depends on extracting energy from atomic fusion (pp. 225-231). If the experiments now going on in the technically advanced countries are successful, there will eventually be a flood of new power.

In Western civilization, the average man has at his disposal power undreamt of by previous generations. The driver of even the most modest family car has at his command many times the power available to the aristocrat of a century ago in his horse-drawn carriage. The farm worker with his tractor has incomparably more power than the farmer with his horse-drawn plow. An industrial worker in the average machine shop has under his control about ten horsepower to drive his machine. The pilot of a large supersonic aircraft commands engines developing hundreds of thousands of horsepower. It has been calculated that every man, woman, and child in the United States today commands, directly or indirectly, as much power as would be produced by 100 slaves.

This fortunate situation is far from being common in the world as a whole. Most of the people of Asia and Africa do not enjoy anything like the standard of living of the West. The economy of these "have-not" countries must be much the same as it was in the West before the Industrial Revolution. That is, they have a peasant economy in which most of the population spend their

With the development of the steam engine in the 18th century, the heat from fire was for the first time harnessed to provide power. The engine shown left is James Watt's rotative steam engine, developed in 1784. Apart from small changes, the engine was hardly improved for 50 years.

lives working with their hands to get a poor living off the land. It is, perhaps, an over-simplification to blame their poverty only on a shortage of power. But this shortage is certainly one basic reason for a low standard of living. Increased power could improve agriculture, start factories, improve communications, and "prime the pump" for the start of a better life for millions of people.

One of the reasons why many underdeveloped countries are short of power is that they have little or none of the fossil fuels (p. 42) that are so abundant in the West. (It is a curious fact, by the way, that these fuels are confined almost entirely to the Northern Hemisphere.) Other means of power production will have to be found for these countries. This is where the more fortunate nations can give generous aid.

This book is about power and the means of producing it. The word "energy" has more than one meaning in common use. Even in science the word is used in several ways—for example, "heat energy," "electrical energy," and so on. In general, energy in these expressions means the capacity for doing work. But in this book we shall adapt this idea and use the word "energy" to describe the raw materials of power production. The word "power" will be used to mean energy that has been converted into a form that can readily be applied to produce *useful* work. The first section of this book deals with the sources of energy that can be turned into power. The second section presents the scientific principles that lie behind the conversion of energy into power. This section also shows how and why different kinds of machines have been developed to meet a particular need while using a particular sort of "raw energy."

The third section looks into the future. The fossil fuels, which form the energy supply for most purposes at present, are of limited extent. These fuels are being used up at a relatively rapid rate, and the time will come when they are all consumed. New ways of producing power are now being investigated, and some of the more promising of these will be described.

Nuclear energy is the greatest power source yet discovered. The power from nuclear fission can destroy cities, but its constructive uses are more promising. Left: A cyclotron, used in nuclear research. It accelerates streams of charged particles to speeds high enough to smash atoms.

1   Energy from the Sun–Income

Before we can get a balanced picture of the energy available for man's use, we must correct a somewhat distorted impression that many people have. We live in an age when most of the energy that supports our industrial societies comes out of coal mines and oil wells. These fuels are being consumed at such a rate that, within a few hundred years, coal and oil may be completely used up. However, it would be wrong for us to panic at this prospect and imagine that mankind will soon be threatened with extinction in an energy-starved world.

The fact is that fossil fuels are only a small part of the natural energy that is there for the taking. This holds true not only now but for at least a thousand million years to come—if man survives that long. For most of his history, man got by without the fossil fuels. He used the energy of the wind and of the rivers, and with these he laid the foundations of the Industrial Revolution. Then he learned how to make use of the steam engine and, later, the internal combustion engine. With these came our vast consumption of coal and oil. But the achievements of the coal and oil era do not prove that the fossil fuels are the only way of meeting energy demands. It is simply that these fuels have monopolized the attention of engineers and inventors. In much the same way, the further development of waterpower—which was only in its infancy when steam engines took over—was neglected in the nineteenth century. There were other, and apparently better, sources of power available.

Now we can foresee the exhaustion of fossil fuels. There is a new interest in other sources of power, including some that have been neglected during the past hundred years. We might say that, after a brief holiday with coal and oil, man is taking a fresh look at the inexhaustible sources of power that have always been with him.

We have talked about water- and windpower, and we have mentioned coal and oil. In neither case have we attempted to explain how these come to exist. There are, as we shall see, some sources of power that come from the earth itself. But such sources are relatively small,

The light and heat from the sun make the earth habitable. In the religion of ancient Egypt, the sun held supreme place as giver of life to mankind. Under Akhenaton (1375-1358 B.C.), it was worshiped as the sole deity. The drawing above, taken from a limestone relief, shows Akhenaton offering a sacrifice to the sun; the sun's rays end in hands that nurture life. Right: Beneath a picture of the sun is represented the earth on the same scale.

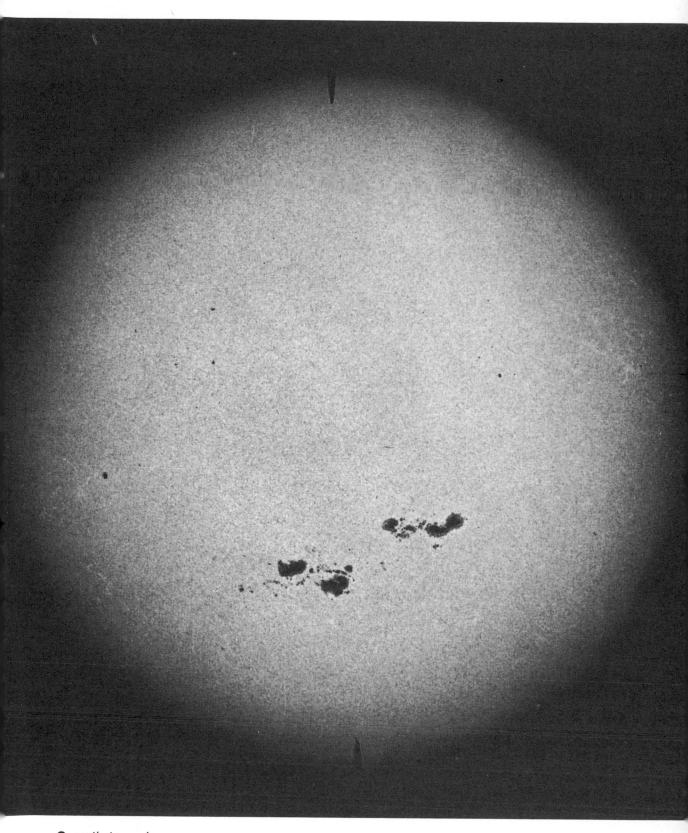

● earth to scale

and by themselves they would not prevent our planet from being a lump of lifeless and frozen matter. We are, in fact, almost entirely dependent on energy originating outside the earth. That energy comes directly from the sun.

We can get some idea of the huge amount of energy that arrives from the sun by expressing it in various ways. For instance, suppose we were to take all the known or estimated deposits of coal and oil and burn them so as to give energy at the same rate as that supplied by the sun. We would use up these deposits completely in three days. Or imagine that the sun itself is a mass of coal and oil burning in the same way as we consume them. If that were so, the sun would have burned to ashes in 8,000 years. But we know that the sun has been shining for millions of years. The most recent discoveries by astronomers and physicists indicate that the sun's age is about five billion years.

Some ancient religions were based on sun worship. Although the worshipers did not know the real story, they were wise to give the sun such a prominent role. It seems fair to say that solar energy sustains all life. So it is worth while taking a closer look at what the sun is and how it works. Although the sun is 93 million miles away, we know a surprising amount about it. The sun's diameter is about 865,000 miles. That is about 109 times the diameter of the earth. Its mass is 333,000 times that of the earth. If sun and earth were made of the same material, the sun would have a mass of a million times that of the earth. Obviously, then, the sun's average density is only about one-third that of the earth. In fact, the sun is not a mass of rock and metal like the earth. The sun, instead, consists almost entirely of the element hydrogen, with about one per cent of heavier elements.

Conditions at the sun's center are almost unimaginable. The temperature there is up to about 20 million degrees Centigrade, and the pressure due to gravity is about one billion tons per square inch. Under such colossal pressure, the atoms of hydrogen—on earth, the lightest of all gases—are packed together so tightly that their density is about ten times that of lead.

Although the pressure concentrates the hydrogen atoms, the temperature is so great that atoms no longer exist in their original form. That is, each hydrogen atom normally contains a nucleus with a positively-charged proton, and a negatively-charged electron outside the nucleus. But in the sun these atoms break up into particles so that the proton of each nucleus and its electron are separated from each other. If the temperatures were to fall, the atoms would re-form again. But as long as the sun's temperature is up to millions of degrees, we have what is called a *plasma*—essentially,

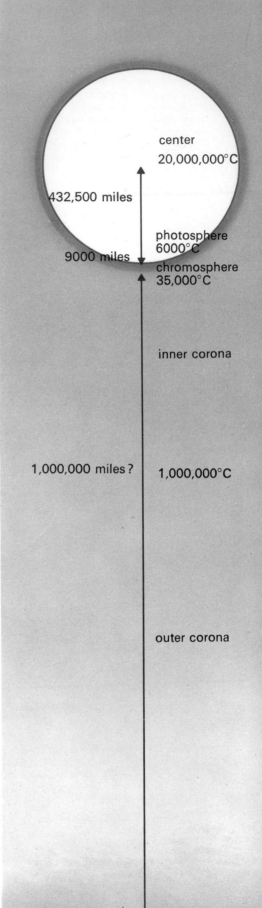

center
20,000,000°C

432,500 miles

photosphere
6000°C

9000 miles

chromosphere
35,000°C

inner corona

1,000,000 miles ?

1,000,000°C

outer corona

Diagram (left) charts data about the sun. The sun's diameter is about 865,000 miles. Its surface is called the photosphere; above this surface, for about 6,000 to 9,000 miles, is the chromosphere. Then comes the corona, which extends perhaps more than 2 million miles into space. The temperature of each atom in the gas of the corona is about 1,000,000°C. But the atoms are spread out so thinly that the gas itself adds nothing to the heat that the earth receives from the sun.

Below: The basic process by which helium nuclei are built up inside the sun. (1) Two protons collide; one becomes a neutron (blue), and the proton and neutron together form a deuteron (heavy hydrogen nucleus). (2) Another proton joins this deuteron, forming a nucleus of the light isotope of helium. (3) Two such nuclei collide and eject two protons. What remains (4) is a nucleus of the common form of helium.

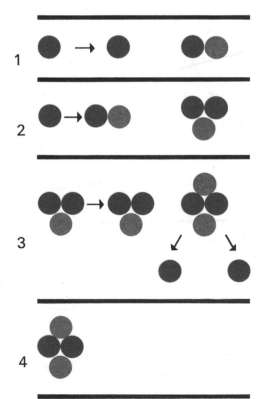

electrically-charged gas. In this state, the temperature and the pressure together permit a regrouping, or *fusion*, of nuclear particles. Four protons combine to form the nucleus of a new element, helium. This regrouping of protons is not, however, a simple joining up of existing particles. There is a slight loss of mass.

Here we come to one of the basic facts of atomic physics. For centuries man had been taught that matter was indestructible. Now we know that mass and energy are interchangeable. Almost everyone has heard of Einstein's famous equation, $E = mc^2$. But how many people realize what it really means? E stands for energy, m for mass, and c for the velocity of light. This simple little equation is "loaded," because c, the velocity of light, is a huge figure—about 186,000 miles per second. In the equation, c is squared. In other words, a very small mass of material is equivalent to a huge amount of energy. A favorite way of illustrating this is to say that a lump of metal the size of a pea contains enough energy to drive the largest ship afloat across the Atlantic. But there is a catch in this statement. It is quite true that the energy in that fragment of metal would be equal to the task—but *only* if all of its mass could be transformed into a form of energy the ship could use. As we shall see later, this is easier said than done.

What goes on inside the sun, as we have said, is a fusion of hydrogen to helium. The loss of mass is the direct cause of the sun's outpouring of energy. Fortunately for us, the fusion process inside the sun goes on at a steady rate. In this conversion of mass into energy, we can see why the sun has shone for millions of years and should continue to do so for at least as long again. The loss of mass is extremely small: It has been calculated that in the past five billion years the sun has lost no more than 2 per cent of its original mass. Indeed, for all practical purposes we can say that the sun is an inexhaustible source of energy.

Experiments with hydrogen bombs show that much of the energy of fusion generates short radiation waves called X rays and gamma rays. Because these waves are so short, they have a very high concentration of energy. They are therefore able to penetrate, for example, thick walls of concrete. Rays of this sort are deadly. If the earth received the full force of this radiation from the sun, life would be impossible. But the outer layers of the sun act as an energy converter. The gases of these layers are heated by the short waves; in turn, the gases give out radiations mostly of longer wave length—that is ultraviolet, visible light, and the longer waves of infrared, or heat. Just over 50 per cent of total radiation is visible light, 4 per cent is invisible ultraviolet, and approximately 45 per cent is infrared.

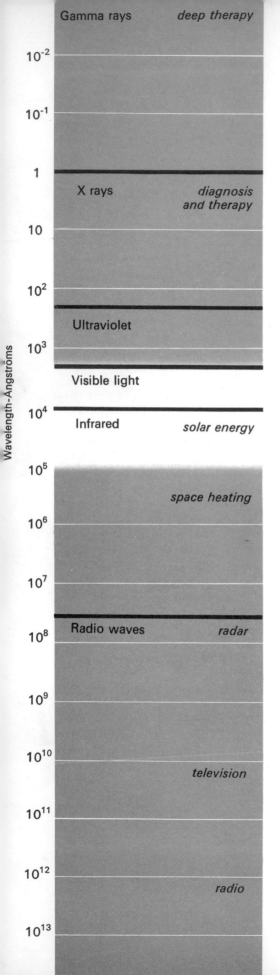

Wavelength–Angstroms

Gamma rays	*deep therapy*
10^{-2}	
10^{-1}	
1	
X rays	*diagnosis and therapy*
10	
10^2	
Ultraviolet	
10^3	
Visible light	
10^4	
Infrared	*solar energy*
10^5	
	space heating
10^6	
10^7	
Radio waves	*radar*
10^8	
10^9	
10^{10}	
	television
10^{11}	
10^{12}	
	radio
10^{13}	

The sun's outpouring of energy in the form of such radiation is equal to the heat and light that would be produced by 4 million million million million thousand-watt electric bulbs. Because the earth is 93 million miles away, no more than 1/2,000,000,000th of the total radiation reaches the earth's upper atmosphere. Now, let us see what happens to the tiny fraction of the sun's energy after it has traveled, in 8 minutes, to the earth. About 40 per cent of the sun's radiation is instantly reflected back into space by the layers of ice crystals, clouds, and water vapor in the atmosphere. Most of this radiation reflected back is the part with the lowest energy, and therefore the lowest penetrating power—that is, the red and infrared portions. Of the remaining 60 per cent of the energy, some heats the atmosphere while the rest travels on until it reaches the earth's surface. This radiant energy provides the driving force for the fluctuations and circulations of the earth's atmosphere. Eventually this energy is also returned to space as degraded, low-energy, long-wave radiation. In this way, a balance is kept between the energy received by the earth and the energy leaving it.

Thus, too, a fairly steady temperature is maintained on earth. We say "fairly steady" because we know that there have been major fluctuations in the earth's temperature in the past. Doubtless there will be others in the

The chart (left) shows the range of the electromagnetic spectrum and the uses to man of the different rays of the sun. All the solar energy that can be utilized for power is concentrated into the relatively narrow band (shown white). Radio waves have a wide range of wave lengths, from 10^8 Angstroms to 10^{13} Angstroms. (1 Angstrom = 1/100,000,000 centimeter.) Radar makes use of the shortest radio waves. Infrared rays have longer wave lengths than visible red light. Right: Photograph taken on ordinary light-sensitive film, and, below, the same subject photographed on film sensitive to infrared rays, which are invisible to the unaided eye.

The sun's total radiation into space amounts to 5.3 million million million million horsepower. Only 1/2,000,000,000th of this reaches the earth, 93 million miles away.

Not all the sun's radiation that reaches the earth's atmosphere actually reaches the earth's surface. X rays and short ultraviolet rays (A) are stopped by the upper atmosphere about 250 miles up. Most of the other radiation, including visible light rays and heat rays, penetrates to the earth's surface, although some of the energy heats the atmosphere itself (B). Eventually the energy is returned to space (C).

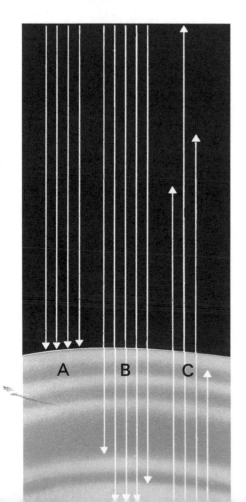

future. The great Ice Ages, and the traces that they have left, bear witness to such changes. Not much is known about the causes of these cold spells, lasting many hundreds of thousands of years. Scientists usually assume that alterations in the energy output of the sun were responsible. But these alterations may work in a way that is unexpected, considering that a huge increase in the size of the polar caps is involved. It has been calculated that an ice age could be caused by an *increase* in the amount of solar energy reaching the earth. This would have the effect of evaporating more water from the oceans in the tropics. Then there would be an increase of cloud cover in the colder regions. This, in turn, would screen those regions and prevent the sun from melting polar ice during the summer. At the same time, the clouds would condense and fall as rain and snow so that the polar icecaps would grow larger and larger. A slight reduction in solar energy could have the opposite effect and reduce the size of the icecaps.

Fluctuations of this sort are, of course, small in proportion to the total energy received on earth. But they illustrate the process of what we call *energy cycles*, which are going on continuously on earth. The essential thing about energy cycles is that they are atmospheric "pockets" into which some of the sun's energy falls. Instead of being instantly re-radiated and lost—as is the 40 per cent that was reflected back into space—the energy that penetrates the atmosphere stays on earth for a while. Here it gets converted several times from one kind of energy to another before it finally escapes as low-grade infrared heat. The length of time that the energy stays within the atmosphere varies from a few weeks to millions of years, according to the kind of cycle that it goes through.

There are two main energy cycles—the weather cycle and the life cycle. The first of these, the weather cycle, is probably more familiar, although it can sometimes be quite spectacular. Light waves are to a small extent intercepted by the atmosphere, and their energy is converted into heat. The air becomes warmer—which is essentially a convenient way of saying that each molecule of air has gained more energy. Each molecule, which is always in motion colliding with and bouncing off its neighbors, now has more motion than before. In short, each molecule needs more room to move about in. The result of such an increase of energy is that air expands. This air becomes less dense than other parts of the atmosphere that may not have received the same amount of heat. When the air becomes hot, it rises; when the air loses heat and cools, it sinks. The result is a series of *convection* currents that, on a large scale, go to make up our wind and weather.

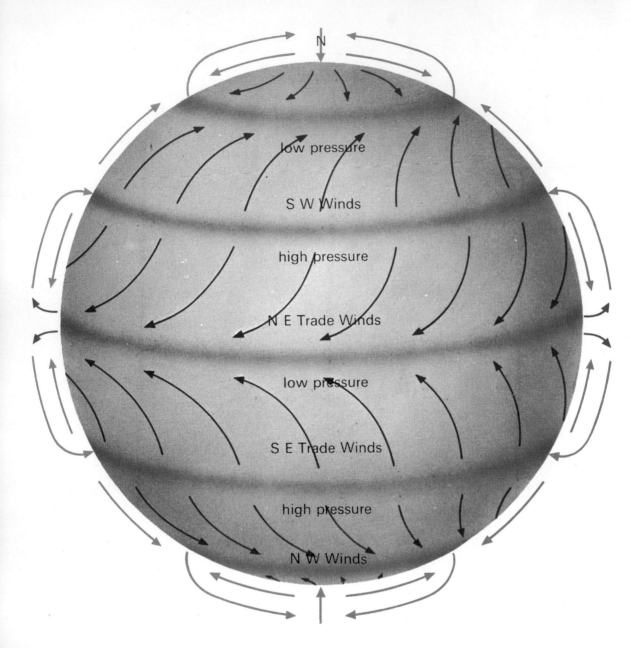

low pressure

S W Winds

high pressure

N E Trade Winds

low pressure

S E Trade Winds

high pressure

N W Winds

Major wind systems of the world. Much more heat from the sun reaches equatorial regions than polar regions because (see diagram left) the sun's rays hit the earth directly at the equator (A), whereas near the poles (B) the same amount of heat is spread over a larger area. Also, the rays reaching the poles lose more heat on the way because they have more atmosphere to penetrate. The air above equatorial regions is heated the most; it expands, rises by convection, and moves outward at high level toward the poles. At about latitude 30°, some of it has cooled sufficiently to return to earth; here part of it drifts back to the equator, while part drifts toward the poles. At about latitude 60°, it meets cold air moving from the poles; it is forced to rise over this and finally reaches the poles at high level. Winds move obliquely because of earth's rotation.

The amount of energy intercepted from sunlight by air molecules is quite small. Most of the light travels on until it hits the earth's surface. Here is where most of the light is converted into heat. Admittedly, much of it is reflected back into the atmosphere by the surface of the sea, which covers 70 per cent of the earth's surface. This reflected light also gives up some of its energy to air molecules. And part of the light is reflected downwards again from clouds and ice crystals. Indeed, the light reflected from the sea's surface may bounce backwards and forwards several times between that surface and the stratosphere before it escapes. The energy finally escapes as light through a gap in the clouds, or it becomes degraded into heat in the atmosphere or on the earth's surface.

These happenings are basic to everything that follows in this book. A fundamental principle is involved and it is this: In nature, every conversion of energy is a change downwards from a high energy level (such as that of the original high energy X rays and gamma rays within the sun) to a low energy level (such as low energy infrared radiation, the form in which most energy finally escapes from earth into outer space). Energy is always "sliding down hill."

What of the solar energy that penetrates to the earth's surface? Some of it is reflected, as we saw, from the sea. The same is true of light reaching the land. But some of the energy is absorbed, and both sea and land are warmed by the light that is absorbed. The sea is warmed in depth. As the light penetrates the top 600 feet or so, its energy is turned to heat in a large mass of water. The land receiving just the same intensity of light energy warms up noticeably only at the surface. Soil and rock below the surface, however, are warmed gradually by conduction.

There is thus a marked difference between the temperature fluctuations of sea and land. The sea warms up gradually but remains at a more constant temperature. The surface of the land warms up more quickly and to a higher temperature, but cools more quickly at night. Both land and sea re-radiate their heat into the atmosphere, and this heat is the biggest source of the air movements that we mentioned above. This accounts for all our winds, from a light breeze to a hurricane. And because land and sea heat up and cool down at different rates, it is on the islands and along coastal regions of the earth that we find more winds of a strength likely to be of interest to users of wind energy.

There is another energy cycle that converts solar energy into a different form. This time the energy is locked up in water. Part of the light energy from the sun is downgraded, as we saw, into heat energy that warms

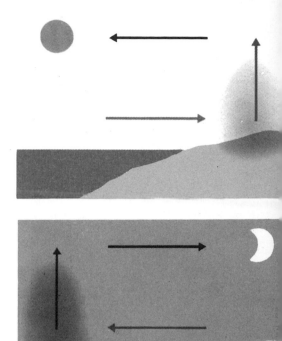

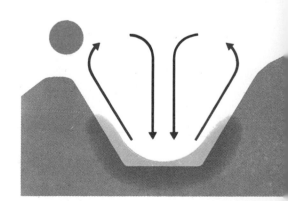

The above diagrams show how land and sea breezes are caused. Land heats quicker than water. Thus, during the day, warm air (red) rises from the land and draws in cooler air from over the sea. At night the reverse process takes place, for land also cools quicker than water. Below: How a daytime breeze is caused in a mountain valley. Heated air rises along the warm slopes, then cools and descends into the valley.

up the oceans, particularly in the tropics. This energy also heats rivers, lakes, and the land itself, which— apart from deserts—contains considerable quantities of water. The warm water is evaporated into the air and rises with the ascending air streams. If the air is warm enough, it can hold a remarkably large amount of invisible water vapor. When the air has risen to a height, expanded, and cooled, it is then super-saturated with moisture, and clouds form. When these clouds cool still further, the water vapor condenses into rain, hail, or snow, and falls back onto the earth's surface.

Most of this water falls back onto the surface of the sea or onto the low-lying land. There is little or no power to be had from such water. What matters to man is the water that dropped onto high ground, such as mountain ranges. Water deposited high up in the mountains has energy because of its position: Sooner or later,

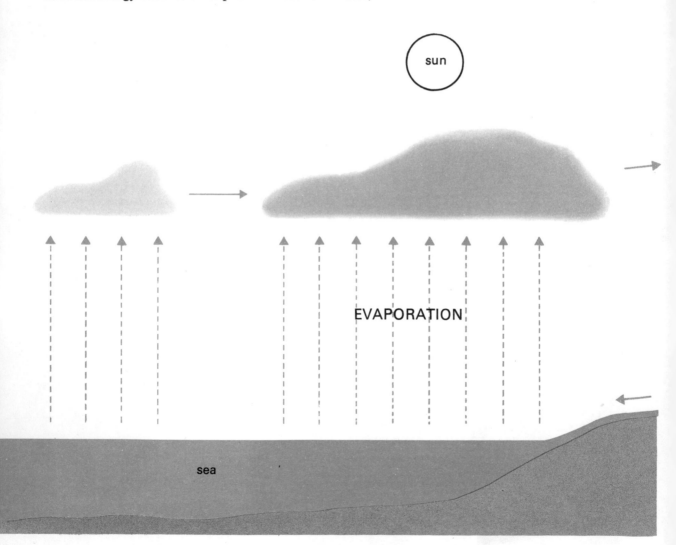

The hydrologic, or water, cycle. The sun evaporates water from rivers and lakes, from the soil and vegetation, and—mainly—from the sea. The water vapor rises with the air and is circulated in air currents. When the air containing the moisture rises to pass over another air mass or a mountain, it cools and cannot hold as much water as before. The water then condenses to form clouds; eventually the water is precipitated as rain, snow, or sleet. Some of this precipitation evaporates very quickly; some penetrates the soil (infiltration); and some runs off the land surface into streams, lakes, or ponds. Of that which penetrates the soil, some returns to the atmosphere by evaporation or by plant transpiration. The remainder penetrates soil and rock, becomes part of the underground water system, and eventually finds its way back to the sea.

water will run down to the sea again. Some of this water, of course, may be evaporated before it reaches the sea. But all the water goes through the same cycle again and again.

We have been tracing the long process by which nuclear energy inside the sun becomes converted to the energy of wind and water on earth. You might well ask what form the energy takes in the wind and water if it is not nuclear energy. Before we can answer that question, we shall have to face some basic concepts of physics. In order to measure the amount of energy available in wind or water, we must first know how much wind or water we are talking about. In other words, what is their weight—or should it be mass? We have to be clear about the difference between mass and weight. Imagine a traveler about to set off on a trip around the world. He is very fond of fruit, so he first stops by a fruitstore to

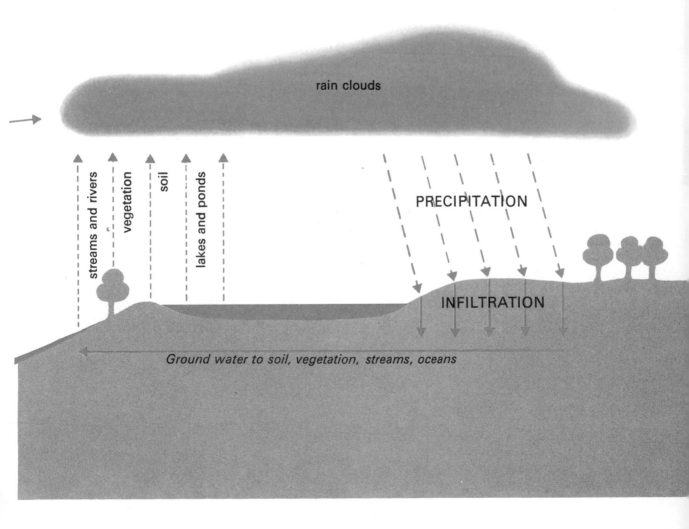

rain clouds

streams and rivers

vegetation

soil

lakes and ponds

PRECIPITATION

INFILTRATION

Ground water to soil, vegetation, streams, oceans

buy a pound of apples. The clerk puts some apples in a bag and places them on one side of an old-fashioned platform balance. On the other side is a piece of metal marked "1 lb." When the clerk gets an exact balance, the traveler takes his apples and goes off. His first destination is an extremely high mountain peak. Now in his luggage he has a spring balance scale and, out of curiosity, he decides to weigh the bag of apples before eating one. (By the way, throughout this imaginary story we must pretend that the apples would not shrink through spoilage or loss of water.) The traveler discovers that his apples weigh just a bit under one pound. He decides to save them to complain to the clerk on his return. But as he proceeds on his trip, wherever he is he weighs his bag of apples on his spring balance. Much to his amazement, the bag always weighs something slightly different. On the North Pole, it weighs a little more than one pound; on the Equator, a little less; on the desert floor, a little more; on mountain tops, a bit less.

By this time, our traveler is quite confused. When he arrives home, he goes straight to the fruitstore to complain. But the clerk puts the apples back on the platform scale and demonstrates that they still balance perfectly with the 1-lb. piece of metal. Indeed, when the traveler uses his own spring scale to prove his point, he discovers that this, too, now registers exactly one pound.

In explaining these mysterious doings we should come to understand the difference between weight and mass. We start by accepting a basic law: The earth's gravitational force exerts an attractive force on all matter on earth. When the bag of apples was hung from the hook on the spring balance, the earth's gravity pulled on the apples. This caused a spring to stretch, and the markings on the scale indicated the force of gravitational attraction. Now this force depends on the quantity of matter in objects and the distance between their centers. In the story, the distance between the center of the bag of apples and the center of the earth was changing slightly as the traveler moved about. Thus, the weight was changing, because the weight of any object on earth is the measure of the earth's attraction for an object. That is why the weight of an object may vary slightly with its location on earth. And if the traveler had gone to the moon with his bag of apples and spring balance, he would have seen a great decrease in weight. Because it is much smaller than the earth, the moon's gravitational attraction is less. An object weighs on the moon only about one-sixth of its weight on earth.

Now, a platform balance scale operates in a different way. It compares the unknown mass of apples with the known mass of metal. The piece of metal is rated as

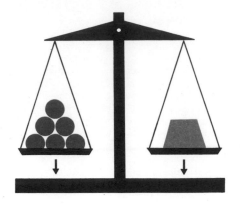

Weight is the result of gravity acting on mass. Thus, apples that weigh one pound at sea level on the earth would weigh only about 1/6th of a pound on the moon, because the moon's gravity is about 1/6th that of the earth. This difference could not be measured by a beam balance (above). Since the mass is the same in both pans, the beam would hang level whatever the gravitational pull.

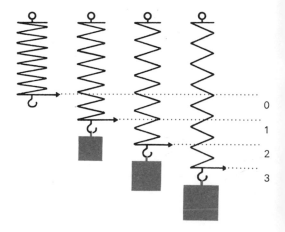

In a spring balance (above), a spiral spring stretches in direct proportion to the load. Differences in gravity will show correspondingly different readings for the same mass. Contrast with the beam balance (top), which merely compares masses.

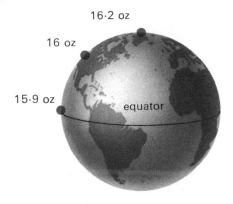

16·2 oz

16 oz

15·9 oz

equator

The earth is not perfectly spherical but slightly flattened at the poles. Consequently, gravitational attraction varies from place to place over its surface. Diagram compares weight of the same mass at the pole, at latitude 45°, and at the equator.

The first man to experience weightlessness outside a space vehicle was the Russian astronaut Alexei Leonov. He left his spaceship on March 18, 1965, as it was circling the earth and "walked" around in space.

so-many pounds (or a fraction) on the basis of a standard metal mass kept by the Bureau of Standards in Washington. Thus, mass is the quantity of matter in a body and, in all ordinary situations, it never changes. Of course, gravity is also affecting the platform balance and its metal mass. But it does not affect the comparison because the apples and the metal mass are always affected by the same force. Had the traveler taken a platform balance on his trip, his bag of apples would always have balanced perfectly with his 1-lb. piece of metal. Indeed, if the traveler went to the moon with the platform balance, the apples would balance perfectly with the 1-lb. mass. The force of gravitational attraction on the moon is the same for the mass of apples as it is for the mass of metal.

Part of the confusion between "mass" and "weight" arises because of the use of words. We say we are "weighing" objects when we are really trying to compare an unknown mass with a standard mass. Then, too, the standard pieces of metal are called "weights" when they are actually masses. Still further confusion comes from the fact that we use the same word for both terms of measurement—"the pound." We should really say that the traveler took one *pound-mass* with him and that whenever he placed it on his spring balance he was measuring *pound-force*.

So far we have been discussing weight and mass in descriptive words. But it is possible to put such matters in quantitative terms—that is, in mathematics. This may be hard for many people to grasp, but this is the way scientists deal with such concepts. So here, as elsewhere throughout this book, we shall indicate some of the basic mathematics involved in these matters. Those who find these sections too difficult may skip over them and learn from the more familiar words.

We can express the relationship between mass and weight, for instance, using one of Newton's laws of motion. This states that if a body is acted upon by a force (F), the acceleration (a) is equal to the value of the force divided by the mass (M) of the body. This law is expressed by the formula:

$$a = \frac{F}{M}.$$

Suppose we place a body of one pound-mass on a frictionless horizontal table and find experimentally the force required to give it an acceleration of one foot per second per second (1 ft/sec²). This force is called one *poundal*. Now let us drop this one pound-mass so that it falls freely under the action of gravity, and measure its acceleration. We find that, if this is done at various places on the earth's surface, this "acceleration due to gravity" varies slightly at the different locations. Let us assign the symbol g ft/sec^2 to this acceleration. We now see that the weight of this one pound-mass is given by 1 multiplied by g poundals. Thus it is that the weight varies slightly from place to place. It is found by experiment that the average value of g is about 32 ft/sec^2, and so the pound-force is defined as 32 poundals. The weight of our one pound-mass is therefore

$$\frac{1 \times g}{32} \text{ pound-force.}$$

In general, the weight W of a mass M pound-mass is

$$\frac{Mg}{32} \text{ pound-force.}$$

If the g in this expression is cancelled with the 32, the number for the mass of a body is the same as the number for its weight.

Let us now go back to think about a one pound-mass of water that, through evaporation, has been drawn up from the sea by the sun's energy and deposited 10,000 feet up on a mountain. The force of gravity on this one pound-mass is one pound-force. Now, scientifically defined, *work is done when a force moves in the direction of its line of action. The amount of work is the value of the force multiplied by the distance moved.* The line of action

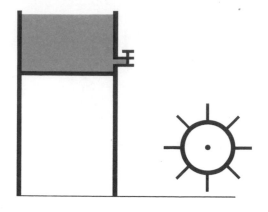

Potential energy is the capacity to do work that a substance possesses by virtue of its position. Thus, water in the tank at the top of the tower next to the turbine has potential energy.

With the construction of this dam across a mountain valley in Switzerland, a store of potential energy has been created that can be drawn upon as required.

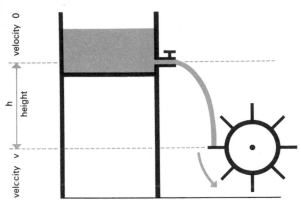

velocity 0

h height

velcocity v

Kinetic energy is the capacity for doing work that matter in motion possesses. Thus, when the stopcock is opened, water falls due to gravity and can be used to drive the turbine. (Letters *v* and *h* are discussed in text.)

Below: When water rushes down these pipes, the potential energy it had when stored at the top is converted into kinetic energy, which drives turbines in the building at the bottom.

of the force on this one pound-mass of water is a vertical line from the mountain height to sea level. Therefore the maximum work that the water can do is one pound-force multiplied by 10,000 feet. This equals a force of 10,000 foot pounds. The definition of energy in mechanics is *the ability to do work*. Thus, in its position 10,000 feet up the mountain, the one pound-mass of water has energy equal to 10,000 foot-pound-force. This kind of energy, which exists because of position, is called *potential energy*. In general, if a body of weight *(W)* and mass *(M)* is at a height *(h)* above some given level, its potential energy is expressed by the formula:

$$Wh = \frac{Mgh}{32} \text{ foot-pound-force.}$$

This helps to explain the energy of a stationary particle of water. But what of the energy of motion, such as in the wind? Let us see if we can relate the energy of motion to the potential energy we have already dealt with. If our one pound-mass of water at 10,000 feet were to fall freely under the action of gravity, its potential energy would be reduced progressively as it fell. One of the basic principles of science, however, is the law of conservation of energy: Energy is never destroyed but is converted into some other form. Thus it follows that the potential energy of the water must be progressively converted into another form. And, indeed, as the water falls, its velocity steadily increases. This energy due to motion is given the name *kinetic energy* (Greek *kinesis* = movement). If we can find how the velocity of falling water is related to the height fallen, we can establish a relationship between potential and kinetic energy.

Suppose that the velocity of the water after it has fallen distance *h* feet is *v* feet/sec. Its acceleration will be *g*, the acceleration due to gravity, which we shall assume to be constant. The average velocity over the distance is the change in velocity divided by two. That is,

$$\frac{v}{2} \text{ feet/second.}$$

The time taken for the descent is distance divided by velocity,

$$\text{or } h \div \frac{v}{2} = \frac{2h}{v}.$$

Now, acceleration equals change in velocity divided by time,

$$\text{or } v \div \frac{2h}{v} = \frac{v^2}{2h}.$$

But the acceleration is the acceleration due to gravity *g*. Thus,

$$\frac{v^2}{2h} = g, \quad \text{or } v^2 = 2gh.$$

If we go back to our formula for potential energy as $\frac{Mgh}{32}$, we can now replace *gh* with $\frac{v^2}{2}$, and get $\frac{Mv^2}{2 \times 32}$.

This is the formula for kinetic energy. Let us write these out again.

$$\text{Potential energy} = \frac{Mgh}{32}$$

$$\text{Kinetic energy} = \frac{Mv^2}{2 \times 32}$$

Notice that potential energy depends upon *g*, but kinetic energy does not.

The earth and everything on it is moving. All this movement suggests that everything on earth has a considerable energy of motion. But since everything is moving at the same speed and in the same direction we cannot make use of that energy. But if one thing is moving *relative* to another, it has energy that man may be able to make use of. Put a windmill in the path of the wind. The wind moves in relation to the windmill, which stands still on the ground.

Imagine a given mass of air, say 10 pounds, moving at 30 miles an hour, or 44 feet per second. The kinetic energy of that air is

$$\frac{10 \times 44^2}{2 \times 32}.$$

We express the energy in terms of the work that it could do in one second, so that the result of this equation is 302 foot-pounds-force per second. In other words, the "package" of wind that we are considering has enough energy to raise a weight of 302 pounds-force a height of one foot in one second. This is the way we measure

Above: The water wheel has a potential of about 2 to 6 horsepower, the windmill a potential of from 2 to 8 horsepower. Both were used in the Middle Ages, but their importance as power-producers was eclipsed by the steam engine, developed during the 18th century. Early steam engines had a horsepower potential of from 7 to 100.

Below: Red indicates areas of greatest windpower potential throughout the world.

power, and a unit of power expresses the amount of work that can be done in a given period of time. Horsepower, which we have mentioned in the introduction, is one such unit of power. The value of one horsepower was determined experimentally by James Watt, who wanted to compare his new steam engines with a familiar source of power, the carthorse. By harnessing a horse to a weight suspended over a pulley he found that the horse could raise a weight of 550 pound-force one foot in one second. The horsepower as a unit of power has been widely used ever since.

Returning to our imaginary windmill, we can now see what happens if ten pounds-mass of air traveling at 30 miles per hour gives up its energy to the windmill's sails. It will provide power for the mill at a rate of 302/550 horsepower — that is, about 0.55 horsepower. But that is an ideal figure. It assumes that the air gives up *all* its energy to the mill's sails, which would mean that the air was brought to a complete standstill. But if this happened, the air that followed along behind it would have to push it out of the way before it could also act on the windmill. If all the following wind is not to be slowed down, the energy required to push the first ten pounds out of the way would be exactly the same as the energy that the wind yielded to the mill.

This is not, of course, the way it works, but the imaginary situation that we have described points to a fundamental fact in the conversion of energy into power. You can never extract *all* the energy from any source, and there will always be losses. Just what these losses are and how we can keep them as small as possible will be told on pp. 109-121. For the moment, we can say that a windmill — like any other way of converting kinetic energy into power — can rob the wind of only a part of its energy.

Now let us look at windpower from another point of view. When a strong wind is blowing, we can often see clouds moving across the sky in the same direction as the wind moves at ground level. This tells us that this particular kind of energy from the sun takes the form of air currents that are hundreds, and possibly thousands, of feet deep. And yet we can intercept only the energy that is close to the ground. We cannot build windmills thousands of feet high because they would topple over. Thus, of all the energy in the wind, we can only hope to use a very tiny fraction indeed. And this fact illustrates another general principle: At every stage in the conversion of the sun's energy into usable forms, the energy is scattered and, so to speak, thinned out. The best we can do is to try to catch a small fragment of the total.

Potential energy is not directly usable; it has to be converted. For example, the water, because of its

Top: A simple windmill used to obtain salt by pumping sea water into salt pans where it evaporates. Bottom: A Greek windmill utilizing coastal winds. Small sails work best in high winds.

energy, is able to flow downhill. In doing so, it acquires kinetic energy. It is this energy of motion that drives a water wheel or the blades of a turbine. Because water is 810 times denser than air, water in motion is a more compact, or concentrated, form of energy than air. To be precise, ten pounds of air at sea level occupies 130 cubic feet, but ten pounds of water occupies 0.16 cubic feet. Thus, water is easier to store, handle, and control.

But one fact in particular makes water more useful than air: Water that has been drawn out of the sea and deposited on mountains has potential energy first and kinetic energy second. The question is how we can make the best use of this potential energy. If we trace the careers of rain or snow falling on a mountain range, we find that two very interesting and important situations develop. One is on high mountains, where much of the water is locked up temporarily as snow throughout the winter. In regions such as the Swiss Alps, the biggest *precipitation* (a term that refers to the fall of both rain and snow) occurs in the autumn and winter. Thus, the water's energy of position is preserved until the gradual thaw of the spring and early summer releases the water to run downhill. This is most important, because it means that a heavy snowfall does not mean an uncontrollable torrent of water. Of course, there are places where the spring thaw causes sudden, heavy flooding. But such places tend to be on lower ground, where the potential energy is not so attractive to the would-be user.

The other important situation results when rain falls on the lower slopes of hills and mountains. There the water soaks into the ground, runs through cracks in the rocks, and takes time to drain downhill. The result again is that the flow of rivers in the valleys is much more steady than the rainfall that created them.

There is still another feature of water in mountainous regions that is of practical interest. The valleys down which the water flows are themselves the product of the water's own energy. Over the centuries the run-off of water has excavated a deep trench by carrying away the rock and soil. In doing so, water has hollowed out two sides of a storage tank, or reservoir. It only remains for engineers to build a third side, in the form of a dam. Man can then store vast quantities of water.

The purpose of damming up a valley is simply to conserve potential energy. If the river water is actually in motion, it is in the kinetic state. Like the wind, it must be used instantly; if there is too much water to use all at once, we must let it go by. But if we hold the water in the static condition, we can store it and its energy until we want to use it. The potential energy remains intact, and the only losses are those due to the continuous evapo-

Right: A Swiss mountain valley that has been cut by rushing water and now provides a good site for the building of a dam. Photo below shows a valley with a dam across it; a store of potential energy has now been created.

Below: Hydroelectric power potential (red) of the continents, and the proportion that has been developed (black). Africa's enormous potential is important because the continent is short of other power resources.

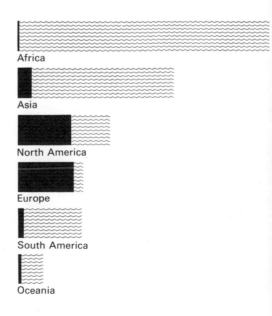

Africa

Asia

North America

Europe

South America

Oceania

ration from the surface. Such losses can be serious in tropical climates. But as long as there is a surplus of water—that is to say, more water flowing than can be converted into power—dam building can be well worth while.

The quantity of energy available at any given moment is proportional to the difference in the level of the water above and below the dam. To a large extent, dams are independent of the fluctuations in the water supply caused by seasonal rain or snow fall. Dams store enough water to enable us to keep their power-producing machinery in continuous use all the year round.

Water storage is a good example of a way in which we can snatch a small fraction of energy from the continuous operation of the solar energy cycle. As we shall see later (p. 130), it is sometimes even worth while expending energy to pump water uphill and to store this water for use when the demand for power is at its peak.

Summing up, we realize that there are two main situations in which it is worth considering water as a source of energy. The first is where energy of position is high and the quantity of water is small. The second is where the energy of position is low but the supply of water is great. In other words, a pound weight of water falling 1,000 feet does the same amount of work as 1,000 pounds falling one foot.

Today we are using about 10 per cent of the water-power that could be exploited. This may seem a very small amount. But the fact is that, although the energy costs nothing and is constantly renewed by the sun, the engineering works needed to harness that energy are extremely costly. Indeed, such works are worth undertaking only in places where there is a large *concentration* of energy. Of course, man now has the means of converting water energy and transmitting it over long distances in the form of electrical energy. But there is a limit beyond which such a project ceases to be economically worth while.

Waterpower accounts for only one per cent of man's total consumption of energy. This will surely increase in the years to come. But it illustrates how small is the share of the sun's energy that we can intercept before it is radiated again into outer space and lost forever.

So far we have seen how the small fraction of the sun's energy that reaches the earth gives rise to energy cycles in air and water. The energy that arrived in the form of light is, as it were, sidetracked temporarily into other forms. These cycles are purely *physical*—that is, they bring about changes of state in air and water. But there is another energy cycle of equal importance, and this is a *chemical* one.

All life on earth depends ultimately on the continued

growth of plants. Man, in common with carnivorous animals, may eat meat as part of a mixed diet. But the animals that man eats have themselves been nourished on vegetable food. This is equally true of marine animals. The fish we eat have lived and grown by eating smaller animals. These smaller animals have themselves depended on a supply of waterborne vegetation called phytoplankton. We can generalize and say that the source of energy for our own needs, as living machines, comes originally from vegetation. We can go further and say that vegetation, whether on land or in the sea, grows in daylight. Hence all foodstuffs finally depend on energy from the sun.

Despite years of research, scientists still do not understand exactly how solar energy is converted into chemical energy. We call the process *photosynthesis* (from Greek words meaning "light-putting-together"). In its simplest form, the process is the joining together of molecules of water and carbon dioxide to form a sugar called *glucose*. This—a chemical compound of the kind classed as a carbohydrate—is living matter's basic raw material and energy source. We have said that scientists do not know exactly how this build-up of simple molecules into a complex sugar takes place. We can say, however, that, starting with six molecules of carbon dioxide and six of water, a plant cell can produce one molecule of glucose and six of oxygen. We can also say that light —that is, visible rays of the spectrum—is needed. Finally, we know that the "go-between" for light and the chemical process is one of several green or yellow pigments that are known collectively as *chlorophyll*. This substance converts light energy into some other form of

The process of photosynthesis is the unique source of all organic matter, and all life depends on it. The light energy from the sun is taken up by the pigments of cells containing chlorophyll— as, for example, in leaves—and is partially converted by photosynthesis into stored chemical energy.

Below: Six molecules of carbon dioxide (carbon, black; oxygen, red) and six molecules of water (hydrogen, blue; oxygen, red) are synthesized by sunlight into one molecule of sugar, while six molecules of oxygen are released.

sunlight

chlorophyll

From the glucose made in photosynthesis, together with water and mineral salts from the soil, plants make all the other molecules they need. Thus, the basic fuel sources of wood and coal are ultimately derived through photosynthesis.

The diagram below lists various chemical compounds synthesized by a green plant from glucose, water, and minerals.

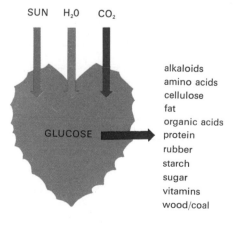

SUN H₂0 CO₂

GLUCOSE

alkaloids
amino acids
cellulose
fat
organic acids
protein
rubber
starch
sugar
vitamins
wood/coal

energy that is needed to force two compounds (carbon dioxide and water) to combine to form glucose. This process may be expressed as a chemical equation:

$$6\,H_2O + 6\,CO_2 + energy = C_6H_{12}O_6 + 6\,O_2$$

We should not assume that life elsewhere would have to depend on the same basic chemical reaction. For all we know, there may be other solar systems with other planets that sustain life on quite different chemical systems. On earth, however, all the energy that we need for life, growth, and movement derives originally from this single process.

We humans have a double interest in the products of photosynthesis. In the first place, we take the vegetable and animal products and use them directly. Our second interest is based on the fact that vegetation makes use of the basic carbohydrate molecule (glucose) to build up still more complex molecules. These form the "skeletons" of all vegetation—those structural elements that enable plants to stand up above the soil's surface. These plant parts consist of more complex carbohydrates such as cellulose, and lignin (Latin *lignum* = wood). The sun, of course, supplies the energy needed to bring about this build-up from glucose.

If we take a closer look at the nature of glucose we find that here, once again, the sun's energy has been converted into potential energy. As we saw, two compounds—carbon dioxide and water—are the raw materials of photosynthesis. These compounds have no natural tendency to combine together. They are forced to do so, and energy from outside supplies that force. What happens, as we saw, is a rearrangement of the original atoms; glucose is synthesized, and oxygen is left over. But the energy is not lost; it is now inside the glucose. The sugar molecule is an arrangement of atoms, that, to use a simple comparison, is like a wound-up spring. Given the right conditions, the spring will unwind, releasing its energy. The presence of oxygen is one right condition. It is no accident that the number of atoms of oxygen originally set free by photosynthesis is exactly the number required for the reverse reaction. Another condition is the presence, in living cells, of a number of organic catalysts called *enzymes*. These chemical compounds help to break down the glucose without themselves being consumed in the process. The energy locked up in glucose is liberated when this reaction takes place:

$$C_6H_{12}O_6 + 6\,O_2 = 6\,H_2O + 6\,O_2 + energy$$

Actually the breakdown of glucose in living matter takes place in more than twenty stages. What is important to us in this book is to remember that all the energy—and

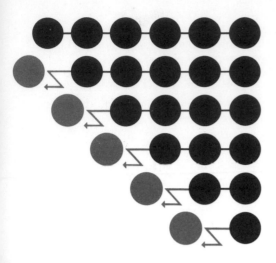

Above: In decaying matter, organic molecules (black) break down by stages, and each stage yields a little energy. The process is, in fact, burning; but it is a slow natural process and takes place at low temperatures. By contrast, fire (below) is uncontrolled combustion. The molecules break up rapidly, yielding sudden free energy in the form of heat. The total energy yield from either process for a given quantity of matter is the same.

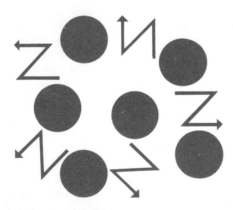

no more and no less—that went into the original synthesis of the glucose comes out again in its breakdown.

In living plants the energy in glucose is liberated in recombining with oxygen at quite low temperatures. In warm-blooded animals like ourselves, the recombination occurs at slightly higher temperatures. This process is called *oxidation*. If conditions are right, oxidation can take place at much higher temperatures, without the help of enzymes or other catalysts. This form of oxidation is familiar to us as burning. This is what happens with the more complex carbohydrates that make up plant structures. Put in familiar terms, if wood is hot enough and there is a ready supply of oxygen, it burns. Once started, it goes on burning until oxidation is complete and all the "built-in" solar energy has been released as heat.

We can look on vegetation as a storehouse of potential energy, ready to be turned into heat. Everyone has observed that living vegetation or timber burns less easily than the same material when dry. This is because living matter contains a high percentage of water. And water, as we shall see in more detail later (p. 110), requires a great deal of heat to raise it to the temperature at which it boils away.

Here, then, in the world's continuous production of vegetable matter, we have a constantly renewed supply of "canned" solar energy. We can use the supply by burning it. If vegetation remains unused, it dies and ultimately rots down into its original components. When this happens, the original solar energy emerges as heat just as surely as in burning. We are usually not aware of this happening except in special cases such as a badly constructed hayloft or a compost heap properly made up of garden refuse. There are, however, some special situations (p. 46) in which vegetation does not disintegrate completely after dying. One such case occurs when vegetation undergoes the process of pickling in the absence of oxygen.

How much solar energy is converted into "energy of vegetation"? Plants are not very efficient users of sunlight. Only about one per cent of the light that falls on plants is used, and the rest is reflected as visible light and infrared waves. Even so, vegetation that grows on the earth's surface in about three and one-half days would, if it were all burnt, satisfy man's fuel requirements for a whole year. Wood, of course, has been used for thousands of years as a source of heat for domestic comfort and for cooking. In some places it is still used for providing heat for conversion into power. But, generally speaking, wood is unsatisfactory as a fuel. It provides less heat per unit of weight than other fuels such as coal and oil. Furthermore, the remaining great forests of the

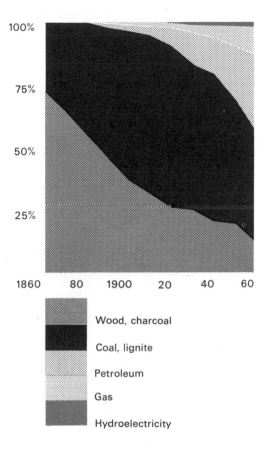

100%
75%
50%
25%

1860   80   1900   20   40   60

Wood, charcoal

Coal, lignite

Petroleum

Gas

Hydroelectricity

Graph shows world consumption of main energy sources (as percentages of the total) from 1860 to 1960. Wood and charcoal have declined as producers of energy, while oil, gas, and—quite recently—hydroelectricity have become prominent. Below: A circular stack of wood undergoing slow partial combustion to produce charcoal. As a source of energy, charcoal has now only local importance, although some metallurgical operations still use considerable quantities.

world are far from the industrial centers of population, where power is in greatest demand.

The supply of solar energy, some of which is daily "sidetracked" into vegetation, is spread out over some 190 million square miles of the earth's surface. If we could concentrate this energy and make use of it where it was most needed, all our energy demands could be comfortably met. There seems little prospect that this can ever be done. But we can be encouraged by the possibility that some day we shall find a way of making direct use of the process of photosynthesis without the intermediary of a growing plant.

But whatever we may achieve in this direction will be limited. Photosynthesis, as we saw, uses only one per cent of the solar energy that reaches the ground. The quantity of energy reaching the earth is fantastically large. In two and one-half minutes, we receive enough energy to satisfy our present needs for a year—if only we could find a way of catching and converting it. Ironically, the places where sunshine is almost continuous—and thus solar energy is most abundant—are desert areas. By their very nature, arid areas are remote from industrial urban areas where power is most needed. Suppose that we can devise ways of collecting solar energy in, let us say, the Sahara Desert. We shall then be faced with enormous and costly problems of transmitting it to the centers of population.

The direct use of solar energy, as we shall see (pp. 222-225), is worth while in situations where other sources of energy are lacking and where power produced from the process is used on the spot. But the problem of large-scale collection of solar energy remains unsolved. For the moment, we can say that the best prospect would be to make use of solar energy in the same form in which it originally arrives. For instance, it may be possible to convert light waves from one form of energy to another. Light waves do just that, of course, in photosynthesis. But that process passes their energy through an intermediate stage that involves a wasteful chemical action.

2 Energy from the Sun – Capital

The physicist, as we have seen, recognizes two forms of energy—potential and kinetic. But anyone concerned with natural resources can think of energy as divided into two other categories—*income* and *capital*. (Think of salary or pay as income, and an inherited bank account as capital.) Income energy is the constant, inexhaustible supply of radiant energy from the sun that reaches the earth in a variety of forms. Energy capital, which we shall consider in this chapter, is in some ways the opposite of income. It consists of the familiar fuels such as coal, oil, and gas, which represent convenient local concentrations of energy. Unlike energy income, capital energy is relatively easy to convert into power. But, also unlike income, capital energy exists in only limited quantities.

Until about two centuries ago, wood was man's most important fuel. (This is still the case in many underdeveloped countries.) It was not until the early eighteenth century that Europeans began to use coal in large quantities for smelting iron. This important application for coal stimulated mining technology and led to the invention of the steam engine, which was used first to drain water from coal mines and other mines. Steam power, once harnessed, soon found a huge range of other uses in the expanding Industrial Revolution.

Oil from natural seepage spots was used in the Middle East in pre-Christian times. But the first modern oil well—which was in the United States—was drilled only in 1859. It was not until the invention of the internal combustion engine, toward the end of the nineteenth century, that the oil industry began its great and still-continuing period of expansion. Well over 90 per cent of the power produced today comes from coal and oil. Most of the remainder comes from gas and waterpower. At present, coal produces about three times as much power as oil, but oil is gradually becoming more important as a source of power.

Coal, oil, and gas are essentially forms of potential energy. Although they differ greatly in physical form, their value as fuels depends on certain features they all share. They owe their existence to living matter—either

Coal and petroleum are the major sources of energy capital: 90 per cent of power produced today comes from them. Above: A fossilized leaf in a piece of coal. Coal comes from plants buried millions of years ago; when burned, it releases energy originally received from the sun. Right: Looking up the shaft of a modern oil derrick. With the invention of the internal-combustion engine in the 1890's, oil suddenly became a major power-producing commodity.

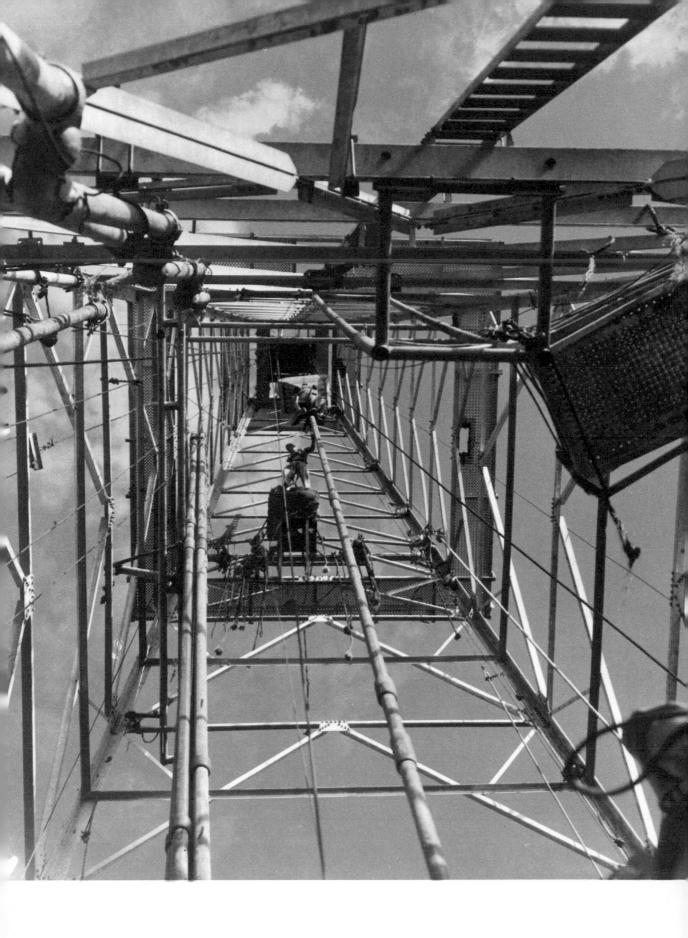

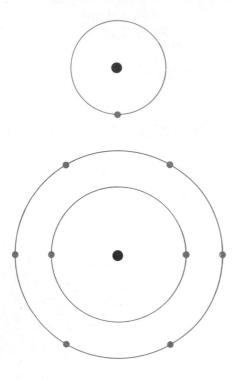

A hydrogen atom has one electron, an oxygen atom has eight. When two hydrogen atoms combine with one oxygen atom to form a molecule of water (below), both hydrogen atoms share electrons with the oxygen atom.

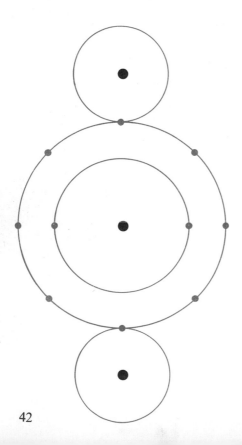

plant or animal—that was originally formed and nourished by the radiant energy of the sun. Because they are derived from living matter, they are known as *fossil* fuels. When we burn a piece of coal, drive an automobile, or cook food on a gas stove, we are using energy from sunlight that shone upon the earth perhaps 200 million years ago.

The only way of releasing the stored energy of these fossil fuels is by combustion. Then the energy reappears as heat. A whole family of devices called heat engines has been developed for converting this heat energy into useful power. (The most important of these will be discussed in Chapters 5 to 8.) Parallel with the development of these engines, thermodynamics—the science that deals with heat and power—has grown to assist the engineer. (A broad outline of this branch of physics is given in the Appendix, p. 242.)

Because of their organic origins, coal, oil, and gas contain the chemical elements of which living matter is formed. This means mainly hydrogen and carbon. Fuels burn when their hydrogen and carbon atoms chemically combine with oxygen. This chemical reaction cannot take place at normal atmospheric temperature. Some external heat must be applied before the chemical combination can take place. Once combustion has started, however, enough heat becomes available to produce a "chain reaction." The fuel continues to burn until most of its heat energy has been exhausted or its supply of oxygen is removed.

In order to understand the source of heat in these fuels, we must know something about their atomic structure. All atoms consist of a nucleus composed mainly of positively charged particles, called *protons*, and uncharged particles, called *neutrons*. The nucleus is surrounded by negatively charged particles called *electrons*, each having a mass about 1/1800th of that of a proton or neutron. In diagrams, we usually show these electrons as revolving, or orbiting, around the nucleus. When two atoms of hydrogen combine with one atom of oxygen to form a molecule of water, the linkage between the atoms occurs in these electron orbits. The electrons now move more slowly and in smaller orbits than they did in the original free atoms. The electrons in the water molecule therefore possess less energy than in the free atoms. This "lost" energy emerges as heat. The energy stored by the electrons in the original hydrogen atom is thus potential energy that can be released at any desired time and converted into heat energy.

The composition of a fuel can be discovered in terms of its percentage of hydrogen, carbon, and other constituents. It is then possible to calculate the weight of oxygen required for the complete combustion of one

A bomb calorimeter, right, is used to determine the heat of combustion of various substances. A known quantity of the test substance (for example, coal) is placed in a crucible inside a steel "bomb," which is then sealed. Oxygen is added through the central valve, and the bomb is then immersed in a large calorimeter containing water. The substance is ignited by passing an electric current through a thin wire suspended in it. Heat evolved during combustion causes a rise in temperature of calorimeter, this rise is noted and the heat involved worked out. Below: Caloric values, in Btu per pound, of various fuels.

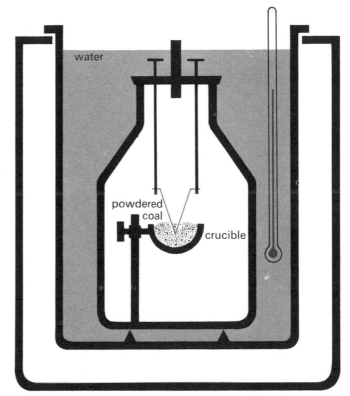

water

powdered coal

crucible

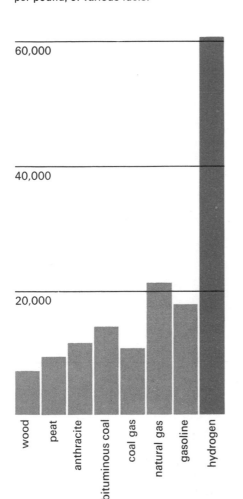

60,000

40,000

20,000

wood

peat

anthracite

bituminous coal

coal gas

natural gas

gasoline

hydrogen

pound of that fuel. Calculations show that between 12 and 16 pounds of air are required for the combustion of one pound of a typical fuel. (The exact amount depends on the exact composition of the fuel.) On the earth's surface, fortunately, air is free of charge. Only the fuel has to be paid for.

There is a standard for rating the quantity of heat liberated by the combustion of fuels. It is based on one pound of a solid or liquid fuel, or one cubic foot of gaseous fuel, and is called its *caloric value*. Since gases change in volume considerably with variations of pressure and temperature, the cubic foot must be measured at some standard temperature and pressure. It is possible to estimate the caloric value of a fuel by multiplying the caloric values of its constituent elements by their proportions in the fuel. This theoretical value will be slightly higher than the actual caloric value of the fuel because some energy is used in separating the chemical compounds in the fuel. The unit of heat is known as the British Thermal Unit (Btu). One Btu is the amount of heat required to raise the temperature of one pound of water 1°F. The caloric value of hydrogen is 61,500 Btu per pound; that of carbon is 14,200 Btu per pound. Hydrogen is thus a very valuable part of any fuel. The percentage of carbon in coals varies from 80 per cent to over 90 per cent. Fuel oils, on the other hand, contain more hydrogen (about 10 per cent) and less ash (or incombustible matter). Thus, fuel oils usually have a higher caloric value than coals. Typical values are about 18,000 Btu per pound for oil, and 12,000 to 15,000 Btu per pound for coal. The caloric value of coal gas is approximately 500 Btu per cubic foot. Natural gas has a caloric value of about 1,000 Btu per cubic foot.

The exact chemical composition of coal is complicated. Fortunately this does not have much effect on its use. Crude oil, or petroleum, on the other hand, is a mixture of certain well-known organic chemical compounds. Most of these organic compounds are hydrocarbons—that is, compounds formed by the chemical combination of hydrogen and carbon. The capacity of an element to combine with others depends upon an element's *valency* (Latin *valere*—"to be strong"). The number of atoms of other elements with which an element can combine is limited by the number of valency "arms" that each atom possesses. Each element has a fixed number of arms, and each arm is able to combine with one arm of another element. (Of course, the arms have no physical existence. The valency of an element actually depends on the arrangement of the electrons orbiting in an atom.) Carbon has a valency of four; hydrogen has a valency of one. Thus, the simplest hydrocarbon compound consists of one atom of carbon with four atoms of hydrogen. This compound is called methane, and its chemical formula is CH_4. Another simple hydrocarbon is formed by two atoms of carbon and four of hydrogen. In this case, two of the valency arms of each carbon atom attach themselves to two arms from the other carbon atom. This leaves a total of four arms for the hydrogen atoms. This compound is called ethylene (with the chemical formula C_2H_4). The double linkage between the carbon atoms introduces a strain in the bonding of the molecule. Ethylene is therefore less stable than methane. A possible third variation has two carbon atoms linked together by three of their valency arms. This leaves only two arms for hydrogen atoms. This hydrocarbon is acetylene (formula C_2H_2), a highly unstable compound.

Methane (CH_4) is an example of what is called a *saturated* hydrocarbon. It is called "saturated" because it has "absorbed" (that is, combined with) the maximum possible number of hydrogen atoms. Ethylene and acetylene, on the other hand, are unsaturated. More than one of the valency arms of each of their carbon atoms have combined with another carbon atom. More complicated compounds are formed by adding more carbon atoms to the first one. If two carbon atoms are linked together by one valency arm each, six arms are

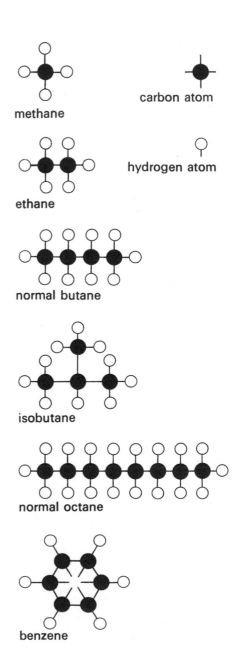

methane

carbon atom

ethane

hydrogen atom

normal butane

isobutane

normal octane

benzene

left. A hydrogen atom can be attached to each of these six arms. This is ethane, another saturated hydrocarbon (with the chemical formula C_2H_6). Similarly, three carbon atoms produce propane (C_3H_8) and four carbon atoms produce butane (C_4H_{10}). Then follow a whole series of hydrocarbons—pentane, hexane, heptane, octane, and so on. Most of the constituents of petroleum consist of these saturated hydrocarbons. Methane and ethane are gases. So are propane and butane, but these two are more easily liquefied. They are the main constituents of the gas fuel that is "bottled" for ease of transportation.

As the hydrocarbon molecules become bigger, with longer chains of carbon atoms, so the liquids become heavier and thicker. When more than about 25 carbon atoms make up the chain, the material becomes solid at ordinary temperatures. In what is known as the "catalytic cracking process," at an oil refinery (p. 64), these longer chains are, in effect, broken. A heavy oil is transformed into a lighter one. In some cases, the products of the cracking process may contain a proportion of unsaturated hydrocarbons. These less-stable compounds have important uses in the chemical industry.

Another stable combination of carbon and hydrogen is benzene, which consists of six carbon atoms linked together to form a hexagonal, or six-sided ring. This linking absorbs three valency arms from each carbon atom. One hydrogen atom is attached to the other valency arm of each carbon atom. The benzene ring may be combined with another hydrocarbon molecule by removing one hydrogen atom. One end of a carbon chain can then be attached to the carbon valency arm that has been freed. Such compounds, in which the benzene ring is present, are called *aromatics*. Aromatics are more stable than the usual unsaturated compounds so they are quite acceptable constituents of fuel oils and gasolines.

At the beginning of this chapter, we mentioned that coal, oil, and gas can be traced back to plant or animal life. As we shall see later, there is still some uncertainty over exactly how oil and natural gas are formed. But on present evidence it seems reasonable to regard all three

Left: Molecules of heavy oils, like that shown in top photo, have long chains of carbon atoms. In cracking, these chains are broken, producing a lighter, thinner oil, as in lower photo.

as fossil fuels. When, where, and how did these fuels form? Most scientists agree that the earth is about 4,500 million years old. By examining and comparing rock layers and the fossils embedded in them, geologists have managed to piece together the broad outlines of earth's history during the last 600 million years or so.

Consider the earth's age and the period of time required for the formation of coal seams. Man's recorded history (the last 6,000 years or so) and the 300 or so years that coal has been extensively mined then seem insignificant moments in time. It is easier to understand this if we compress the time scale into more manageable proportions. Imagine that the earth's 4,500 million years represent one calendar year, starting on January 1. On this time scale, the Carboniferous Period (the most important coal-forming period) began on December 5 and lasted eight days. Man's recorded history started about 40 seconds before midnight on December 31, while the last 300 years are represented by about the final two seconds of the year. Scientists believe that the earth is still in its youth and should be fit for human habitation for twice or three times its present age. Even if mankind is lucky enough to survive as long as this, it is certain that he will not be using fossil fuels to supply his energy needs in that far-distant future. At our present rate of consumption, for instance, coal supplies will not last much more than a few hundred years.

Much of the coal mined by present-day industrial countries dates from the Carboniferous Period. This began about 345 million years ago and ended about 280 million years ago. The other major coal-forming periods of geological time were the Cretaceous (136 to 65 million years ago) and the Tertiary (65 to about 2 million years ago). In each of these periods, the regions that now contain coal deposits had warm or mild and very humid climates. Such a climate favored the rapid, dense growth of huge swamp forests choked with trees and ground vegetation. As each generation of trees grew to maturity, died, and fell, new growths sprang up to take their place. As a result, great layers of vegetation were laid down during the many millions of years that these climatic conditions lasted. Eventually, however, the climates of these regions changed. The forest growth ceased, and the dead vegetation was overlaid by mud and other sediments that erosion carried down from higher land. As the load of sediments increased, the vegetation was steadily compressed into the hard, black substance we know as coal. In some parts of the world this process was repeated several times. The result was a number of seams of coal, each sandwiched between layers of sediment. The type of coal occurring in a particular seam depends on such factors as the nature of the plants from

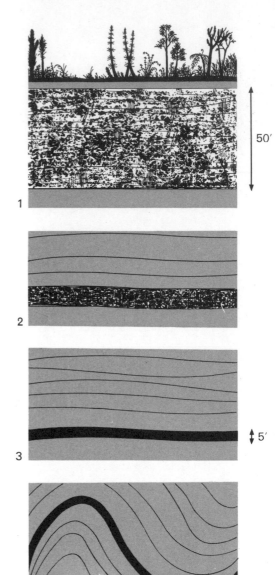

Diagrams show how anthracite has been formed over millions of years. Vegetable matter becomes trapped in a swamp (1) and only partially decays. Under its own weight and the weight of sediment deposited on top, it becomes more and more compressed and forms peat, then lignite (2), and finally coal (3). The original 50 feet of vegetation has now become about 5 feet of coal. Coal is finally turned to anthracite by the pressure and heat of buckling (4).

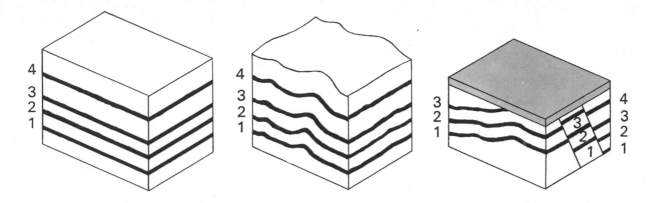

Three types of carboniferous strata (coal seams are marked black). Left: Undisturbed horizontal strata. Center: Buckling of seams due to folding. Right: A complex pattern of seams formed by folding and faulting. Note that the surface has been worn away by erosion and has subsequently been covered by overburden (red) deposited by sea. If the seams are too irregular they may be difficult or even impossible to mine.

Chart below details changes in composition that occur at different stages in the formation of anthracite from wood. The percentage of carbon (black) increases; at the same time the percentages of oxygen (gray) and hydrogen (red) decrease.

which it was derived and the extent to which the plants decayed before burial under sediments. Later geological events, such as the movement and folding of the layers above and below the seam, also affected the type of coal.

In the great coalfields of the world, the original layers of decaying vegetation must have been immensely thick. Such layers represent many thousands of generations of trees. It is estimated that a depth of ten feet of vegetable remains goes into the making of a one-foot layer of coal. In some coalfields in the United States, the seams are more than 100 feet thick; in other regions, however, seams are only a few inches thick.

Not all the coal beneath the earth's surface is recoverable, of course. The best thickness of a seam for mining is about five to ten feet. Seams less than 14 inches thick are not an economic proposition; very thick seams are difficult and may become dangerous if worked to exhaustion. Another factor that reduces our usable reserves of coal is that much of the coal in a mine must be left as pillars to support the roof. Many seams of good

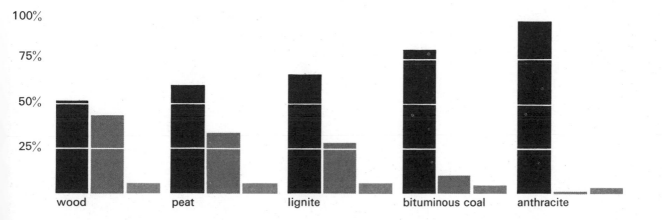

When coal lies close to the surface, the *open-pit* method of mining is used. A large drag-line removes the top layers of earth, exposing the coal, which is then torn out of the ground and loaded into trucks.

If the coal seams lie close to the side of a hill, they can be mined through shafts driven horizontally. This is called *drift* mining.

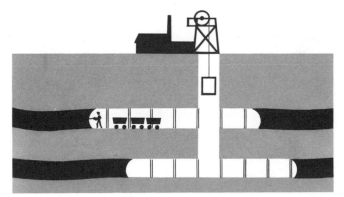

If the seams are deep beneath the surface, *shaft* mining is used. Bituminous coal is usually found in fairly level seams and can be mined by pushing out galleries from the main shaft.

Anthracite seams are twisted and broken (see page 46). Consequently, galleries must be driven at various angles to reach the coal.

Left: Mechanized mining of a thick pitch-coal seam in a German coal mine. Coal falls from the cutting machine onto a conveyor belt.

Greek miners, depicted on a clay tablet of the sixth century B.C. Ore is hacked away with a pick and collected in baskets. In the center hangs a primitive lamp, with its wick protruding from a vase. Right: Exploitation of cheap juvenile labor in mid-19th century England.

Below: A mine in France in the 16th century. The system of tunnels and shafts is well developed. All power is muscle-power.

La Rouge myne de sainct Nicolae

Below: A mechanized mining system
already in use in pits today. Nearly
all the operations are controlled
by one operator at a control
console, like that pictured at right.
First the coal-face ends are cut; then
the shearer-loader moves along the
whole length of the coal-face cutting
out a 20-inch slice of coal and loading
it on to the conveyor. The coal-face
wall may be over 170 yards long. When
the slice has been cut, the whole coal
cutting and conveying machinery is
advanced 20 inches and the cutter
begins another slice. The lower photo
shows the shearer; the coal-face is on
the left, while on the right is the
cable-carrying equipment that rolls
and unrolls the power cables and hoses.
The photo also shows the roof supports,
which are advanced by remote control.

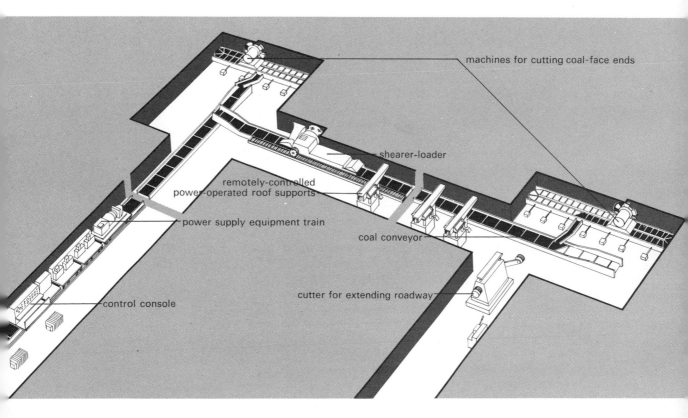

machines for cutting coal-face ends

shearer-loader

remotely-controlled
power-operated roof supports

power supply equipment train

coal conveyor

control console

cutter for extending roadway

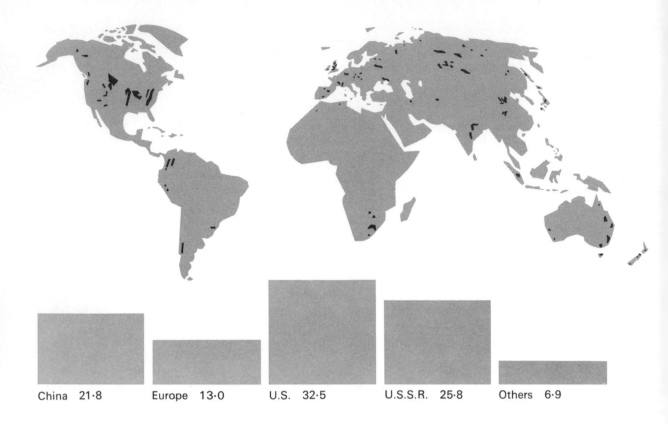

| China 21·8 | Europe 13·0 | U.S. 32·5 | U.S.S.R. 25·8 | Others 6·9 |

coal cannot be mined because they are flooded by water seepage from above. Finally, some seams cannot be mined because they dip at a sharp angle, owing to folding or faulting that occurred after the coal beds were originally deposited.

For all these reasons, therefore, the estimates of known and assumed coal reserves (shown on this page) are likely to be optimistic. Still, they reveal a number of important facts. Most of the coal reserves, for instance, are in the Northern Hemisphere—mainly in North America, Asia, and Europe. The United States has larger reserves than any other country, followed by the Soviet Union, China, the United Kingdom, and Germany. At present rates of production, the United States has enough coal to last for several hundred—perhaps up to 1,000—years. The United Kingdom and Germany have enough for about 200 years. There are other solid fuels derived from compressed vegetation, such as peat or lignite. But their reserves are small in comparison with coal and could not extend these time limits by more than a small per cent.

Map shows principal coalfields throughout the world; coal deposits are concentrated in the northern hemisphere. Diagram plots coal resources; figures are percentages of total resources (which exceed 2,300,000,000,000 metric tons).

Right: Mechanized surface mining of peat in central Ireland. Peat is undercut, chopped into brick shapes, and perforated; it is then allowed to dry before it is transported to a peat-fired power station (top right). Peat blocks are pulverized before being blown into the boiler furnace.

It is indisputable that coal originated from vegetable remains. The origin of oil is less certain. It is probable, however, that oil was formed from the bodies of small marine animals and plants that were deposited on the sea bed. These organisms became overlaid and compressed by sedimentary matter, and were subsequently converted into hydrocarbons—probably with the help of naturally occurring catalysts.

This may explain *how* the oil forms. It does not explain why oil occurs in some places and not in others. Special conditions are needed to produce an oil reservoir large enough to be tapped commercially. Basically, this is what happens. Oil, being a liquid, can pass through or around many of the sedimentary layers on land or beneath the sea. It will naturally tend to migrate upward toward areas of weaker pressure. The first stage in the development of an oil well occurs when the oil comes up against an impervious layer of rock that it is unable to penetrate. In many cases, the oil may be able to flow horizontally until it finds a way around the impervious layer. But if the oil is forming during a period of mountain-building, the rock layers may be contorted by

Lower diagram shows a typical landscape and indicates where oil may be found. Upper diagrams show these locations in more detail.

(1) A dome of rock strata—formed during folding—is one of the commonest types of oil trap. Many of the world's greatest oilfields are of this type. The oil (black), as it seeps upwards, is trapped by the impervious rock that slopes down on either side. Note that the oil rises above the water (blue) that usually seeps upward with it.

(2) A fault-trap occurs when a fracture in strata brings a layer of porous rock against a layer of impervious rock. This movement creates a pocket in which oil can collect.

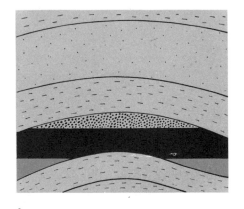

1

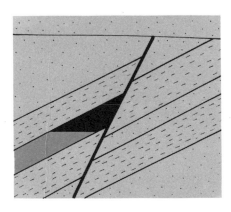

2

strong folding
major faulting

gentle folding
some faulting

movements of the earth's crust. In this case, the oil may be trapped in one of two ways. First, both the oil-bearing layer and impervious layers above the oil may have been folded to form a dome. The oil, usually floating on water, then rises toward the dead end at the top of the dome. If natural gas is present, which is often the case, this rises to the uppermost part of the dome. The second way occurs if the layers are inclined at an angle to the horizontal, but do not form a dome. Then it is possible for oil to be trapped by a fault, caused by earth movements cutting across the layers. This may have the effect of bringing the lower end of the inclined, oil-bearing porous layer across the end of an impervious layer. Thus an oil reservoir may be produced. A bore hole put down into either of these reservoirs of oil would produce an oil well. The pressure of the underlying water is sufficient to force the oil up through the bore hole.

Early methods of oil drilling were haphazard and wasteful, for little was known of the geology of oil-bearing rocks. "Wildcat" wells were bored by men taking a gamble, and most of these wells produced no oil at all. The oilfields of the early days were a forest of

(3) A stratigraphic trap develops when nonporous sediments are deposited on top of other, broken, strata that may be oil-bearing.

(4) A salt dome occurs when a plug of salt under pressure pushes up the strata. Very often the salt breaks through the strata, and oil may accumulate in the sloping porous layers surrounding the plug.

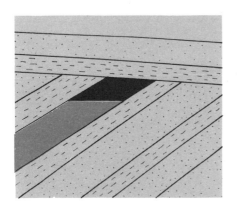

3

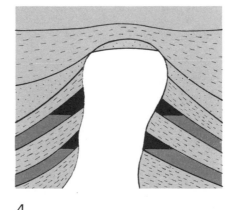

4

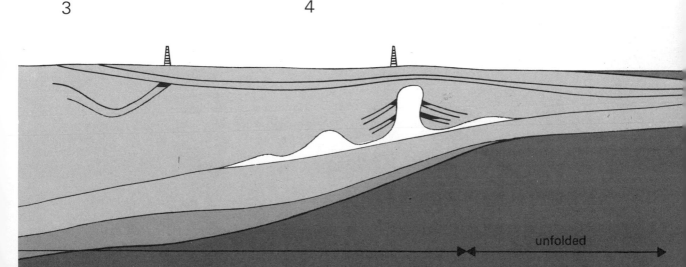

unfolded

hopefully-placed drilling rigs, in contrast with the much fewer, but scientifically located, rigs in modern fields. Prospecting for oil is a very different proposition from mapping the extent of coal seams. Oil usually occurs in isolated individual pockets, while a coal seam may run for many miles. The services of highly skilled geologists and geophysicists are vital in discovering oil.

The search for oil in an untapped area usually starts with an aerial and ground reconnaissance. This results in photographs and maps of the detailed shape of the land. From these, geologists are able to produce conjectural drawings showing how the rock layers may lie beneath the surface. From such drawings they can judge whether or not the layers are likely to include oil traps.

Such preliminary surveys are usually supported by geophysical measurements. One such method consists of careful measurement of the tiny differences in the force of gravity over the area. These differences are ex-extremely small—only a few millionth parts of the force of gravity at sea level—and very delicate instruments are therefore required. The principle behind this method is based on the formation of a dome, as previously described. The denser rocks in the lower part of the earth's crust are brought nearer to the surface. Thus they exert a slightly greater gravitational attraction than the

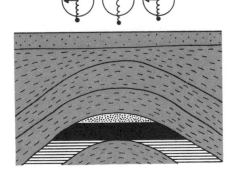

Looking for oil. Ground reconnaissance (top) sorts out those areas where oil may be buried. One instrument used is the gravimeter (left), which can measure tiny differences in gravity. Diagram above shows how such variations may indicate presence of oil.

lighter rocks nearby. Sometimes, however, the domes are produced by a large column of salt, which may be thousands of feet thick. These salt domes produce a slightly smaller force of gravity than the heavier surrounding rocks. Thus, the geophysicists may be looking for a gravitational force slightly greater *or* slightly smaller than the local average.

Seismic soundings are another survey method. This consists of producing artificial earthquake waves by firing a high explosive charge beneath the surface. The waves are reflected at different speeds and different directions according to the density and angle of inclination of the underlying layers. The system of operation is to arrange a number of pick-up points along the surface at known distances from the point at which the explosion is detonated. Instruments at these pick-up points record the times at which the waves return to the surface after being reflected by the rock layers, and convey this information electrically to a recording truck. Usually several shots are fired from different positions while the pick-up points remain fixed. The recordings from the pick-up points give a good idea of the depths and inclination of the reflecting layers.

The final result of these surveys is the drilling of a test bore hole. An important part of this work is the exami-

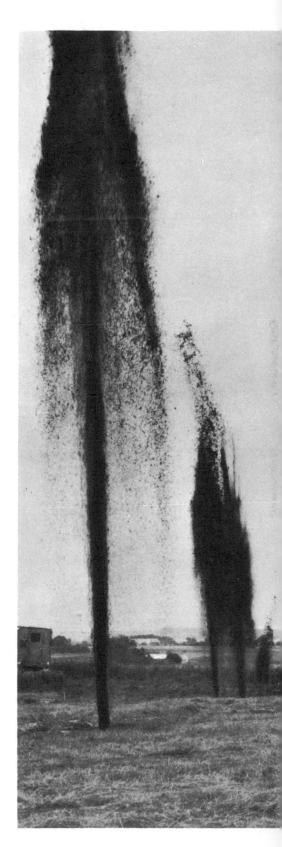

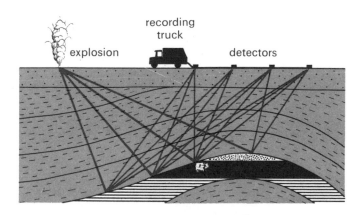

Diagram shows how an explosion, detected at various points, can indicate arrangement of rock strata beneath the surface. Often a number of explosions are fired simultaneously (right). The reflected shock waves are recorded on long sheets of paper (above).

An oil well is drilled with lengths of steel pipes, called the "drill string." At the lower end of the string is the cutting tool (the "bit" —like the one below left); at the upper end is a square pipe called the "kelly." The drill string is suspended in the derrick and can be raised or lowered by means of the drilling line. The string is turned by a rotary table with a square hole in it through which the kelly passes. The table is turned by the draw-work engines. As drilling proceeds, the whole string is slowly lowered. The string is hollow; liquid mud is forced down it, out through holes in the bit (see diagram below right), and then upwards outside the string, taking the cuttings with it. When the top of the kelly is almost down to the rotary table, drilling ceases. The mud flow is stopped, the kelly unscrewed, and a new 30-foot length of pipe is added to the top of the string. The kelly is then put back and drilling is resumed. When the bit is worn out and has to be changed, the whole drill string is removed from the hole. The pipes are stacked inside the derrick in 90-foot lengths, and when the bit has been replaced, the string is reassembled. The hydraulic blowout preventer guards against sudden explosions if the drill hits fluids under high pressure. Well-depths of 2,000 to 10,000 feet are common. The present record (1958) is 25,340 feet.

Opposite page: Top picture shows a typical scene of 50 years ago as competing companies frantically drilled for oil in Signal Hill, California. Lower picture shows a present-day oilfield in New Jersey. All the derricks are owned by one company.

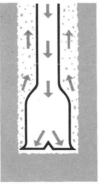

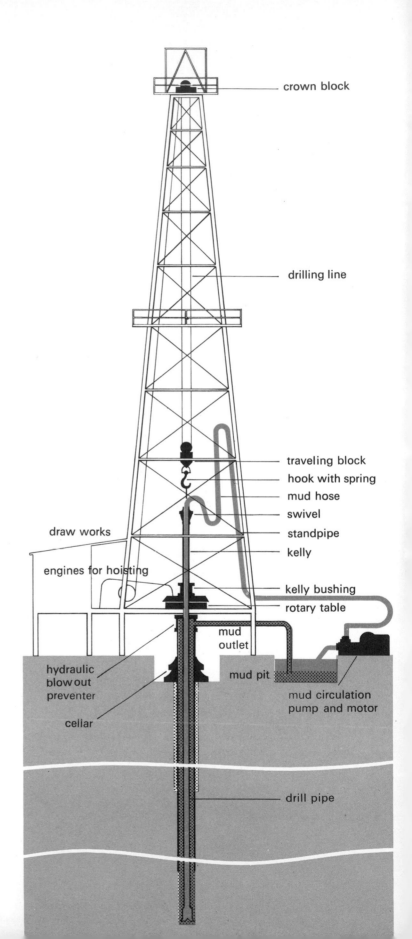

crown block

drilling line

traveling block
hook with spring
mud hose
swivel
standpipe
kelly

draw works

engines for hoisting

kelly bushing
rotary table

mud outlet

hydraulic blow out preventer

mud pit

cellar

mud circulation pump and motor

drill pipe

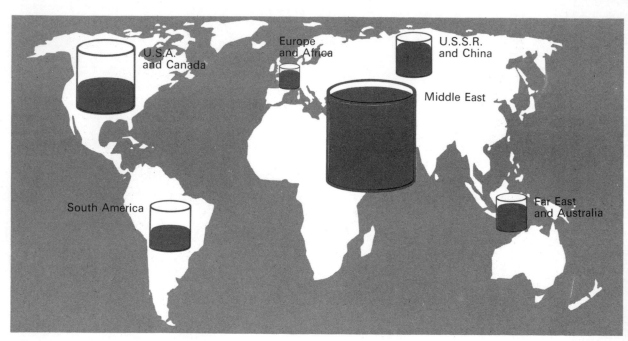

U.S.A. and Canada

Europe and Africa

U.S.S.R. and China

Middle East

South America

Far East and Australia

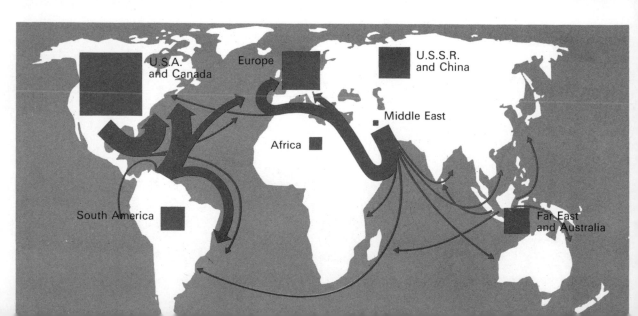

U.S.A. and Canada

Europe

U.S.S.R. and China

Middle East

Africa

South America

Far East and Australia

nation of the rock removed by the drill from various depths. This will either confirm or disprove the geological surmises that have previously been made. If oil is finally struck, the well is put into production and other drillings are made to develop the oilfield. But it often happens that no oil is found. Then further drillings may be made in the area. The more precise information about the rock layers obtained from the original boring often helps in the selection of alternative sites.

There are two main oil-producing areas in the world. One is in the United States and the Caribbean area. The other is in the Middle East, including the southern part of the Soviet Union. Most of the crude oil produced in the Middle East must be conveyed to the more densely populated areas of the world, and so a considerable transportation problem is involved. The oil is usually shipped to the oil-consuming countries by tankers.

Unlike coal from the mine, the petroleum that siphons up from the oil well has to go through a number of processes before it can be used industrially. This is because petroleum is a mixture of a whole range of hydrocarbons. Petroleum must first pass through a refinery where the various grades of oil are separated by *fractional distillation*. In principle, this process consists of boiling the petroleum and passing the vapor through a cooling tower. The temperature in the tower is regulated, being hottest at the bottom and coolest at the top. This causes the fraction, or kind of oil, with the highest boiling point to condense first. Those with lower boiling points condense later—that is, higher up the tower. Each fraction is tapped off into side channels and stored separately.

The lightest liquid fraction is gasoline, which is a very volatile liquid suitable for use in automobile engines. The next lightest fraction consists of white spirit and solvents, which are used in paint manufacture and dry cleaning. Then comes kerosene, for a familiar range of domestic purposes, and also for fuel for jet engines. Gas oil, the next fraction, is a less-volatile, yellowish liquid, used as fuel for diesel engines and for domestic central-heating plants. There is also a heavier, even less volatile form of diesel oil used mainly in large, slow-speed marine engines. Finally, the residue, known as furnace oil, is a very dark, viscous liquid, used in various industrial processes, for large heating boilers, and for marine and power-station boilers.

The proportions of these various fractions vary according to the nature of the petroleum and are not influenced by the distillation process. Sometimes these proportions conflict with the demand for the various products. In the very early days of oil refining, for example, the main demand was for kerosene. The auto-

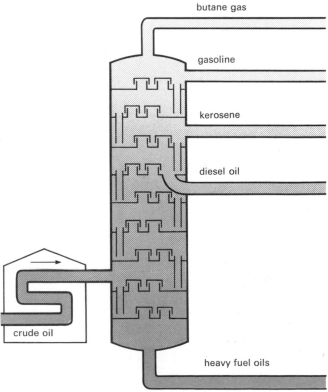

butane gas

gasoline

kerosene

diesel oil

crude oil

heavy fuel oils

Above: The Tabangao oil refinery on Luzon Island in the Philippines. It processes over a million tons of crude oil a year. Diagram right shows how oil is refined. The crude oil is taken in through a heater, and in the tower the hot oil vapors condense at different temperatures. The heavy fractions condense at the bottom, the lighter fractions higher up the tower. Each fraction is drawn off separately.

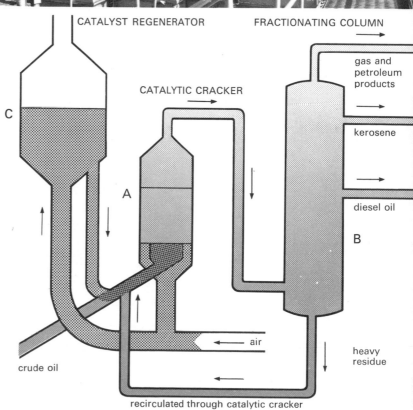

CATALYST REGENERATOR   FRACTIONATING COLUMN

CATALYTIC CRACKER

C

A

B

gas and
petroleum
products

kerosene

diesel oil

air

crude oil

heavy
residue

recirculated through catalytic cracker

Diagram right shows the cracking of heavy oils, using a catalyst—a substance that speeds up a chemical change without itself being consumed. With the aid of the catalyst, the heavy oil is cracked in a pressure vessel (A) and fractionated at B. At C the catalyst is cleaned, ready for re-use. Photo above shows cracking apparatus at a refinery in Essex, England.

mobile was then in its infancy, and large quantities of
gasoline were thrown away. The pendulum has now
swung the other way, and the demand for gasoline exceeds that for some of the other fractions. This problem
has been overcome by processing some of the less-
marketable heavier fractions through a catalytic cracker.
The term "cracking" very aptly describes this process.
In general terms, the heavier fractions consist of molecules having more atoms than do the lighter fractions.
In the cracking process, these molecules arc broken
down into smaller units, thus producing the more volatile liquids needed for heat engines.

In addition to its use as a fuel and as a source of energy,
oil is now being used as the raw material for the quite
new, but already huge, petrochemical industry. Among
the familiar products of this industry are synthetic fibers
and a whole range of plastics.

Since oil occurs in isolated pockets, and not in continuous seams like coal, it is very difficult to estimate
how much oil is still left in the ground. The oil companies spend large sums annually on exploration, as
they must if they are to remain in business. New wells
are continually being found and brought into production. It is estimated that proved reserves are sufficient

Below: Modern oil refineries, like
this one in Louisiana, work 24
hours a day processing crude oil
into literally hundreds of different
products. Right: Drilling for oil in
the bed of the Persian Gulf.

for about another fifty years at the present rate of consumption. It seems that the prospects for oil are no better, and are probably worse, than those for coal.

Another source of oil, which has so far been largely ignored, is oil shale. This material occurs at or near the surface in various parts of the world, and consists of a limestone rock impregnated with oil. Recovery of the oil is difficult, and the expenses involved in extracting it are high. But as supplies of other fuels diminish, the oil companies will undoubtedly turn to this source. Probably enough oil could be obtained from oil shale to meet our present total energy requirements for about five years.

Natural gas is one of the most important energy sources with which we supplement our diminishing reserves of coal and oil. Natural gas is closely associated with oil, both chemically and in its geological distribution. As we have seen, methane, propane, and butane, three of natural gas's most important constituents, are formed like oil when atoms of carbon combine with atoms of hydrogen. Natural gas is often found in the dome-like layers that harbor oil, although quite often such layers contain gas only. This gas is a very rich fuel compared with the gas produced from coal. Coal gas is made by heating coal with a limited quantity of air. In addition to combustible gases (mainly hydrogen, carbon monoxide, and methane), coal gas contains a high proportion of nitrogen from the air used in the gasifying process. Natural gas contains no nitrogen and is all combustible gas. Thus, a cubic foot of natural gas liberates more heat when it burns than does the same quantity of coal gas.

If the source of natural gas is within reasonable distance of the consumer, a pipeline system can be used, just as for coal gas. Many parts of the United States do get natural gas from sources many hundreds of miles away. Under other circumstances, the only practicable solution is to compress the gas and store and convey it in refrigerated pressure vessels as a liquid. When a control valve at the top of the vessel is opened, the liquid returns to its gaseous state, ready for use. Ships fitted with large pressure tanks now bring natural gas from the Sahara oilfield to supplement the coal-gas supplies of several European countries.

Experts are, necessarily, as uncertain about the total world reserves of natural gas as they are about reserves of oil. New sources are frequently found, and the search continues apace. Recently, for instance, oil companies have discovered new sources of oil and gas in the North Sea. Exactly how long the natural gas reserves will last remains in doubt, but the prospects are not likely to be much better than those for oil.

Map shows principal pipelines for conveying natural gas in Western Europe, and also the route taken by methane carriers supplying the United Kingdom and France from Algeria.

Below: The construction of a French tanker now in service carrying natural gas in liquid form from Algeria to Le Havre. Its capacity is about 25,000 cubic yards; its length 650 feet.

power stations

coke ovens and
gas works

industrial users

house coal

railways
other domestic uses
exports

gasoline

kerosene

diesel oil
and distillates
residual
fuel oils

lubricating oils
other products

Modern technological societies depend upon coal, oil, and gas. The demand for electricity grows enormously year by year. So, therefore, does the demand for the fuels that help to produce it. Petroleum products are the main fuel used in transportation by road vehicles and has largely replaced coal as a fuel in railways and shipping. As we shall see in Section 2, oil is the only practical fuel for aircraft—another greatly expanding market for fuel. Domestic central heating, already well established in North America and parts of Europe, is spreading to other parts of the world as standards of living rise. Coal, oil, gas, and electricity are all used in this application.

Against all this must be set a fact: In many countries, the best coal seams have already been exhausted and the richest oil wells are beginning to run dry. New reserves of both these fuels may still be found in underdeveloped areas of the world. But the general picture remains—an insatiable, ever-growing demand chasing a rapidly diminishing supply. In succeeding chapters, we shall take a look at some alternative sources of energy that may supplement, and eventually replace, our traditional fuels.

Divisions in top diagram compare amounts of coal used by various consumers; the diagram refers to no particular country but gives typical values for Western Europe. The largest proportion of coal—nearly one-third—is used for electricity generation. Lower diagram compares quantities of the various products obtained from crude oil.

Graph shows rate of increase of production of coal, oil, natural gas and hydroelectric power from 1860 to 1960. Note that the soaring output of oil and gas continues unchecked, but that rate of increase of coal production began to waver after 1910, due to increased labor costs and to competition from oil and gas. Compare this with graph on page 39 showing proportions of the different fuels consumed, expressed as percentages of the total.

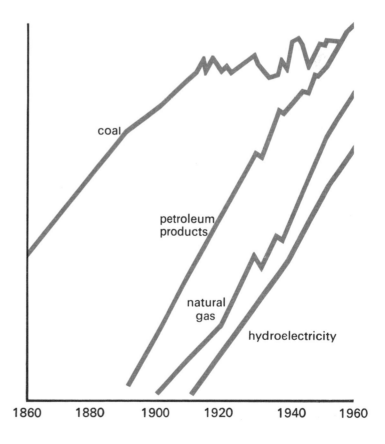

coal

petroleum
products

natural
gas

hydroelectricity

1860   1880   1900   1920   1940   1960

3 Energy from the Earth

In Chapter 1 we discussed energy of motion, or kinetic energy. We were then thinking in terms of wind and water. We saw how water could have potential energy when stored high above sea level in a dam. But as soon as water was released and started to flow downhill under the influence of gravity, its energy was converted into kinetic energy.

Moving water, however, is only one instance of a mass in motion. A moving solid body also has kinetic energy, but this can take two different forms. One is the energy of a body moving in a straight line; the other is the energy that a body has because it is rotating round its own axis. If, for instance, we hold a bicycle wheel up by its axle and spin it by hand, the wheel rotates. In an ideal situation (where there was no friction and no air resistance) it would go on spinning forever. This is in keeping with Newton's first law of motion, which says that a body will either remain at rest or (as in the case of the wheel) move at the same speed unless acted on by a force. The wheel is a mass in motion; therefore, it has kinetic energy.

We are interested in extracting useful power from energy. If the energy is kinetic, we must interfere with it in some way, so as to convert all or part of the energy into some other form. It is obvious that, if we can interfere with a moving body by applying a force to it, we can alter the amount of its energy. If we apply a force that is in the same direction as the body's motion, we shall increase its energy. If we do anything that tends to slow a moving body down, we will get energy from it. At the same time, the energy that the moving body loses will be reflected in its reduced speed.

Now let us see how we can apply these ideas to our own planet. The earth, as we have said, is orbiting around the sun at a speed of 18 miles per second. The earth's mass is $5.9. \times 10^{21}$ tons (5,900 million million million tons). The kinetic energy of the earth's orbital motion is so huge that figures become meaningless. But the earth is also spinning on its own axis. The rotating earth has so much kinetic energy that, if we could find a way of tapping it, we could obtain all our present energy requirements—at a cost, of course, of slowing down its

Waves breaking over rocks are a continual reminder of the great energy involved in the ebb and flow of the tides. The tidal mill above, built on the Rhone River, France, in the 1890's, was one of many devices that attempted to utilize this energy, the water wheel being raised and lowered with the tide. However, most such devices were inefficient, and it is only recently that schemes have been devised that can harness tidal energy with any real success.

rotation. The slowing down, however, would be so slight that a year's deceleration would add no more than 1/500th of a second to the present length of a day. (At present the earth completes one rotation in 23 hours 56 minutes and 4.08 seconds.) But we are unlikely to be able to apply an external force to the earth so as to extract this energy.

However, there is an external force that acts on the earth—the force of universal gravitation. Although we do not know exactly what gravitation is or how it works, we are able to talk about it in terms of what it does. It was Isaac Newton who first set forth the law of gravitation, stating that the force of gravitational attraction between two bodies is directly proportional to the product of their masses and inversely proportional to the square of the distance between their centers. Now, the sun's mass is almost 30 million times that of the moon. But the gravitational force that the sun exerts upon the earth is only about 167 times that of the moon, because the sun is so very much farther away. What is more, because the sun is so far away, its attractive pull acts in a fairly constant and uniform way on all the earth's ocean waters. That is, the *differences* of pull are relatively small. The moon, however, is so close that its mass is constantly changing its position relative to various parts of the earth. Thus the moon becomes the principal agent in exerting an attractive pull on the earth's oceans. We know the results of this force as the tides.

It is easy enough to say that gravitational attraction of the moon pulls the water beneath it to cause a high tide. But this would account for only one of the two high tides that occur in each period of about 25 hours. The moon is opposite each point of the earth only once in that period. Yet at the same time there is a high tide near the point opposite the moon, there is also high tide at the point on the exact opposite side of the earth. To explain this requires a fuller understanding of what causes tides.

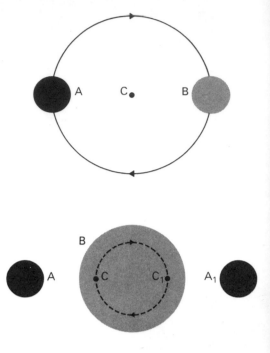

Top: If two bodies of equal mass (A and B) rotate about each other, their center of mass (the point around which they rotate—C) is midway between them. Lower: If one body is much larger than the other, the center of mass will be inside the larger body (C when the smaller body is at A; C_1 when it is at A_1).

Below: How the tides are raised on the earth. The direct gravitational attraction of the moon pulls up the water on that side of the earth nearest to the moon (at A). The high tide at B, on the opposite side of the earth, is caused by centrifugal force, as the moon and the earth swing around each other about point C.

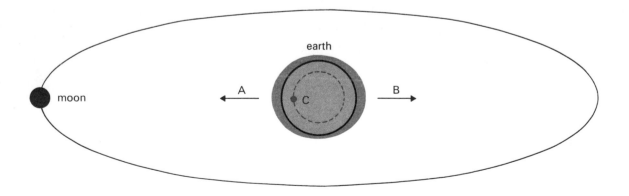

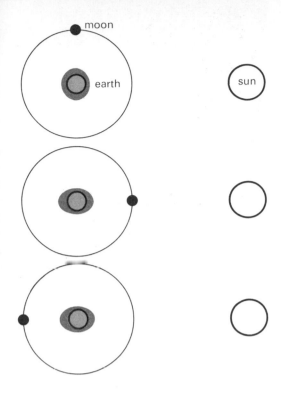

When the moon and sun are at right angles to each other (top diagram), the moon's gravitational attraction is somewhat offset by the sun's gravitational pull, and tidal range is thus diminished; these are the *neap* tides. Center: When the sun and moon are on the same side of the earth, they pull together and *spring* tides are experienced.
Lower diagram: Spring tides also occur when the sun and moon are on opposite sides of the earth.

A tidal range of, let us say, 5 feet at the 30-mile wide mouth of an estuary builds up as the estuary narrows. It would be 15 feet where the estuary is 10 miles wide, and 75 feet at 2 miles wide. Friction, however, reduces these figures considerably.

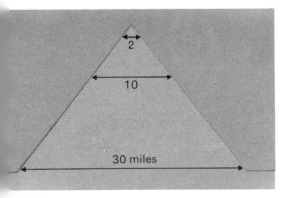

We speak of the moon orbiting around the earth. But the fact is that the moon does not orbit around the earth's center. Rather, the moon and the earth together swing around their common *center of mass* about every 29 days. This center of mass can be found by imagining the earth and the moon to be connected by a weightless rod and then calculating the point at which earth and moon would balance each other. The mass of the earth is about 80 times that of the moon's. Thus, the point of balance will not be in the middle of the rod but will be nearer the earth's center. The point is actually inside the earth—about 1,000 miles from the earth's surface. The whole earth is also spinning around on its own axis. All this while, the point of the common center of mass is changing its position, although it remains about 1,000 miles beneath the surface. It is always located in that part of the earth that is closest to the moon and the moon's gravitational force is greatest at this point. The ocean water thus rides in a "hump" known as high tide.

Now, the part of the ocean on the exact opposite side of this "hump" is the point farthest from the moon. The attraction of the moon, in other words, is least, because —as we saw with Newton's law—gravitational force declines with distance. This opposite point is also farther from the center of mass around which the earth and moon are revolving every 29 days. Thus, this point is going farther and faster than other parts of the earth and it undergoes the greatest centrifugal force. Since the centrifugal force here exceeds the gravitational attraction of the moon, the water also rises in a "hump" on this side of the earth.

We can now explain why each part of the earth experiences two high tides about every 25 hours. As the earth spins, its surface travels around, carrying the ocean waters with it. But the two tidal "humps" stay at fixed points opposite the moon. So it is that the tides surge up and down the shores of land that are carried underneath them. Friction, inertia, and other effects of rotation delay those surgings so that the high tide is not exactly under the moon—there may be a lag of up to six hours, in fact.

The sun's gravitational pull is also acting on the earth to produce tides. However, the sun's effect on the tides is only about one-half that of the moon's because the great distance (between the sun and the earth) means that there is a smaller *difference* in the sun's pulling force during the revolutions of the earth. About twice a month, the sun and the moon are in alignment—that is, they are either on the same side or exactly opposite each other in relation to the earth. Thus, their effects reinforce each other and the tides coincide. So it is that about every two weeks we experience the larger tides known as *spring tides*. When the moon and sun are at right angles to each other—in relation to the earth—the two forces are working against each other. Then we have the smaller tides known as *neap tides*.

The alternate rise and fall of water produces long slow waves that spread out in all directions from the equator. But these tidal bulges produce no noticeable effect in the middle of the ocean. Even at islands in mid-ocean, the spring tides rise only about 4 feet, while neap tides are about 2 feet. But at shores where there are bays and river mouths, the tides may pile up to considerable heights.

When these waves run into a funnel-shaped arm of the sea, such as the English Channel, the result is a more extreme rise and fall of tide. Even higher tides occur when these same waves run up into a narrowing channel. On the other hand, seas that are virtually land-locked, such as the Mediterranean and the Baltic, experience little or no tide.

Anyone who has watched the rise and fall of the tide must have been impressed by the energy involved in this phenomenon. Vast quantities of water are raised quite considerable heights (in Canada's Bay of Fundy up to 52 feet, and about 2 feet less in Britain's Bristol Channel) only to be released again six hours later. The source of this energy is the kinetic energy of rotation of the earth. The effect of the tides is to slow down the speed of rotation of the earth, lengthening the day by about one second every thousand years.

The possibility of using tidal energy for power production has fascinated engineers for centuries. Here and there can be found relics of ancient tide-mills. Interest in this source of energy has been revived in recent years, and there is one full-scale development to be described in Chapter 6. The problems of harnessing tidal energy are, however, formidable, because of the very nature of this form of energy.

Tidal energy differs from the energy of water flowing along a riverbed because tidal flow is intermittent. The

Above: Work in progress on the Rance tidal power project (see map below left), which will utilize the tides of up to 30 feet to drive turbines. The power station is expected to produce 540 million kilowatt hours per year.

Map below left shows tidal ranges (in feet) near Rance and throughout the English Channel. Below: Lines plot rise and fall of tide for one location on three different (not consecutive) days. Note that tidal range (vertical scale) and time of peaks vary.

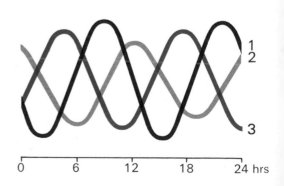

The Passamaquoddy tidal project, at the eastern boundary between Canada and the United States, plans to make use of two pools. By filling the high pool at high tide and emptying the low pool at low tide, a maximum water-level difference would be created. Release of the high-pool water could then be held to coincide with peak power demand. On the diagram, L indicates locks, FG the filling gates, and EG the emptying gates.

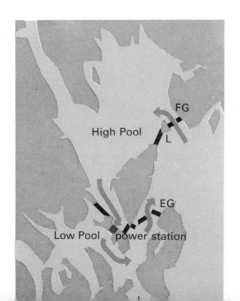

incoming flood tide flows for about six and one-half hours, followed by the same duration of the outgoing ebb tide. Conversion of this energy to useful power can be obtained during only part of these time intervals. Machinery would work discontinuously, and power output is thus spasmodic. Also, the times of high and low water occur 50 minutes later every day. It is very seldom that the period of maximum power production will coincide with the period of greatest public demand.

Another difficulty is that the available difference in water level is usually small. This difference in elevation between two bodies of water—as in high and low tides—is called *head*. There are only a few places in the world where the range of tide is as much as 50 feet. Even this is a much lower value than is found in most river hydro-electric projects. Further, the available head will vary from day to day over a two-week period, as the tide changes from springs to neaps and back again. Where the spring tide is 50 feet, the neap tide will not be much more than 35 feet. The power output will therefore also vary in proportion.

Ways have been suggested of overcoming some of these problems. But it does seem certain that such projects can only be economic in the few places where the tidal range is high and where geographical conditions

are suitable. Tidal power is therefore unlikely to make a vital contribution to our dwindling energy resources.

The earth possesses another store of energy of which some use is already being made. This is the heat that flows from the earth's interior to the surface.

It is known from measurements made in mines that the temperature of the earth increases by 16°F. for every 1,000 feet of depth. Until fairly recently, this was taken to imply that the temperature of the central core was of the order of 5,000°F. A more recent and reasonable theory is that the earth's heat comes from the decay of radioactive material about 20 miles deep. (This "decay" is, of course, a form of atomic *fission*, or a breaking down of the nucleus.) Earlier theories assumed that the earth's store of heat was the remains of the heat present when the earth was formed by condensation of the extremely hot primeval gases. If this were the true explanation, all this heat would long since have been radiated to outer space, and the center of the earth would be as cold as the surface. The radioactive explanation seems more acceptable, since this involves a continuous production of heat.

The total amount of energy coming to the surface of the earth is surprisingly large. If this energy could all be used, it would be sufficient for about five times our present energy requirements. Unfortunately the energy

The sole source of energy for the power stations at Larderello in northwest Italy is steam, which gushes from specially-drilled wells and is used to drive turbogenerators. The plants produce enough power to operate most of Italy's railway system.

Below: Natural steam contains many impurities; therefore, the steam is passed through a heat-exchanger, which boils clean water to drive the turbines.

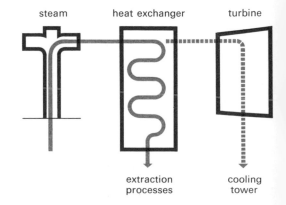

steam   heat exchanger   turbine

extraction processes   cooling tower

Hot-water springs near Reykjavik, Iceland, discharge low-pressure steam that has been utilized to provide the town with central heating.

The power stations at Wairakei, in the North Island of New Zealand, utilize the energy of steam geysers that have long been tourist attractions. At present the project is producing 192,000 kilowatts (750,000 horsepower).

per unit surface area is low, averaging about half-a-horsepower per acre. Obviously the large-scale recovery of energy of such low intensity is out of the question.

There are, however, certain regions of the earth where the heat flow is much increased. These are the volcanic areas. In such places, hot springs, geysers, and even jets of steam spouting from the earth may be found. Some of these natural phenomena have been put to work. The largest and most successful of such projects is the Larderello steam wells, about 50 miles from Florence, Italy. This site has been developed over the last sixty years, first by using steam that emerged naturally from the earth, and later by boring wells to 2,000 feet deep. A large continuous flow of steam is now being drawn off and is used for the generation of electricity.

There are other places in the world where similar phenomena exist. One of the most famous of these is Wairakei in a region of New Zealand, that has hot water lakes surrounded by snow-covered mountains. Here, there is a natural steam vent from which issues a continuous supply of steam. New Zealand is fortunate in having some large rivers from which most of its power requirements are supplied. But as the demand for power grows, even more attention may well be given to this natural source of energy.

The only other large-scale utilization of the earth's heat is to be found in Iceland. This island is completely without coal or oil, and the climate is extremely cold. Fortunately for the inhabitants of the capital, Reykjavik, an area about ten miles from the city has been found where there is an abundant supply of natural hot water. This hot water has been piped to the city and is sufficient to provide central heating for every building in it. This must be regarded as a fair reward for the 30,000 people who live in that cold climate for they would otherwise have to pay for expensively imported fuel. The Icelandic thermal springs do not, however, produce steam at a temperature that makes it worth while for conversion into power.

These uses of the earth's heat are interesting and provide cheap power for those countries fortunate enough to possess them. They can, however, add very little to the world's total sum of energy resources. Someday, however—although it is unlikely—someone may discover a way of deliberately tapping the earth's heat.

We have just said that the earth's heat is probably produced by the gradual decay of radioactive material in the earth's crust. In using this energy, we are taking advantage of a natural and uncontrollable source of atomic energy. But use of atomic energy in a controlled way is being rapidly developed, and we shall now consider this in more detail.

4   Energy from the Atom

In our survey of natural sources of energy, we have mentioned two kinds of atomic energy—fusion in the sun and fission in the earth's crust. Any explanation of how the sun or the earth generates heat by fusion or fission would have been impossible 60 or so years ago. But so much has been discovered about the world of physics in the twentieth century that phenomena that were once mysteries are now easily explained. Much more important, the new knowledge has come, it seems, just in time. Modern physics opens up a vista of energy supply for the future that should relieve us of anxiety for many centuries to come.

Today the fact that there is energy to be had from within atoms—either as explosive weapons or as sources of useful power—is part of our daily life. What has happened since the end of the nineteenth century is so startling that it dwarfs almost any previous leap forward in scientific knowledge. The discovery of nuclear energy was not the work of one brilliant man. It was the result of a series of discoveries, each of which led to further research. Let us look first at the situation as it was toward the end of the last century.

Scientists had by then produced what appeared to be a satisfying and almost complete framework of knowledge. The motion of the planets could be explained, and even their future movements predicted, by Newtonian mechanics. Indeed, these calculations had reached such perfection that the existence and position of the planet Pluto was predicted before it had actually been observed through a telescope. What is more, the science of mechanics could also be applied to terrestrial objects, which obeyed the same laws as the stars and the planets.

At the other end of the scale of size, most of the elements had been identified, and their behavior in combining with others into compounds had been investigated. The concept of atomic weight—the ratio of the weight of any atom to the weight of an atom of a particular element—was introduced by John Dalton in the first decade of the nineteenth century. By the end of the nineteenth century, the atomic weights of all then-

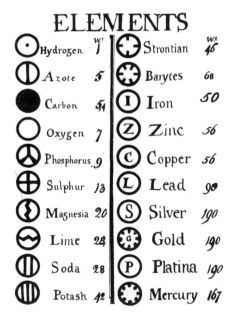

Symbols for atoms, and the first list of atomic weights, drawn up in 1808-1810 by the English scientist John Dalton. His ideas marked the beginning of modern atomic theory. Right: A "swimming pool" research reactor belonging to the Danish Atomic Energy Commission.

known elements had been determined. But the smallest particle of matter was still believed to be the atom (Greek *atmos* = uncut, indivisible), a belief that could be traced back more than two thousand years.

There were two closely related branches of physics that had made great strides in the nineteenth century. These were electricity and magnetism, both intimately connected with energy and power. Electricity and magnetism were invisible forms of energy; they could not be touched; and, like gravity (p. 28), they could be described only in terms of their effects. The various kinds of electric and magnetic effects were measured and labeled with the names of the pioneers in this branch of science. The achievements in this field were useful in opening up new ways of converting energy into power (p. 157). Apart from this, the research proved to be vital in two distinct ways to the exploration of the atom. One was that the first slender clue to atomic structure came quite unexpectedly from a purely electrical experiment. The other was that electrical energy in various forms was found to be the ideal weapon with which to assault the hitherto impregnable basic particle, the atom. In fact, the atomic age is the offspring of electricity.

The story begins with an experiment that, on the surface, seemed to have no possible relation to atomic structure. In 1887 William Crookes was investigating the behavior of electricity in air at low pressure. His apparatus was a long glass tube connected to a vacuum pump, with two electrodes, or metallic contacts, sealed into the glass. The electrodes were connected to a source of high electrical voltage. As the vacuum pump lowered the pressure, a green glow developed inside the tube, and a current started to flow. And—most important for our story—a small vane mounted on a pivot inside the tube was deflected. This indicated that it had been struck by invisible particles traveling from the negative electrode (or cathode) toward the positive (or anode) electrode.

The particles that deflected the pivoted vane were called *cathode rays*, and their mass was found to be about 1/1800th of that of a hydrogen atom. This was a shattering discovery. After all, hydrogen was the lightest of all elements. Its atom was naturally considered to be the smallest particle of matter that could possibly exist. Now here was a "sub-atomic" particle, not just a little lighter than the smallest atom, but very much lighter. With one simple experiment, Crookes had upset the beliefs of centuries.

The individual particles of a cathode ray discharge were called *electrons*. Furthermore, the electrical charge of an electron was measured and found to be always the same. It thus became plain that the strength of an electrical charge depends on the number of electrons pres-

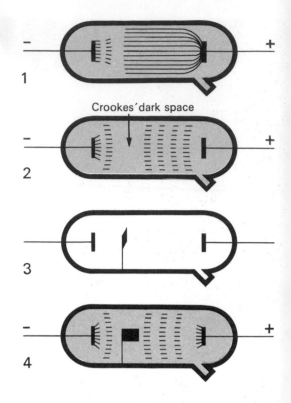

Crookes' experiment in 1887 involved imposing a high voltage on gases in a glass tube. When the tube was full of air, no current flowed. But as air was extracted from the tube, the gas became ionized and carried a current (1). As pressure was further reduced, the glow in the region of the cathode faded away, leaving a "Crookes' dark space" (2). Crookes then showed that a small vane pivoted in this space (3) rotated as though struck by particles (4) leaving the cathode. Particles were later shown to exist and to be about 1/1,800th the size of hydrogen atoms.

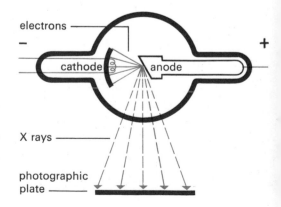

If a stream of electrons passes at high speed from the cathode to the anode within a vacuum tube, most of their energy is converted into heat, but a fraction is emitted as X rays.

ent. It also became evident that an electric current flowing through a conductor—such as air—was, in fact, a stream of electrons. Whatever gas was used in Crookes tube experiment, the same electrons were to be found. The inescapable conclusion was that all matter contains negatively charged sub-atomic particles.

The Crookes tube is now an almost forgotten museum piece. But its grandchild is with us today in the form of the cathode-ray device we call a television tube. The discovery of electrons, however, was not the only benefit that came from the Crookes tube. Under certain conditions, the stream of electrons striking the wall of the tube produced an emission of invisible rays that had extraordinary powers of penetration. These X rays, as they were called, were discovered by Wilhelm Roentgen working in Würzburg, Germany, in 1895. X rays were soon found to have a much shorter wave length than visible light. The importance of X rays for examining objects that are opaque to visible light rays is a story in itself. But what made their discovery important at this time was that, when X rays were found in other situations, they were easily identified and not to be confused with other sorts of radiation.

The next episode comes with the discovery by a French physicist, Henri Becquerel. He found that certain ores of uranium also gave off radiations that penetrated solid matter. Further researches in France, notably by Pierre and Marie Curie, resulted in the isolation of a much more radioactive substance, which was called *radium*. The situation now became a little more complicated than it had been with the X-ray tube. These radioactive substances were emitting several kinds of radiations at the same time. These were named *alpha*, *beta*, and *gamma* rays, after the first three letters of the Greek alphabet. To begin with, all that was known was that the radium was emitting rays that were far more penetrating than X rays. But Ernest Rutherford, in England, sorted the rays out. The gamma rays turned out to be extremely short radiation waves, shorter even than X rays. Like all other electromagnetic waves, they were unaffected when they were passed through a magnetic field.

But the other (alpha and beta) rays turned out not to be radiation waves at all. They were streams of particles that *were* affected by a magnetic field. The alpha rays were slightly deflected in one direction, and the beta rays much more markedly in the opposite direction. This difference was fortunate, because it made it much easier to separate and identify them. But what was even more important was that the deflection of these "rays" by a magnetic field was evidence that they too were sub-atomic particles. The alpha rays were first thought to be

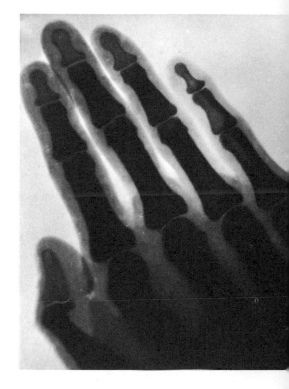

An early X-ray photograph (1896). X rays pass through flesh but are stopped by denser bones. Careless exposure to X-ray radiation can be dangerous. Photographs like the one above were sometimes obtained only at the expense of burns that were persistent and healed with difficulty.

Using natural radioactivity to take a photograph. Pitchblende, which contains radium, is placed over a metal key resting on a photographic plate wrapped in black paper. When the plate is developed (lower picture), a picture of the key appears.

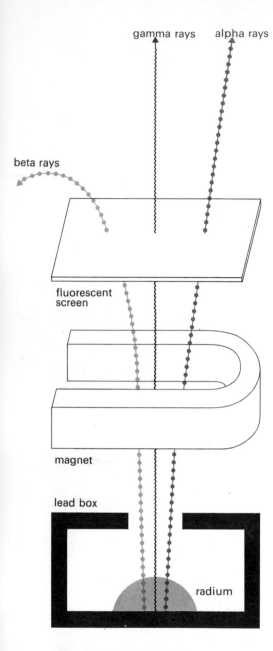

gamma rays   alpha rays

beta rays

fluorescent screen

magnet

lead box

radium

When Rutherford passed the radiations from radium through a magnetic field, he found that they split up into three beams. Alpha particles were deflected slightly; beta rays were deflected in the opposite direction and to a much greater extent; gamma rays were not deflected at all.

positively charged hydrogen or helium atoms. Although this idea had to be revised later, the very fact of their existence was the first indication that one element might emerge from another. The old atomic theory, in other words, was dealt another blow. Later it was found that alpha rays were streams of helium atoms without their electrons. The beta rays turned out to be the familiar cathode rays, or streams of electrons. As beta rays, however, the electrons travel very much faster than those in the Crookes tube.

Rutherford had been much impressed by the penetrating power of alpha particles, (no longer called "rays"). In the true spirit of scientific curiosity—"let us see what happens if we do such and such"—he aimed a stream of these particles at a piece of thin metal foil. Two things happened, and both of them gave valuable information. One was that those alpha particles that passed through the foil were slightly deflected from their original straight-line path. This could mean only that they were being influenced by some other positively charged body. Furthermore, so many particles pierced the foil that Rutherford was forced to one conclusion. What appeared to the eye as a sheet of solid metal was, in fact, made up of very small positively charged cores surrounded by a great deal of empty space. At this point, in 1908, the word *nucleus* moved into the vocabulary of physics. Rutherford adopted "nucleus" (plural, nuclei) as a label for the central core of the atom.

The second thing revealed was that some of the alpha particles must have been traveling directly towards a nucleus. These particles were promptly returned along their original path by a very large repulsive force. By comparing the number that were bounced back with the number that penetrated, Rutherford calculated that a bounced particle must have approached the nucleus to within one million-millionth of a centimeter. That distance was one ten-thousandth of the accepted diameter of the atom. Here was confirmation that the atom consisted almost entirely of a massive, positively charged nucleus. Around the nucleus orbited very light, negatively charged electrons, present in such numbers as to make their total charge equal to that of the nucleus. The limits of the electrons' orbits were considered to define the diameter of the atom, but most of the space inside was empty. It is tempting to think of an atom as being like the solar system, with the sun as the nucleus and the planets as the electrons. But there is one great difference between the two systems. In our solar system, the planets orbit in a predictable path that is more or less in one plane, or dimension. But in the atom, the electrons must be imagined to be orbiting in all three dimensions simultaneously and in no fixed route.

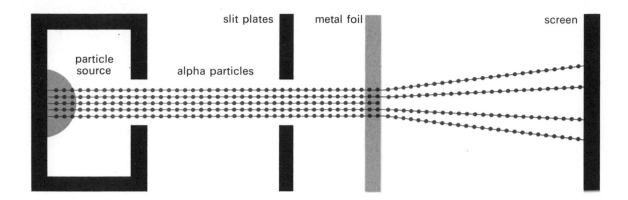

slit plates   metal foil   screen

particle source

alpha particles

Rutherford studied the behavior of alpha particles by directing a stream of them at thin metal foil. He found that most of them passed through and were slightly deflected from their original straight line. But what was surprising was that some particles were repulsed by the foil and returned along their original path.

From the above experiment Rutherford deduced the existence of the nucleus— the central core of atoms. He concluded that the deflections were caused by the alpha particles approaching a positive charge—and the nearer they approached, the greater their deflection. Those particles that met the positively-charged nucleus head-on were turned back along their original path. Thus, the atom appeared to consist of a tiny core containing a positive charge, around which orbited negatively-charged electrons. Most of the atom, in fact, consists of empty space.

By 1911 the structure of the atom had really begun to take shape in men's minds. Basically it was as we have described—a nucleus around which orbited one or more electrons. We now know that the *chemical* properties of an element depend on the number and arrangement of electrons. We also know that an atom's *physical* properties, including almost all the mass, are concentrated in the nucleus. Before we put aside the electrons we must first take a brief look at one more discovery in which they helped to provide evidence.

The atom of the simplest and lightest element, hydrogen, consists of a single electron orbiting around the lightest possible nucleus. Evidently this nucleus must itself be an elementary particle of matter, and we call it a *proton* (Greek *protos* = first). Now, take the next heaviest element, helium. This has two electrons, and therefore the nucleus must carry a positive charge of two.

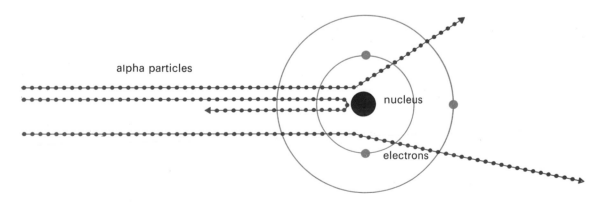

alpha particles

nucleus

electrons

But helium's atomic weight is four. The nucleus must contain two protons, in order to balance the electrons, but that accounts for only half its atomic weight. Physicists were thus forced to assume that there must be two other particles in the helium nucleus. These particles would have the same mass as protons, but carry no electrical charge, either positive or negative. In fact, the particles turned out to be electrically neutral, and they were appropriately named *neutrons* (Latin *neuter* = neither).

Next in the series of elements comes lithium, which has three electrons, and therefore three protons. We find that naturally-occurring lithium actually has an atomic weight of 6.92. According to our own argument, all atomic weights should be multiples of the atomic weight of hydrogen—which is one—and therefore they should be whole numbers. This is no place to go into the details of how this difficulty was resolved. But the conclusion is that, while the number of protons in each element's atom (called the *atomic number*) is always the same, the number of neutrons can vary. A few atoms in natural lithium have three neutrons, making a lithium of atomic weight six and called lithium 6. But most of the remaining lithium atoms (actually, 92 per cent) have four neutrons, making lithium 7. The sum of the atoms of lithiums 6 and 7 makes up the lithium 6.92 that we find in nature.

It is thus possible for an atom of a single element to exist in more than one form. When this happens we call the atoms *isotopes*, (Greek *isos* = "equal," *topos* = "place"—that is, equal place in the table of atomic numbers). Almost all atoms exist as isotopes. Hydrogen, for example, has two other isotopes—deuterium (also known as heavy hydrogen) and tritium. Isotopes play a part in our story for a particular reason. All the isotopes of an element behave the same in chemical reactions, because all isotopes of the same element have the same number of electrons. Therefore isotopes cannot be sorted out from one another by chemical means. The only way in which they can be separated is by taking advantage of their very small differences in atomic weight.

We find that all atoms, except the simplest form of hydrogen, must have a more or less complicated nucleus. If we are to discover its properties, we must attack the nucleus and try to break it down into its component parts. Basically, we can investigate the nucleus only by hitting it hard in the hope that something will happen. It is as if the protons and neutrons of a nucleus were like a solid mass of cannon balls glued tightly together. One way to explore the heap would be to bombard it with other projectiles of similar size, traveling at varying

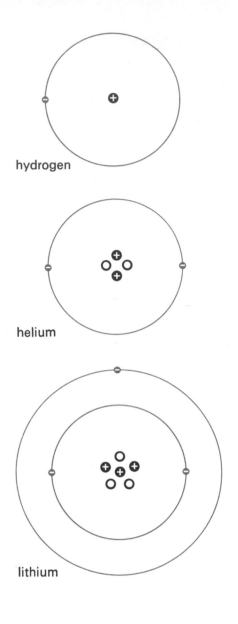

hydrogen

helium

lithium

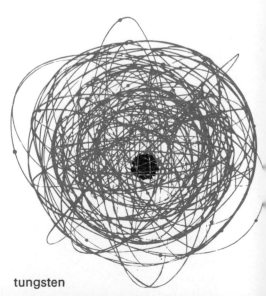

tungsten

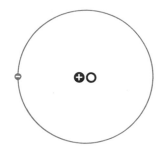

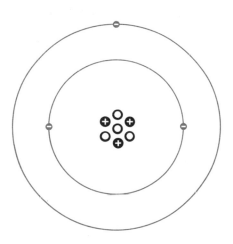

Opposite page above: A hydrogen atom
has a nucleus consisting of one
positively-charged proton; around this
orbits one negatively-charged electron.
An atom of helium has a nucleus of 2
protons and 2 neutrons (uncharged
particles), orbited by 2 electrons. The
lithium atom shown has 3 electrons,
3 protons, and 3 neutrons, but
most lithium atoms have 4 neutrons
(see text). The nucleus of the tungsten
atom (opposite below) includes 74
protons and is surrounded by 74 electrons.
Above: Isotopes are atoms of the same
element having the same atomic number
but different atomic weights. Deuterium
is a hydrogen isotope; its nucleus
contains 1 proton and 1 neutron.
The lithium isotope shown has
4 neutrons.

speeds. We could then judge from the effects of bombardment how much energy was needed to dislodge one ball out of the heap. We could also study the effect of shooting a ball that penetrated the heap without breaking it.

Such nuclear "artillery practice" is popularly known as "atom smashing." It is obvious that the shots fired must be small enough to pass through the almost empty space surrounding each nucleus. They should not be so large, either, as to smash the whole nucleus in such a way that we cannot see what has happened. Yet electrons are far too small and light to make any impact on a nucleus. The only available "bullet" that can be shot at a nucleus is another sub-atomic particle. In effect, scientists are forced to use small nuclei or parts of nuclei in order to explore the nucleus of the atom. The ammunition at physicists' disposal can be summed up as follows:

Proton: the nucleus of a hydrogen atom—positively charged

Deuteron: the nucleus of "heavy hydrogen," an isotope

Alpha particle: the nucleus of a helium atom.

Remember that we are speaking of target practice on nuclei that are far too small to be seen, using projectiles that are even smaller. How, then, can scientists judge the effects of bombardment? The answer is that they can study nuclear particles as they study electricity—by observing their effects. There are several ways of doing this. One is by using the extremely simple but ingenious cloud chamber, invented by C. T. R. Wilson in 1899. This device takes advantage of the fact that a gas saturated with water vapor can easily be made supersaturated by lowering the temperature. This can be done in the cloud chamber by reducing the pressure. When the gas-vapor mixture is in this condition, water will condense around any small particle, particularly if it is electrically charged. Then, a charged sub-atomic particle is made to pass through this cloud mass. It collides with thousands of gas atoms and leaves them electrically charged, or ionized, along its line of flight. Water vapor immediately condenses on the ionized atoms. The path of the particle thus appears as a streak, which can be photographed before it dies away.

This simple device does various things. First, it reveals the path of a charged particle. Second, the length of the path tells us how far such a particle can travel in that particular mixture. Third, the cloud chamber shows clearly if the path is straight or curved, the latter perhaps under the influence of a magnetic field. Finally, if one

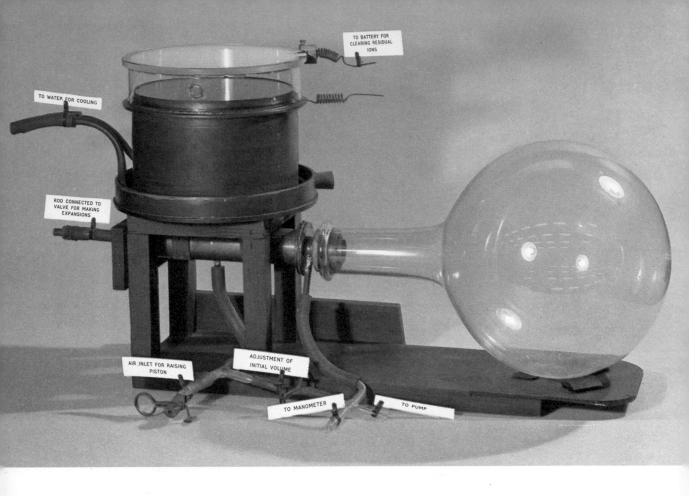

TO BATTERY FOR CLEARING RESIDUAL IONS

TO WATER FOR COOLING

ROD CONNECTED TO VALVE FOR MAKING EXPANSIONS

AIR INLET FOR RAISING PISTON

ADJUSTMENT OF INITIAL VOLUME

TO MANOMETER

TO PUMP

particle collides with another, giving rise to yet a third particle, the collision and the results of the collision are clearly shown.

These effects enabled Rutherford, in 1919, to observe the consequences of exposing water-saturated nitrogen gas to a barrage of alpha particles. He found that some of the alpha particles collided with nitrogen atoms. As a result, there appeared atoms of hydrogen (where none had been before) and also atoms of an isotope of oxygen. This was the first time anyone had "split the atom." In this instance, the alpha particle—that is, a helium nucleus with 2 protons and 2 neutrons—did not merely knock a fragment off the nitrogen nucleus (with its 7 protons and 7 neutrons). The alpha particle was absorbed into the nitrogen nucleus, which then had 9 protons and 9 neutrons. Next, a proton shot out leaving 8 protons and 9 neutrons. The proton picked up a free electron, and became a hydrogen atom. The remaining nucleus formed an atom of oxygen, with 8 protons and 9 neutrons—atomic weight: 17. The atomic weight of ordinary oxygen is 16, and oxygen 17 is an isotope.

This experiment showed that it was possible to change one element into another by "atom smashing." It also led to experiments with other elements, and one of these

The original cloud chamber used by Wilson in his experiments at the turn of the century.

Below: Photograph taken using a cloud chamber. It shows the trails of alpha particles; one particle has met a nitrogen nucleus and the forked path shows the result (see caption opposite). Newly-formed oxygen shoots off in one direction (heavier track) and an ejected proton shoots off in another direction.

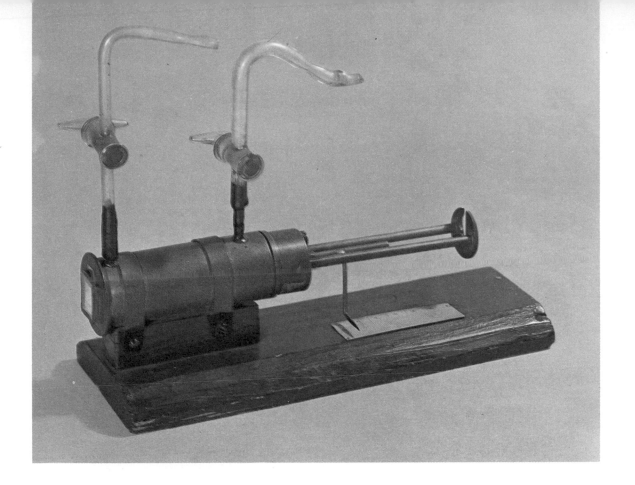

The apparatus used by Rutherford to break up the nuclei of nitrogen atoms. Diagram below shows what happened. An alpha particle—a helium nucleus with 2 protons and 2 neutrons—was absorbed into a nitrogen nucleus, which then had 9 protons and 9 neutrons. A proton shot out, picking up a free electron and becoming a hydrogen atom. The remaining nucleus became an atom of oxygen; its atomic weight was 17 (it had 8 protons and 9 neutrons) and it was an isotope of ordinary oxygen.

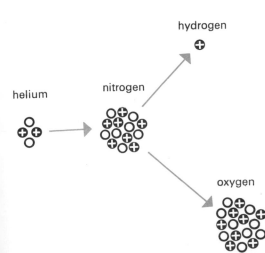

produced a surprising result. When aluminum was bombarded by alpha particles, protons were released. But the energy of the protons (measured by the distance they traveled in the cloud chamber) was *greater* than the energy of the original alpha particle. In other words, matter was being converted into energy. If this experiment could be repeated on a large-enough scale, here was a source of energy that could possibly be turned to practical use.

The importance of this, and many similar experiments, lies in the fact that energy from breaking up the nucleus of an atom could for the first time be produced *artificially*. The emission of energy from natural radioactive substances such as radium was already known. The rate of emission, however, was too slow to be attractive as a source of power.

In these early experiments, the alpha particle ammunition came from radium material. In common with the other two available particles (protons and deuterons), the alpha particle was at a disadvantage because it was positively charged, and so is the nucleus that it is attacking. This means that the attacking particle would naturally be repelled by the nucleus. Therefore, the velocity of the particle must be enormous to overcome the repulsion and to score a direct hit. Radium's alpha particles had just such velocity, but they were emitted at random and only a few reached the target. If only a larger number of particles could be aimed precisely at nuclei, much more might be discovered.

The proton was an obvious choice for the particle to be used in such an advance. It was already known what happens if an electric discharge is passed through hydrogen gas at low pressure. The single electron of each atom is stripped off, leaving a positively-charged nucleus or proton. The next step would be to accelerate these protons to a speed high enough to penetrate the nuclear target. Here is the point in our story where the new electric and magnetic technologies were essential if further progress was to be made.

Two members of Rutherford's research team, John Cockcroft and Ernest Walton, constructed a vacuum discharge tube (illustrated in diagram on this page). The tube consisted of two main parts. One part was a small discharge tube that produced a supply of protons. The other was a large tube carrying highly-charged electrodes arranged in such a way that the protons were accelerated in a vacuum towards the target.

This time the target was lithium. The effects of bombardment were observed on a special fluorescent screen, which would light up if struck by a sub-atomic particle. This experiment—a milestone in nuclear physics—showed two things. First, it showed that artificially-produced protons could split open an atom just as surely as could natural alpha particles. Lithium's nucleus contains 3 protons and 4 neutrons. The bombarding proton entered the nucleus, which then became—but only temporarily—a nucleus of the element boron (with 4 protons and 4 neutrons). This in turn split into two helium nuclei, or alpha particles. The second result was that the alpha particles had just as much energy as those that were naturally shot out of uranium. Thus, the bombardment of lithium resulted in the emission of particles with far *more* energy than the proton that had caused the break-up. The question at once arises: Where did all the energy come from? We can get the answer quite easily by adding up the atomic weights. One lithium atom—weight 7.018—plus one hydrogen atom—weight 1.008—equals a weight of 8.026.

But the final product was two helium nuclei, each of atomic weight 4.004, for a total 8.008. Where is the missing 0.018? It was turned into energy, the energy of action of the alpha particles. This experiment in 1932 was striking proof of a statement that had been made by an obscure clerk in the Patent Office at Berne, Switzerland, back in 1905. This man, Albert Einstein, had produced, in his spare time, a complicated mathematical

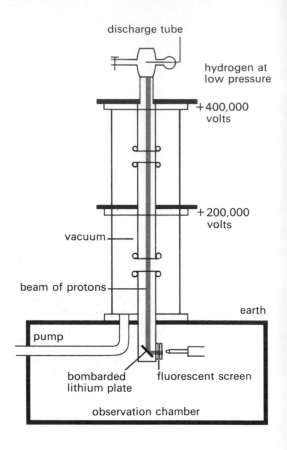

Diagram of Cockcroft and Walton's discharge tube, in which protons were accelerated to high velocity and directed onto a lithium target. Diagram below shows how the proton entered the lithium nucleus, which then became the nucleus of boron (4 protons and 4 neutrons) and at once split into 2 helium nuclei (alpha particles). Between them these nuclei carried 50 times more energy than had been given to the compound nucleus by the proton. The energy came from the disintegration of a tiny quantity of matter.

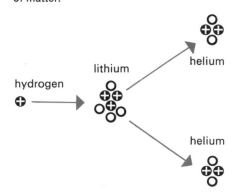

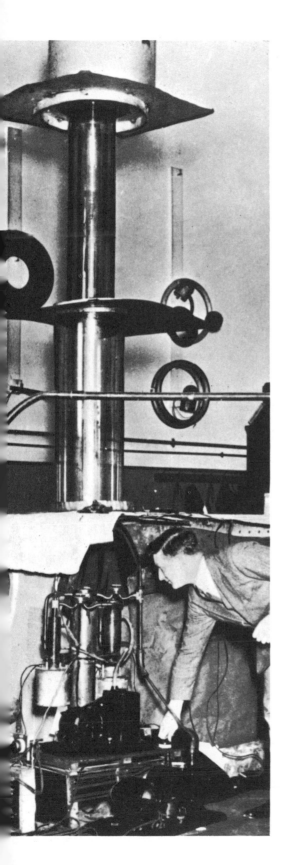

Left: The discharge tube used by
Cockcroft and Walton to bombard
lithium with protons. Below:
Cockcroft in the Cavendish Laboratory,
Cambridge, photographed in 1932.

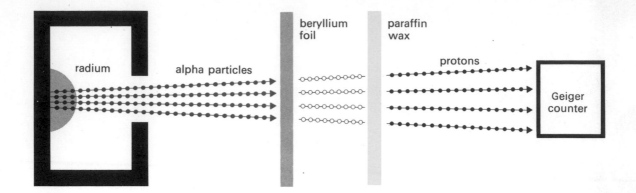

radium · alpha particles · beryllium foil · paraffin wax · protons · Geiger counter

The discovery of the neutron. In 1932, Rutherford and Chadwick bombarded beryllium with alpha particles and found that uncharged particles were emitted. These particles could be deduced only at second hand—from their ability to knock protons out of paraffin wax. Even thick lead placed between the beryllium and the paraffin wax did not significantly reduce the number of protons recorded by the Geiger counter. The only particle that could pass through lead and yet still give so much energy to protons was the neutron. Hitherto such a particle had only been imagined by Rutherford as having the same mass as a proton, but no electrical charge. Diagram below shows what happened: An alpha particle hit a beryllium nucleus, producing an unstable nucleus (of 6 protons and 7 neutrons). Immediately 1 neutron shot out, leaving a nucleus of carbon. Figures give atomic weights; the .006 is the loss of mass that occurred during the process. This mass was turned into energy and given to the emitted neutron, and accounts for the neutron's ability to knock protons from the paraffin wax.

paper. We know this paper's thesis as the Theory of Relativity. Einstein claimed—although not as part of his main thesis, but rather as a sideline—that matter and energy *must* be different manifestations of the same thing. Therefore, matter and energy are interchangeable. Further, Einstein stated that the conversion from mass to energy required that mass be multiplied by the square of the velocity of light. We mentioned a formula, $E = mc^2$, in our discussion of the origins of solar energy (p. 21). Here, in this lithium bombardment experiment 27 years after Einstein's paper, was the experimental proof of his theory. The alpha particles did indeed have the energy equivalent to the mass that had disappeared.

We have been talking about neutrons as a necessary part of most nuclei. But their existence was initially a piece of brilliant deduction by Rutherford. Now, in the same year as the lithium experiment, Rutherford and James Chadwick found a way of proving their existence. They bombarded the element beryllium with alpha particles from the radioactive element polonium and found that *uncharged* particles were being produced. These particles could pass through an inch of lead. But even after doing so, the particles were still powerful enough to knock protons out of a layer of paraffin wax. Note that the particles could not be observed in a cloud chamber or on a fluorescent screen, because they carried no charge. They could be observed only by their secondary effect—that of displacing and setting in motion positively charged protons from the wax. What actually happened in this experiment is worth showing in detail. So much of the rest of the story of nuclear energy depends on the deductions that can be made from its results.

An alpha particle (2 protons, 2 neutrons) smacked into a beryllium nucleus (4 protons, 5 neutrons) to form a nucleus (6 protons, 7 neutrons). This did not hold together—in other words, it was *unstable*. One neutron shot out with considerable energy, leaving a nucleus (6

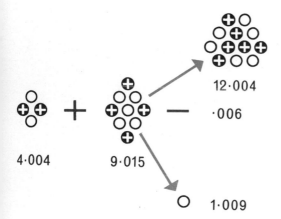

4·004   9·015   12·004   ·006   1·009

protons, 6 neutrons) with the atomic weight of 12—in fact, a carbon atom. If we add up the masses of all the particles, we find a loss of mass of 0.006 (see diagram, p. 88). This loss accounts for the energy with which the protons traveled out of the wax.

This experiment was interesting enough in that it showed that it was possible, by bombardment with alpha particles, to convert beryllium into carbon. But its real importance lies in its proof of the existence of the uncharged particle that we call a neutron. The elusive neutron, which had previously to be assumed, actually exists. Because it carries no charge, it is neither attracted nor repelled by a nucleus. Because it is "neutral," the neutron can penetrate a mass of dense atoms, such as lead, without being deflected by nuclear charges. If it scores a direct hit on a nucleus, it either bounces off and continues its journey, or sticks to the nucleus. If it does the latter, it can upset the "balance of power" in that nucleus and make it unstable. Most nuclei are, as predicted, composed of two particles—protons and neutrons—in almost equal numbers in the lighter elements (except the simplest form of hydrogen, which has only one proton). But the heavier elements have proportionately more neutrons; the commonest form of uranium, for instance, has 92 protons and 146 neutrons. Some elements exist in which the proportion of neutrons to protons results in some form of internal strain. Such elements tend to break up, and we call such unstable elements *radioactive*. But in breaking up, these elements do not simply discard excess neutrons. True, they sometimes do this, as we shall see. But their radioactivity takes other forms as well, such as the emission of gamma and X rays, alpha particles, beta particles, and heat.

It may help to keep our minds clear at this stage by stating that, from now on, we are interested in two main things: neutrons, how they behave and what they can do for us; and the heat energy that comes from the breakdown of nuclei. These are the main goals of our search. However, we shall have to keep track of other phenomena such as emissions of alpha and beta particles, gamma and X rays. Scientists cannot prevent these dangerous and unwanted by-products so they must take precautions against them.

During the early 1930's, the Italian physicist Enrico Fermi was investigating the heaviest element, uranium. He wanted to see if it was possible to make extra neutrons stick to uranium, and so produce a new element heavier than any known on earth. Since the heaviest elements already contain a large number of neutrons, there was a sporting chance that an additional neutron or two might produce a completely new element. While Fermi was busy with this project, he made an extremely

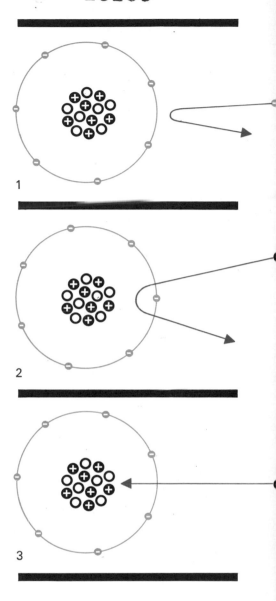

Diagram summarizes behavior of sub-atomic particles. (1) If electrons are directed at an atom, they are repelled by the negative charge of its orbiting electrons. (2) If protons are fired at the atom, they can penetrate the electrons but are repelled by the positive charge of the nucleus. (3) Only a neutron, which has no charge, can penetrate right to the nucleus.

important discovery: Neutrons have a far greater chance of being captured by a nucleus if their original velocity is *reduced*. Neutrons do not need to have the high velocity that will overcome the repulsion of a positively charged nucleus. In fact, neutrons tend to score more hits when traveling much more slowly than the high energy neutrons emitted in the beryllium bombardment experiment (which we have just described).

The question then arose: What is the best way of slowing down neutrons? Fermi knew that there were nuclei of certain elements whose atomic weights are even numbers (that is, their nuclear make-up consists of equal numbers of protons and neutrons). Such nuclei have the power of bouncing neutrons off without absorbing them. But the effect of the bounce is to slow, or decelerate the neutrons. These elements are hydrogen, helium, carbon, and oxygen. Not only were they effective by themselves, but compounds made up of these elements were also useful as decelerators. Fermi found that the rate of capture of slowed-down neutrons could be increased as much as a thousandfold. This discovery was immensely helpful to Fermi in his immediate attempt to make what he called a *transuranic* element— that is, an element with an atomic number greater than that of uranium. It was to be even more important later, and we shall come across these slowing-down compounds again under a new name of *moderators* (p. 95).

Fermi's search for a heavier element was successful. By grafting a neutron on to the nucleus of uranium 238 he produced a new element, plutonium 239. But at the same time, he also found that uranium—when bombarded by neutrons—disintegrated into much lighter elements. These elements seemed to have the same properties as barium (with an atomic weight of about 138) and strontium (with an atomic weight of about 88). Here was something totally unexpected. It had been known for some time that a naturally radioactive element such as radium (atomic weight: 226) very slowly decomposed into lead (atomic weight: 207), a relatively small change in atomic weight. But for an atom of uranium to break instantaneously into two much smaller elements—this was something new.

It was seven years before the mystery of Fermi's contradictory results was finally cleared up. Again the story switches to another country, this time to Germany. There Otto Hahn and Fritz Strassmann in 1939 proved that one of the products of disintegration of uranium was, in fact, barium. What had confused the issue was that Fermi's experiments had been done on *natural* uranium. This material is itself a *mixture* of isotopes. Of the raw material, 99.27 per cent was uranium 238; nearly 0.7 per cent was uranium 235; and there was a tiny per-

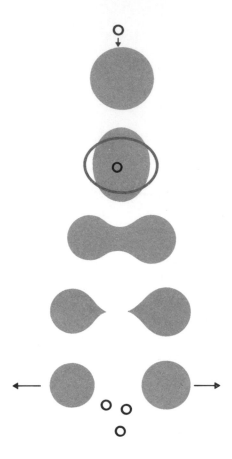

Nuclear fission. A neutron enters a uranium nucleus, and the compound nucleus splits into two roughly equal fragments. Two or three neutrons are also emitted.

Natural uranium is a mixture of two isotopes, U-235 and U-238, the ratio being about one U-235 atom to every 140 U-238 atoms. Only U-235 is fissionable, for U-238 absorbs neutrons without producing fission. Since there is so much U-238, it will absorb the neutrons emitted from an atom of U-235 before they meet other atoms of U-235.

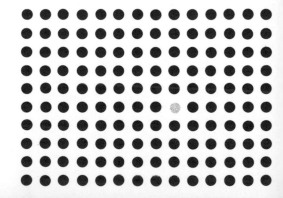

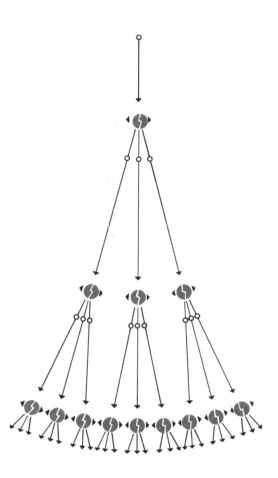

In natural uranium, the neutrons emitted by the fissions of U-235 are captured by U-238 atoms. If, however, there were no U-238 atoms, each of the emitted neutrons might hit a U-235 atom, produce fission, and in turn release more neutrons. Such an idealized chain reaction is illustrated above. The fission of a U-235 atom produces three neutrons, each of which splits another U-235 atom; each of these fissions produces three more neutrons, and so on.

centage of uranium 234. We can forget that last isotope and concentrate on the first two.

What had caused the confusion was that uranium 238 was converted to plutonium 239. But the uranium 235 was split into two roughly equal fragments, of which one was definitely identified as barium. At last we have arrived at *nuclear fission*. It is vital to understand that this is not the same as radioactive decay, such as occurs in radium. In fission, the nucleus—disturbed by the capture of an extra neutron—breaks into two roughly equal halves. These halves fly apart with great velocity, which means that the break-up is accompanied by a release of energy. The loss of mass for each split atom works out at 0.23. That is 13 times greater than the loss in the lithium experiment. This was the most energetic conversion of mass into energy that man had ever encountered.

But that was not all. Every fission of a nucleus also gave rise to two, and sometimes three, fresh neutrons. Each of these neutrons could lodge in the nucleus of another atom of uranium 235. Thus, under ideal conditions, the first neutron may cause fission in one atom. Three neutrons, by-products of this fission, may split three more nuclei, releasing 9 neutrons. Nine neutrons may split nine nuclei, releasing 27 neutrons, and so on. This *chain reaction* can take place in a fraction of a second. If we remember that each fission also produces a great deal of energy, it is plain that an extremely violent explosion can result. As we all know, the fission bombs dropped on Hiroshima and Nagasaki in 1945 were the most devastating instruments of destruction that man had produced to that time.

We have just said that such a chain reaction would take place under ideal conditions. We now have to look at these conditions and see how they can be reached if we want to produce power in the form of a "big bang." We start with natural uranium, containing over 99 per cent uranium 238 and only 0.7 per cent uranium 235. As it exists in nature, this mixture of isotopes is useless. The uranium 235 atoms are constantly breaking up, and each fission produces more neutrons. But the uranium 235 atoms are scattered so widely in the mixture that the chances of a neutron hitting another uranium 235 atom are very small indeed. Furthermore, the heavier isotope uranium 238 has an "appetite" for neutrons. This means that most of the neutrons emitted by uranium 235 will be absorbed long before they reach another uranium 235 atom. But even if scientists succeed in assembling a mass of pure uranium 235, they cannot be sure of getting a chain reaction unless the mass is of certain size. In a lump of pure uranium, each nucleus occupies proportionately as much space as a housefly in the center of a room 20 feet long, 15 feet wide, and 8 feet high. On the same scale, a neutron would be equivalent to an airgun fired at random into the room. A shot's chances of hitting the fly are very small indeed. Obviously the neutron must travel a very long way through an assemblage of nuclei before it finally scores a hit. If the lump of uranium is too small, a neutron may even escape into the outer air without ever hitting it.

There is thus a certain minimum, or *critical*, size of uranium, below which a chain reaction cannot take place. Contrariwise, if the mass is above this size, there is a rapid chain reaction and the mass explodes violently. Thus, if an explosion is desired, men have to carry the uranium to the desired location in the form of two lumps of sub-critical size. Then the two lumps are brought together to form a mass that is greater than the critical size. Even so, as soon as the chain reaction starts, the mass of uranium heats up rapidly and expands so that the atoms are soon further apart than they were before the chain reaction started. Scientists solve the problem by enclosing the bomb material in a heavy metal case that resists the expansion for a fraction of a millionth of a second and thus allows the chain reaction to develop. In a successful uranium bomb explosion, the chain reaction continues until some seventy generations of neutrons have been produced—that is, until the first neutron that started the chain has multiplied into 10^{21} neutrons (a thousand million million million), in the incredibly short time of one-millionth of a second. Even this, and all the fission that goes with it, is not enough to cause an explosion that is outstandingly better than the detonation of a similar weight of TNT. But if the mass can be contained until the 71st generation of neutrons has emerged—making the total neutrons about two and one-half times the huge number we have just mentioned—then the explosion is indeed catastrophic.

You may well ask: "Why pay so much attention to explosions?" There are two reasons. One is that, in describing the mechanics of an atom bomb, we learn something about the behavior of uranium and its neutrons. The second reason is that, even if we are against using nuclear bombs for military aims, there still remains the possibility of using them for peaceful purposes. In the field of civil engineering there may be great advantages in blasting rock that has to be excavated. For instance, this kind of explosion is so rapid and violent that it can pulverize huge masses of rock, so that the rock can be handled far more easily than in the form of huge broken boulders. Another peaceful possibility is in mining, where there are substances in rock formations that could be leached out, or dissolved, in water once the rock has been pulverized. A third way in

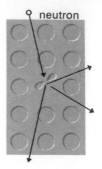

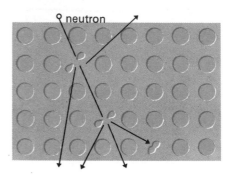

Top diagram: In a small piece of uranium-235, the neutrons released during fission escape before hitting other atoms and causing further fission. However, beyond a certain size —the *critical* size—many neutrons may escape; but at least one neutron per fission will cause another fission (lower diagram), and a chain reaction will take place, producing a violent explosion. Below: An atom bomb. Two pieces of U-235 of sub-critical size (upper) are brought together quickly by a small explosive charge (lower). Critical mass of U-235 then explodes.

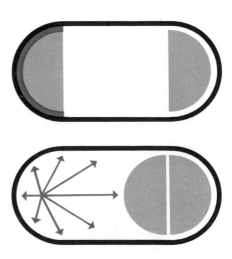

Right: Using nuclear energy for non-military purposes. Pictures are from a film of an underground hydrogen bomb explosion that was used to produce a quarter-mile-wide crater.

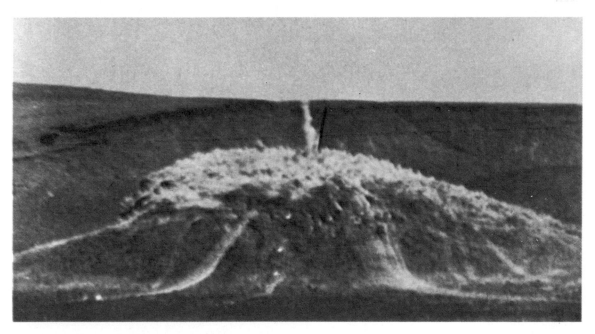

which atomic bombs could be useful is in heating heavy oils that are trapped in sand deposits. A case in point would be the Athabasca tar sands in Canada, estimated to contain 10,000 million tons of very heavy oil. This oil is at present inaccessible. But if "cooked" by an underground explosion, it could be pumped to the surface. This could considerably increase the amount of our available oil resources.

So much for the uncontrolled chain reaction of a bomb. As we said, this kind of ultra-rapid chain reaction can be obtained only with pure uranium 235, (although pure plutonium can also be used). The separation of pure uranium from its isotopes is costly and difficult. Fortunately we do not need such costly material for a nuclear device that is designed to produce heat energy in a controlled way. Scientists can use natural uranium containing only 0.7 per cent of the fissionable uranium 235 and still get a chain reaction. What they do is to take advantage of the fact that the two uranium isotopes capture neutrons when these are traveling at different speeds. As the graph on this page shows, uranium 235 captures slow neutrons more effectively than it captures fast ones. Uranium 238, on the other hand, catches far fewer neutrons at either fast or slow speeds, but there is

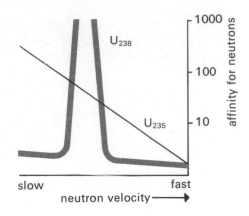

Uranium-235 captures slow neutrons much more readily than fast ones (black diagonal line). Uranium-238 (blue) captures very few neutrons at fast or slow speeds, but there is a small range of medium speeds at which neutrons are captured very readily.

Below: Diagram shows the function of the moderator. Thin rods of natural uranium (gray) are separated by blocks of carbon (black). The neutrons from the fission of a U-235 atom (dark blue) have a good chance of escaping from the uranium before being absorbed by U-238 (light blue). In the carbon they are slowed down so that when they arrive at the next uranium rod they are moving slowly enough to be captured by another U-235 atom. As diagram above shows, there is a greater chance of a slow neutron being captured by U-235 than by U-238. Thus the chain reaction continues.

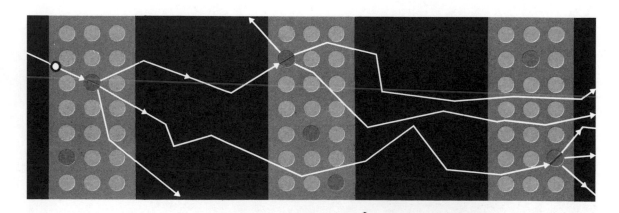

○ uranium-235

○ uranium-238

O neutron

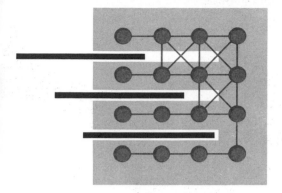

A nuclear reactor: Rods of uranium (blue) are embedded in a moderator such as graphite (gray). Black bars are control rods made from a substance such as cadmium, which absorbs neutrons very rapidly. Blue lines show paths of neutrons produced by fission. By adjusting the penetration of the rods, the speed of the chain reaction can be finely controlled. To stop the reaction, the rods are pushed right in, so that more neutrons are absorbed than are needed to keep the reaction going.

How plutonium, which is fissionable in the same way as U-235, is made from U-238. The U-238 absorbs a neutron forming U-239, which is unstable. It emits a beta ray and leaves another unstable residue, called neptunium. This also emits a beta ray and forms plutonium. The numbers preceding the symbols are the number of protons in the nucleus, called the atomic number. Emission of a beta particle (electron) converts a neutron into a proton, increasing the atomic number by one.

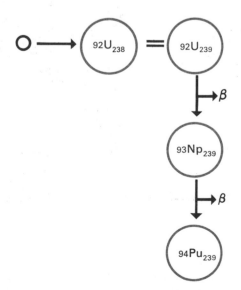

a narrow band of medium speeds at which it captures neutrons very intensively. Thus, scientists must arrange matters so that neutrons—which begin their life at very high speeds—can be slowed down past this critical speed. Then there will be a much greater chance of promoting a chain reaction in the uranium 235 component of the uranium mixture. Better still, scientists have devised a way of keeping most of the neutrons out of the way of uranium 238 atoms *while* they are being slowed down. This ingenious trick makes use of Fermi's discovery (p. 90) that certain substances can slow down neutrons without absorbing them. We call these substances *moderators*. There are several useful moderators, but we can show the process best by taking pure carbon as a typical one.

Uranium is formed into rods about one inch in diameter. These rods are arranged in a bed of carbon blocks so that each rod is separated from its neighbors by a distance of seven inches. What happens is this. An atom of uranium 235 splits and, on the average, gives out 2.5 high-speed neutrons. Because the uranium rod is thin, the chances are that all these neutrons will escape out of the rod before being captured by a uranium 238 nucleus. The neutrons are now safely out of the uranium mixture and wander about in the moderator. There the neutrons rebound off carbon atoms and progressively lose speed. By the time the neutrons arrive at the next rod, their speed should be low enough for their capture by a uranium 235 nucleus. Of course, when this happens, there will be another fission, and more neutrons will start on their journey. Even so, a small proportion of neutrons will be captured by uranium 238 nuclei but these also make themselves useful because they convert uranium 238 into plutonium, which is fissionable in the same way as uranium 235. Thus any plutonium that is made simply adds to the stock of fissionable material in the rod.

The assembly of uranium rods and a moderator is called an atomic *pile*, or *reactor*. There are now a great number of reactors of different designs, each with a special purpose. The primary purpose of a reactor is to produce heat energy. At first the energy is kinetic, in the high velocity of the liberated particles. These collide with atoms in the uranium rods, their metal casing, and in the moderator. Their kinetic energy is converted into heat, which must be removed as fast as it is generated. The various ways of doing this are described in Chapter 6 (pp. 139-149).

The reactor we have just described is called a *breeder* reactor. Its main purpose is to produce heat energy. At the same time, it "breeds" fresh fissionable plutonium out of the otherwise useless uranium 238. It would, of

The atomic power station at Marcoule, France, uses uranium fuel. Photo shows reactor's loading face; the fuel is loaded through the holes. Enclosing circular wall is pre-stressed concrete.

On this page are shown four types of nuclear reactors. The graphite-moderated reactor, right, is derived from Enrico Fermi's reactor. The fuel rods of natural uranium (blue bars) are enclosed in a moderator of pure graphite (black) and cooled by carbon dioxide or other suitable gas, which enters by the lower pipe. The gas is heated by the reaction and leaves by the upper pipe. Its heat is then used to raise steam in a conventional boiler, so as to drive an electricity-generating plant.

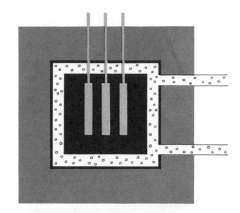

In a fast breeder reactor, the central core (blue square) is made almost entirely of U-235, which means that no moderator is required. The core can be cooled by gas or liquid sodium, which enters by the lower pipes. Heat can then pass via heat exchangers (side coils) and be used to produce electricity. Stray neutrons are absorbed in a blanket of U-238 (blue lines) and convert the U-238 into plutonium, which is used to fuel other reactors.

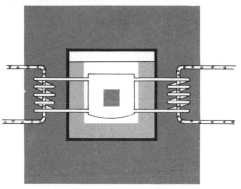

The boiling water reactor uses natural uranium, which has had its proportion of U-235 enriched artificially to about five per cent. The core (blue square) is surrounded by a tank of water; the heat released by fission makes the water boil. The resulting steam is used direct for electricity generation. Enriched uranium costs more than natural uranium, but the reactor is smaller and cheaper to build than the gas-cooled, graphite-moderated type.

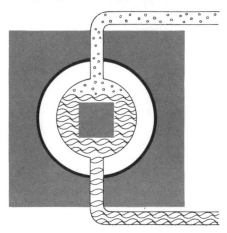

A swimming pool reactor is a low-power reactor that uses fuel rods of enriched uranium. The rods are suspended close together at the bottom of a deep pool of ordinary water or heavy water (the oxide of deuterium, an isotope of hydrogen). The water acts as a moderator, but also cools the reactor, and the depth of water protects the operator from harmful radiation. Such reactors are used chiefly to examine the effect of radiation on various materials, which are lowered into the water.

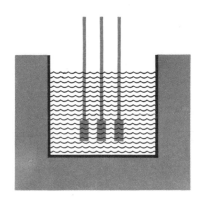

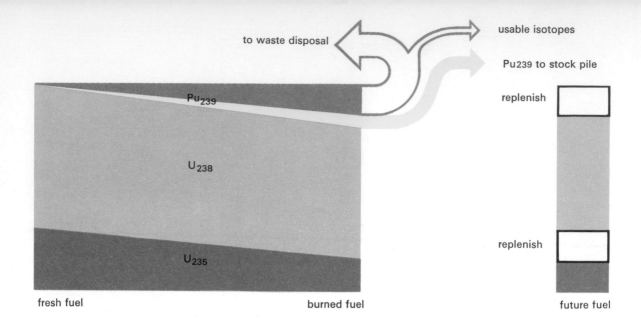

usable isotopes

Pu239 to stock pile

Pu$_{239}$

U$_{238}$

U$_{235}$

fresh fuel

burned fuel

replenish

replenish

future fuel

course, be marvelous if the reactor could breed plutonium as fast as it consumed uranium 235. If this happened, all the original uranium mixture would be used in producing heat energy. But, as we have seen more than once already, there are inevitable losses in any process that converts one form of energy to another. An atomic reactor is no exception.

One source of loss is that not all the neutrons are used profitably. Some neutrons will escape altogether through the outer walls of the reactor. This can be partly prevented by making the reactor as big as possible. (The volume of a substance increases as the cube of its size. But its surface area—in this case, the path of escape of neutrons—increases only as the square.) Then again, some neutrons are captured by the metal containers in which the uranium rods have to be sealed. Finally, one out of every five uranium 235 nuclei that capture a neutron does not split. This nucleus turns into still another isotope, uranium 236, which is stable and thus useless as an energy source. The table on this page shows the fate of the 25 neutrons that arise, on the average, from the fission of 10 atoms of uranium 235.

We also have to consider the by-products of fission. As we said, uranium 235 breaks down into isotopes of medium atomic weight. These are themselves highly radioactive, giving out beta and gamma rays. These are highly dangerous to life, which is why all materials in a reactor are handled by remote control. This threat also explains the heavy shield that surrounds reactors. But some of the fission products themselves have a strong attraction for neutrons; they absorb the neutrons and

This diagram shows what happens to the fuel in a present-day reactor. Starting with a small percentage of U-235 in U-238, the U-235 decreases. But it does not vanish completely and can be recovered for use in new fuel elements. Some waste is produced, but also some useful isotopes, as well as plutonium. Note that the fissionable material— U-235—has to be replenished as well as the U-238.

The fission of ten U-235 atoms produces, on the average, 25 neutrons. Chart below gives a rough idea of the fate of 25 such neutrons.

● ● ● ● ● ● ● ● ● ●	cause 10 more fissions
● ● ●	convert U^{235} to U^{236}
● ● ●	captured
● ●	escape
● ● ● ● ● ● ●	breed 7 Pu atoms

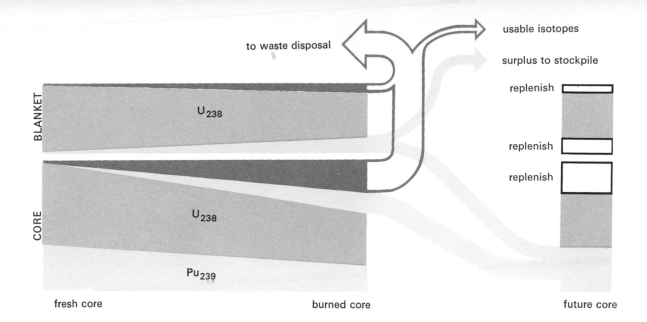

BLANKET

U$_{238}$

CORE

U$_{238}$

Pu$_{239}$

to waste disposal

usable isotopes

surplus to stockpile

replenish

replenish

replenish

fresh core   burned core   future core

The so-called breeder reactor is at present the subject of intense research. It might actually produce its own fuel. An experimental reactor of this type consists of a core of plutonium and U-238, and a blanket of U-238. In the reaction, some of the uranium is converted into plutonium and this more than makes up for the amount of original plutonium that is consumed. Thus only the U-238 has to be replenished.

On the next two pages are the portraits of 18 physicists who contributed directly or indirectly to the advancement of atomic physics. The captions mention only the specific achievements that aided the search for nuclear energy; they do not include each person's many other achievements.

prevent them from splitting uranium atoms. Therefore, as these fission products accumulate in the reactor, the rate of useful fission slows down. It becomes necessary to remove the uranium rods and extract the fission products chemically. The purified uranium is remade into rods and used again.

But in spite of these disadvantages and difficulties, a nuclear reactor is an excellent source of energy. One pound of uranium is equivalent to 2,000 tons of coal—assuming that the energy in both cases is converted into heat and then into electric power. Another way of assessing the concentrated energy in uranium is to say that the world's present power requirements for a year could be satisfied by only 750 tons of uranium.

Uranium is thus an immensely concentrated source of energy. When we consider the amounts available, we can safely think in terms of only thousands of tons, rather than the millions of tons that we use as a yardstick of coal and oil reserves. The most recently published figures (1962) show over 500,000 tons of uranium oxide in North America (U.S.A. and Canada), 1,000,-000 tons in Sweden, and over 200,000 tons in South Africa, with small quantities in other countries. No figures are available for the Soviet Union and Red China. If we take a figure of 2,000,000 tons as an estimated total (excluding Asia), this would satisfy the world's energy requirements for about 2,500 years at present rates of consumption. Even if some of the total reserves claimed prove to be uneconomic, there is clearly a much greater potential in the use of atomic energy than in fossil fuels.

Wilhelm Roentgen (1845-1923);
German. Discovered X rays in
1895.

Henri Becquerel (1852-1908);
French. Discovered radioactivity
in uranium.

Marie Curie (1867-1934); Polish.
With Pierre Curie, isolated
radium.

Lord Rutherford (1871-1937); New
Zealand. Analyzed the emissions
from radium, and was the first
man to split the atom (1919).

Charles Wilson (1869-1959);
British. Invented the cloud
chamber, 1899.

Niels Bohr (1885-1962); Danish.
Supplied mathematical
explanations of atomic structure
and fission.

Enrico Fermi (1901-1954); Italian.
Built the first atomic reactor,
1942.

Ernest Walton (b. 1903); British.
With Cockcroft, built first
discharge tube for bombarding
atoms artificially, 1932.

John Cockcroft (b. 1897);
British. Pioneered with Walton
artificial acceleration of
protons for exploring atomic
structure, 1932.

Max Planck (1858-1947); German. Formulated the quantum theory of electromagnetic radiations.

Albert Einstein (1879-1955); German. Discovered the interchangeability of matter and energy.

Sir Joseph Thompson (1856-1940); British. Demonstrated the first known subatomic particles—electrons.

Lise Meitner (b. 1878); Austrian. Co-worker with Hahn and Strassmann in achieving first fission of uranium (1939).

Otto Hahn (b. 1879); German. (See Meitner.) Also demonstrated the nature of products of uranium fission.

Irène Joliot-Curie (1897-1956); French. (Daughter of Marie Curie.) With Professor Joliot, discovered radioactive isotopes.

James Chadwick (b. 1891); British. Collaborated with Rutherford to produce nuclear energy artificially.

Ernest Lawrence (1901-1958); American. Pioneer of linear accelerators for atom smashing, especially the cyclotron.

J. Robert Oppenheimer (1904–1967); American. Directed development of first atomic bomb at Los Alamos, New Mexico.

Section 2: Converting Energy into Power

5 Basic Principles

In the preceding chapters, we have looked at some of the most important resources of energy that man has available for converting into power. Before we discuss ways in which this power is generated, we must have some idea of the physical laws that underlie the translation of energy into power.

Apart from our various methods of heating and cooling our immediate surroundings, most of our applications of power are to produce *motion* of some kind. Transport by land, sea, and air; the operation of machines in the manufacture of countless articles of daily use; the raising of coal and other minerals from mines—all these uses of power involve motion. Thus, the conversion of energy into power is largely concerned with kinetic energy, the energy of motion.

We can understand easily enough that falling water possesses kinetic energy. But how do fossil fuels, which are stores of potential energy, fit into this scheme of things? The answer is that the potential energy of these fuels is converted into heat. In turn, heat is used to raise the temperature of a *working fluid*—usually steam or air. (In scientific usage, a fluid can be either a liquid or a gas.) The molecules of a fluid are in a state of constant random motion. When the fluid's temperature is raised, the molecules move faster. Thus, the heat that has been applied to the fluid is converted into kinetic energy. If we are to harness this kinetic energy, we must convert the molecular activity into a more organized form of motion, such as the rotation of a shaft or the sliding movement of a piston. Having achieved this, man must still take steps to apply the work produced to the final objective. An automobile, for example, can be caused to move only by the application of a force external to itself. When the engine turns the wheels, the road exerts a friction force that is in the direction of motion. It is this force that propels the car forward. If there were no friction, the wheels would turn but the car would remain stationary. In order to turn the wheels we provide a transmission system, consisting of shafts and gears that connect the wheels with the engine. The engine is a heat engine in which a fossil fuel—gasoline or diesel oil—is

As water is heated to boiling point, its molecules move faster and faster until they finally escape—as steam. In steam engines most of the kinetic energy of these molecules is converted into power. Drawing above shows an idea for an impulse turbine, devised by the Italian Giovanni Branca in 1629. It used the energy from a jet of steam to turn a paddlewheel.

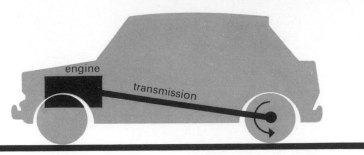

friction force

The force that moves a car along a road is the friction force that the road exerts upon the wheels. If there were no friction, the wheels would simply spin round. The engine converts heat energy into useful work and this is applied to the wheels through a transmission system.

burned. The heat liberated by the fuel is used to increase the kinetic energy of the gases in the engine. The engine converts some of this kinetic energy into useful work.

If this all sounds a bit like the house that Jack built, we have made an important point. The fact is, even a commonplace device such as an automobile involves not one but three interrelated processes. These three processes are typical of all power-producing systems. Energy is first converted into useful work by an engine. The work is then transmitted from the engine to the point at which the power is required. And finally the power is applied to achieve the desired result.

In the example of an automobile, the means of transmission are mechanical. But there are many other ways in which power can be transmitted. In flight, an airplane's direction of movement is controlled by the ailerons and the rudder. Power from the engine is transmitted to the ailerons and rudder, usually by means of a pneumatic system. This system is essentially a pipe containing air, the pressure of which can be increased by an air compressor driven by the engine. For moderate amounts of power, pneumatic and hydraulic (compressed liquid) systems have certain advantages over purely mechanical ones. For instance, pipes can be run through awkward shapes and around corners, thus eliminating the need for gears and couplings, moving shafts, or cables and pulleys.

A hydraulic system of transmitting power, used in car braking. When force is applied to the brake pedal, pressure is exerted on the piston of the master cylinder. Since the brake fluid cannot be compressed, the pressure is transmitted to the braking device at the wheel.

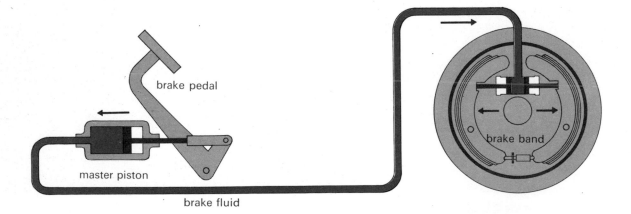

brake pedal

master piston

brake fluid

brake band

If large quantities of power are to be transmitted, particularly over long distances, none of these methods is suitable. Electricity then becomes the only practical source of power. An electric current may be thought of as a stream of electrons moving along a conducting wire —so electricity also belongs to the kinetic category. But, as with other kinds of kinetic energy, it is difficult to store large quantities of electricity. Virtually all the electricity produced in a power station must be used immediately. Most electricity today is produced in power stations with furnaces burning fossil fuels, either coal or oil. In atomic-power stations, there is an atomic reactor that converts atomic energy into heat. But the processes that then follow are identical with those in a fossil-fuel power station.

If the energy source is already kinetic in character— as in the case of water or wind—we do not have to convert it into heat. The engines used for converting water and wind energy into useful work might seem different in kind from those used in power stations using fossil or atomic fuels. The problem, however, is the same—to convert the random kinetic energy of molecules into a more organized, controlled form of motion.

We have seen that, whatever the source of energy, three processes are involved in converting it into useful power. First we produce useful work in an engine; then we transmit this work to the point of use; and finally we apply the power produced, usually with the help of some other mechanical or electrical device. The engines used in the first stage in this sequence are called *prime movers*. It is the principles underlying these engines that concern us in this chapter.

All prime movers involve a *cyclic process*. In such a process, a fluid—water, steam, or some gas—passes through a number of stages and eventually returns to its original condition, ready to repeat the cycle. In this cyclic process, the energy level of the working fluid is

High-voltage cables conduct electricity away from the generating station to where it is needed. When power has to be transmitted over long distances, electricity is the only practical way.

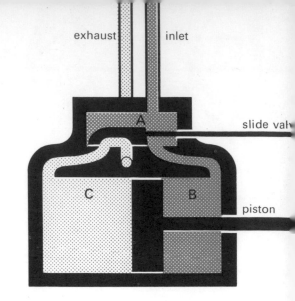

first raised by applying energy from some outside source. In the case of a waterpower plant, this stage is a product of natural events. Solar energy evaporates water from the sea to form clouds that subsequently deposit rainwater on high ground. In a heat engine, this stage involves two processes. The working fluid enters the engine at high temperature in order to increase its available kinetic energy. The fluid must therefore pass through a boiler, where its temperature is raised by using the energy of combustion of a fossil fuel or the heat developed in an atomic reactor. But before the fluid can enter the boiler, its pressure must be raised by a compressor, usually in the form of a pump.

In the next stage, the fluid passes through an engine in which its energy level is all or partly converted into useful work. In a waterpower plant, the engine is a *turbine* (described in detail in the next chapter). From the turbine, the water is returned to its original source, the sea, where it will enter a fresh cycle of evaporation and deposition. In a heat engine, as we saw, the working fluid enters at a high temperature and pressure. The engine converts some of the energy into useful work and expels the fluid at a lower pressure. Unlike the water in a waterpower plant, however, the fluid is not yet ready for another cycle. The fluid's pressure must be raised before

How a double-acting steam engine transforms heat energy into mechanical energy. Steam passes from A to B, pushing the piston from right to left; spent steam passes from C to the exhaust pipe. As the piston moves to the left, the slide valve moves to the right; at this point in time, new steam passes from A to C, pushing the piston back again. Spent steam now escapes from B to the exhaust pipe.

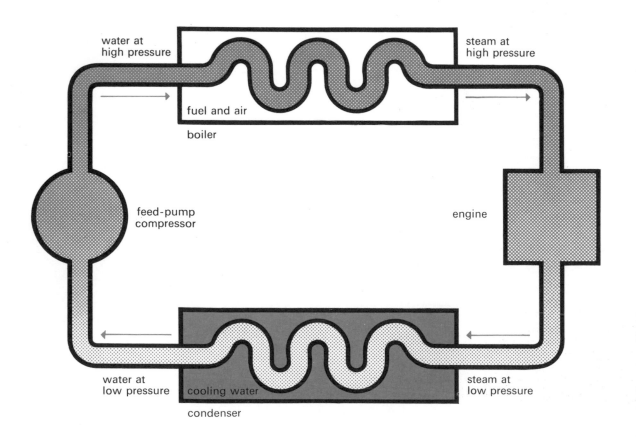

it can re-enter the engine. If we took it straight from the engine and recompressed it, this would require as much work as had been obtained from the engine in the first place. (As a matter of fact, a compressor would require *more* work than the engine could deliver, because some of the work would be wasted in friction losses.)

The only way we can overcome this difficulty is to cool the fluid before it enters the compressor. Less work is required to compress a cold fluid than a hot one. A steam plant (diagram p. 108) is a good example of how this cycle of operations proceeds. The high-pressure steam enters the engine and produces useful work. It is expelled — still in the form of steam but at a lower pressure and temperature — and enters a condenser. Here a flow of cooling water removes heat and converts the steam into water at low pressure. The water then passes to a feed-pump, from which it emerges at high pressure. Next the water enters a boiler, where it is heated. It evaporates into steam and finally re-enters the engine.

In this example, the various units in the complete power plant are separate. But in some power-producing devices, all the processes of heating, expansion, compression, and cooling are carried out in a single unit. The internal-combustion engine of a car is one example of this kind of device. (The term "engine," incidentally, is sometimes used to mean either the whole combination of units or just the power-producing unit. To avoid confusion, we shall use the term "engine" to mean only the power-producing unit. The term "power plant" will be used when referring to the combination of all units through which the working fluid circulates.)

At this point we are once again faced with a small problem of communication. While the basic principles of energy conversion are not difficult in themselves, they are most easily expressed in the form of equations. To non-mathematically-minded readers, these equations will appear formidable at first sight. In fact, they are quite simple to follow and will be fully explained as we go along.

The Law of Conservation of Energy states that energy is never destroyed but is merely changed from one form into another. This law applies to any engine that uses heat, waterpower, or windpower. The engine receives a certain amount of energy (which we shall call E_1) and

The efficiency of a diesel locomotive is about 30 per cent, compared with a steam locomotive's 8 per cent. As with all heat engines, energy is lost through friction, heat, and hot exhaust gases.

Left: Progress of a fluid through a steam plant. Steam enters the engine at high pressure and high temperature. Most of its energy is converted into useful work. It is expelled at lower pressure and then condensed into water, before being forcibly pumped into the boiler, where it is again converted into steam.

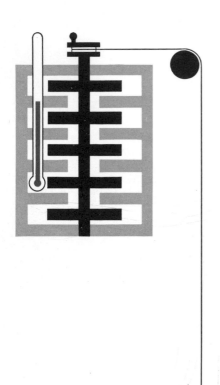

The apparatus that James Joule (above) used to establish relationship between work and heat consisted of a shaft of paddlewheels inside an insulated container of water. A falling weight turned the crank; the friction of the paddles caused a rise in the water temperature, which could be measured.

converts some of this energy into useful work (W). As we saw in Chapter 1, the working fluid passing through an engine must retain at least enough kinetic energy to enable it to leave the engine and make way for the entry of fresh supplies of fluid. This retained energy (E_2) is lost energy so far as productive work is concerned. Also, if the engine uses heat there will be a heat loss (Q) from the hot parts of the engine to its cooler surroundings. To sum up, the input of energy (E_1) reappears as work (W), energy loss (E_2), and heat loss (Q). We can write this in the form of an equation:

$$E_1 = W + Q + E_2$$

This equation applies to all forms of prime movers. But to give it meaning, we must know the numerical value of each of the terms. Looking back to Chapter 1 again, we recall that both potential and kinetic energy are expressed in foot-pounds-force (ft.lbf.) — that is, distance multiplied by force. Yet heat energy is expressed in British Thermal Units, one Btu being the quantity of heat required to raise the temperature of one pound mass of water by one degree Fahrenheit. If we look at the equation again, we see that it will include combinations of potential, kinetic, and heat energies. So we need a conversion factor that gives us the rate of exchange between the foot-pound-force and the Btu.

The English physicist James Joule (1818–1889) made the first experiments on this subject in 1841. His apparatus consisted of a drum containing water, which was churned up by paddle wheels rotated by a crank turned by falling weights. By measuring the work input (in foot-pounds-force) and the mass and rise of temperature of the water, Joule determined this rate of exchange. He called this the "mechanical equivalent of heat." Later experiments with more refined apparatus have put the numerical value of the mechanical equivalent of heat as 778 ft.lbf. equals one Btu. In honor of Joule, the symbol J is used as an abbreviation for the mechanical equivalent of heat. Let us see what this conversion factor means in numerical terms. If one pound of water is dropped from a height of 100 feet, its potential energy is 100 ft.lbf. This is equivalent to

$$\frac{100}{778}\,\text{Btu},$$

so the water's temperature would have risen by only about 1/8°F. A drop of 1,000 feet would result in a temperature rise of ten times this—or only just over 1°F. To raise the temperature of one pound of water from 60°F. to boiling point (212°F.) would require a drop of about 120,000 feet.

Now, the temperatures normally used in heat engines

Top: Part of a seven-cylinder marine diesel engine developing 21,000 horsepower. Bottom: A single-cylinder diesel power unit for a model boat or plane. Both engines work on same principle.

are very much higher than the boiling point of water. Thus we should expect that the heat energy of a pound of fluid (steam or air) entering a heat engine would be much higher than the potential energy possessed by a pound of water in the reservoir of a waterpower plant. We should therefore expect to get much more work from a pound of fluid passing through a heat engine than from a pound of water passing through a water turbine. However, given the same physical size of machine, more pounds of water can flow through a water turbine than fluid through a heat engine. The water is much more dense than the fluid. One cubic foot of water contains 62.5 pounds. One cubic foot of high-pressure steam at a steam turbine's inlet will contain only about one pound. And at the turbine's outlet, where the pressure is very low, one cubic foot of steam contains only about one-thousandth of a pound.

Turning to kinetic energy, we find that high velocities are needed to produce an appreciable rise in temperature. You may recall (from p. 32) that the kinetic energy of an object is its mass multiplied by the square of its velocity divided by twice the value of gravity, or

$$\frac{MV^2}{2 \times 32}.$$

Thus, if one pound of water is moving at 100 feet per second (about 68 miles per hour) its kinetic energy is

$$\frac{1 \times 100^2}{2 \times 32} = 156 \text{ ft.lbf.}$$

This is equivalent to

$$\frac{156}{778} \text{ or } 0.2 \text{ Btu.}$$

At 1,000 ft/sec., its kinetic energy is

$$\frac{1 \times 1000^2}{2 \times 32},$$

which is equivalent to 20 Btu. If we again wished to raise the temperature of one pound of water from 60°F. to 212°F.—this time by moving it very fast and then bringing it suddenly to rest—its speed would have to be 2,750 ft/sec., or nearly 1,900 m.p.h. This helps to explain why wind energy can produce only small quantities of power. It has a low density (one cubic foot of air in normal atmospheric conditions containing only about 0.08 lb.). A *thousand* cubic feet of air will produce only about as much power as *one* cubic foot of water. Thus, a very large windmill is needed to produce a significant power output.

We have shown that heat energy and mechanical energy—and thus work—can, under certain circum-

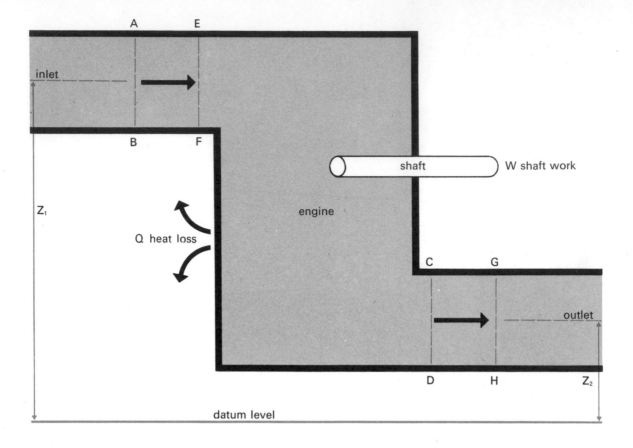

Labels in the diagram: A, E, inlet, B, F, shaft, W shaft work, engine, Z_1, Q heat loss, C, G, outlet, D, H, Z_2, datum level

stances, be interchangeable. We have found that a conversion factor—known as *J*—exists between them. We must therefore take care, in writing our equations, that all quantities of energy, heat, and work are expressed in the same units of measurement. It does not matter whether we work in foot-pounds-force or in British thermal units. Whichever we choose may at first sight look odd. Both systems have certain advantages. We commonly use Btu for heat engines and foot-pounds-force for other prime movers.

To understand what happens to the energy fed into a heat engine, we shall have to break down the equation

$$E_1 = W + Q + E_2$$

into more detail. The diagram (above) represents a heat engine. The engine is very simple because we are not concerned with the details of its construction. Let us suppose that the working fluid (air or steam) enters through the duct at the top left-hand corner. Below the engine is a *datum level*—an imaginary line of zero

Diagram represents a heat engine through which the working fluid flows from left to right. The text discusses the progress of one pound mass of fluid from position ABCD to position EFGH, and the work done by the fluid.

Right: Diagram lists approximate energy losses for a car traveling at 30 mph along a level road. Figures are in percentages. Note that most of the energy is wasted in the cooling system and in the exhaust gases.

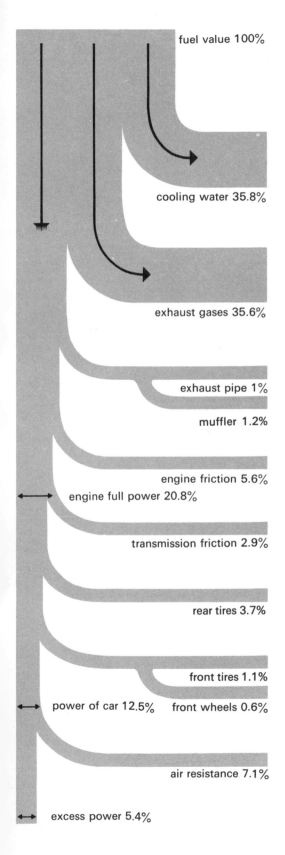

fuel value 100%

cooling water 35.8%

exhaust gases 35.6%

exhaust pipe 1%

muffler 1.2%

engine friction 5.6%

engine full power 20.8%

transmission friction 2.9%

rear tires 3.7%

front tires 1.1%

power of car 12.5%   front wheels 0.6%

air resistance 7.1%

excess power 5.4%

height. From this level we calculate the height of the center line of the inlet duct z_1, and the height of the center line of the outlet duct z_2.

Let us see what happens when one pound mass of working fluid passes through the engine. First, we must draw two imaginary boundaries—AB across the inlet duct, and CD across the outlet duct. These are our starting points; the whole of the engine between these two boundaries contains the fluid. The imaginary boundaries EF and GH are so positioned that two masses of fluid enclosed between AB and EF and between CD and GH would each be one pound. We can therefore imagine the fluid, starting at AB and ending at CD, moving through the engine until it reached EF and GH. One pound of fluid would now have passed through the engine. Suppose that this one pound of fluid caused W Btu of work to be developed at the shaft. The heat loss was Q Btu. Suppose also that the pressure, velocity, and specific volume (that is, the volume of one pound of fluid) at the inlet duct are p_1, c_1, and v_1 respectively. At the outlet duct they are p_2, c_2, and v_2 respectively.

Now, if it is to operate efficiently, an engine must be continuously fed with a supply of fresh fuel and working fluid. So if the fluid at the inlet is to move from AB to EF, it must be pushed by further supplies of fluid coming along behind it. In other words, fluid to the left of AB (in the diagram) has to do work to push it into the engine. This work in effect *increases* the store of energy in the fluid already within the engine. On the other hand, the fluid within the engine has to do work to push the fluid ahead of it from CD to GH at the outlet. This *decreases* the energy available for work at the shaft.

It is quite easy to calculate how much work is done at inlet and outlet. Work, as we know, is force multiplied by distance. The pressure at the inlet is p_1, which represents force per unit area. Thus the total force must be the pressure multiplied by the area of the duct. The work at inlet is therefore pressure (p_1) × area of duct × distance (AE). Now, the area of the duct multiplied by distance AE is the volume between the two boundaries AB and EF. We have already stated that these boundaries enclose one pound of working fluid. The volume is therefore the volume of one pound of fluid—in other words, specific volume v_1. Thus the work at the inlet is expressed very conveniently as $p_1 v_1$; similarly, the work at the outlet is $p_2 v_2$.

At the risk of repetition, we must make sure that we are certain about the meanings of a couple of terms. You will have noticed that the terms pv and W have both been used to define work. The pv terms express the amount of work done in order to move a pound of fluid into or out of the engine. The term W, on the other hand, represents the actual work output of the engine. This is the work that can be used, let us say, to turn a shaft. In the future, then, we shall think of the term W as "shaft work."

If we take another look at our original equation—$E_1 = W + Q + E_2$—it becomes plain that the terms E_1 and E_2 must be made up of four separate items—potential energy, kinetic energy, work, and heat energy. In thermodynamics, heat energy is called *internal energy* and is usually given the symbol u. As we saw at the beginning of the chapter, internal, or heat, energy can be thought of as the *random* kinetic energy of the molecules of a substance. Such heat energy is distinct from the kinetic energy due to the bodily motion of the whole mass of a fluid. In the case of gases, a rise in temperature makes the molecules move faster, and thus more energy is available for release. It is important to realize that, although the individual molecules of a gas are moving at random in all directions, the net result is that the gas as a whole presses on the walls of its container ready to give up energy if an opportunity occurs.

We now have all the information we need to expand our original energy equation into forms applicable to a heat engine (Figure 1, p. 115). E_1 and E_2, we know, are each the sum of the potential and kinetic energies, work at inlet or outlet, and internal energy. E_1 is the sum of these terms at the inlet duct, E_2 is their sum at the outlet duct. Note that J appears below the line in the potential energy, kinetic energy, and work terms. This is because these terms, in their original form, were expressions of foot-pounds-force. By dividing them by the conversion factor J (the mechanical equivalent of heat) the terms are expressed in Btu, which is more suitable for heat engines. The internal energy term, u, is already calculated in Btu and so does not require the conversion factor J below the line.

We can simplify these equations in two ways. First, in the potential energy term, we have g above the line and 32 below the line. If we assume g to have a value of 32 ft/sec^2, the two figures cancel each other out. This leaves z_1 divided by J. Second, the terms for work and internal energy occur together so often in equations of this kind that a collective name, *enthalpy*, has been given to the terms. (Enthalpy is expressed as $h = u + pv$.) Enthalpy is defined as the heat content of a substance per unit mass, and is usually given the symbol h. The revised equation is shown in Figure 2, p. 115.

Now, the engineer's main concern is with the amount of usable power—that is, shaft work—he can get from an engine. So he would probably re-arrange the equation as shown in Figure 3. To put this equation into words, shaft work W equals loss of potential energy

On the opposite page are detailed the stages by which a simple equation is evolved that can be used to give the value of work done by a heat engine. The key to symbols is below, and all the steps are discussed in the text.

c = velocity

E_1 = energy input

E_2 = energy loss

g = force of gravity

h = enthalpy

J = 778 ft lbf/Btu

p = pressure

Q = heat loss

u = internal energy

v = specific volume

z = height of energy source

W = effective work output

plus loss of kinetic energy plus loss of enthalpy minus the heat lost by the engine to its surroundings.

This equation applies to any engine or device through which a fluid can be caused to flow. But in almost every case, the equation can be even further simplified. This is done by omitting some of the terms that, for a given machine, are of only minor importance. For instance, in the heat engine (diagram, p. 112) the change in potential energy due to a difference in height between inlet and outlet is negligible. Thus we can omit the potential energy term altogether. In a heat engine using air or

1

	potential energy		kinetic energy		work		internal energy
$E_1 =$	$\dfrac{gz_1}{32J}$	$+$	$\dfrac{c_1^2}{2 \times 32J}$	$+$	$\dfrac{p_1v_1}{J}$	$+$	u_1
$E_2 =$	$\dfrac{gz_2}{32J}$	$+$	$\dfrac{c_2^2}{2 \times 32J}$	$+$	$\dfrac{p_2v_2}{J}$	$+$	u_2

2

	energy input			energy output
	$\dfrac{z_1}{J} + \dfrac{c_1^2}{2 \times 32J} + h_1$	$=$		$\dfrac{z_2}{J} + \dfrac{c_2^2}{2 \times 32J} + h_2 + W + Q$

3

$$W = \left(\frac{z_1}{J} - \frac{z_2}{J}\right) + \left(\frac{c_1^2}{2 \times 32J} - \frac{c_2^2}{2 \times 32J}\right) + (h_1 - h_2) - Q$$

4

$$W = (h_1 - h_2) - Q$$

steam as a working fluid, the difference between kinetic energy values at inlet and outlet are small compared with the values for internal energy. So, in such a case, we can eliminate the kinetic energy terms.

Figure 4 (p. 115) shows the simple form to which we have reduced our shaft-work equation. Put into words, it states that shaft work equals the difference between the enthalpy at inlet and outlet, minus the heat lost by the engine to its surroundings.

The values for enthalpy at inlet and outlet depend mainly upon the temperature and pressure of the working fluid. For some fluids, the relationships between temperature and pressure are very complex. Steam is an example of such a fluid. But because it is so commonly used in heat engines, engineers have compiled tables that show enthalpy values for every combination of temperature and pressure likely to be met in practice. Thus, if we can make a reliable estimate of heat loss, we can quite easily calculate our heat engine's shaft work per pound of fluid. Air is also a common working fluid. It is used, for instance, in the internal-combustion engine and the gas turbine. Although enthalpy tables are also available for air, its properties are less complicated than those of steam. The change of enthalpy with pressure is quite small where air is involved.

The importance of individual terms in the heat-engine equation is likely to differ from that in the equation for a water turbine. For one thing, relative heat is hardly involved in a water turbine, so we can begin by eliminating the heat-loss symbol, Q. On the other hand, the turbine depends upon the power of falling water, so potential and kinetic energy will play a big part. What about enthalpy? As we have seen, enthalpy (h) equals internal energy (u) plus the product of pressure (p) and specific volume (v). Internal energy depends mainly on the difference in temperature between inlet and outlet. In a water turbine, this change is almost nil, so we can ignore the term u.

$$\text{Thus, } h_1 - h_2 = \frac{p_1 v_1}{J} - \frac{p_2 v_2}{J}$$

The symbol v represents the specific volume of the working fluid expressed in cubic feet per pound (cu.ft/lb). In a heat-engine fluid, this figure may vary considerably according to pressure. Steam has a specific volume of 334 cu.ft/lb at a pressure of one pound per square inch. But steam's specific volume is only about 8.5 cu.ft/lb at 50 pounds per square inch. That is, steam is quite easy to compress. Water can be compressed very slightly, but for all practical purposes we can say that the specific volume of water remains constant at all pressures. Water's specific volume

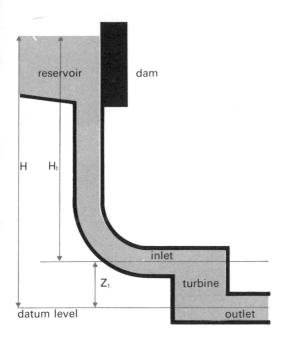

reservoir dam

H H₁

Z₁ inlet

turbine

datum level outlet

Diagram gives some basic data for finding the work output of a water turbine.

Left: The three main kinds of water wheel used for driving generators. The Pelton wheel (top) works best with water at high pressure; the water is directed at the paddles. In the Francis turbine, water is directed by a casing (shown, center) onto all the blades of the rotor (not shown). The Kaplan rotor (bottom) works best with water at low pressure.

is only $\frac{1}{62.5}$ cu.ft/lb, an inconveniently small number. We therefore usually substitute density for specific volume when considering water as a working fluid. Density, which is given the Greek symbol ρ, expresses the mass of a substance in pounds per cubic foot. Since specific volume is expressed in cubic feet per pound, it follows that

$$\text{density} = \frac{1}{\text{specific volume}} \text{ or } \rho = \frac{1}{v}$$

Our term for work (pv) can therefore be written $\frac{p}{\rho}$.

Imagine a column of water of height H (capital letter, to distinguish height from enthalpy) on an area of one square foot. If the pressure at the base of the column is p, then the value of p is the weight of the column of water divided by its area. The weight is volume multiplied by density (multiplied by $\frac{g}{32}$, which we can take to be 1 and therefore ignore). Expressed in symbols, the weight of the water is $H \times 1 \times \rho$. Therefore,

$$p = \frac{H\rho}{1} \text{ or } \frac{p}{\rho} = H.$$

In other words, we can express our work term pv or $\frac{p}{\rho}$ as H, where H is the height of a column of water that would produce the pressure p.

The diagram on the left shows a reservoir, dam head, turbine, and a datum level. H, which is called the *head* of water, is the difference in height between the surface of the water in the reservoir and the outlet of the turbine. This distance represents the total energy input. The potential-energy term z_1 is the height of the inlet fluid above the datum. The datum level is drawn through the center line of the outlet. If this level is regarded as of zero height, it follows that z_2, representing the height of the fluid at outlet, is also zero and can be ignored. H_1, which equals H minus z_1, is the difference in height between reservoir surface and turbine inlet. It represents the pressure of the water at inlet divided by its density. H_2 (not shown on the diagram) is pressure divided by density at outlet.

Our complete equation for the work output of the

Right: The equation for the work output of a water turbine. This is the complete equation and can be simplified, as shown in the text (p. 118).

$$W = (z_1 - z_2) + \left(\frac{c_1{}^2}{2 \times 32} - \frac{c_2{}^2}{2 \times 32}\right) + (H_1 - H_2)$$

water turbine is given on page 117. In words, it states that shaft work equals loss of potential energy plus loss of kinetic energy plus loss of pressure-divided-by-density. Note that J, the mechanical equivalent of heat, has been omitted since no heat is involved. In this equation all the terms represent quantities of foot-pounds-force.

Now, is it possible to simplify the equation to the same extent as we simplified the heat-engine equation? As we have seen, we can eliminate the potential-energy term (z_2) by placing the datum level through the center line of the outlet. Turning to the kinetic-energy terms, we recall that c_1 and c_2 represent the velocity of the working fluid at inlet and outlet. The values of both can be kept small enough to be ignored if the diameters of the inlet and outlet ducts are made very large. If we also ignore energy losses due to friction in the supply pipe, the available head at inlet is given by the simple expression $H - z_1$. The complete equation for the shaft work of the turbine can now be reduced to:

$$W = z_1 + H - z_1 - H_2 \quad \text{or} \quad W = H - H_2$$

This expression is similar to that obtained for the shaft work of our heat engine (Figure 4). Both equations represent ideal cases in which everything possible has been done to reduce energy losses. Obviously, the shaft work is greatest when the negative term (H_2 for the water turbine, h_2 for the heat engine) is as small as possible.

In every type of prime mover, the chief aim is to obtain the maximum shaft work for a given expenditure of energy. Most people can give a rough-and-ready definition of the word "efficiency." To the engineer, however, it has a precise meaning—the ratio of shaft work to energy input. When we compare the efficiencies of particular engines, we must first decide whether we are considering power plants as a whole or merely parts of them, such as the prime movers. In the case of a water-power plant, the energy input should really include the amount of solar energy used to evaporate a given quantity of water from the sea and release it over high ground as rain. The best we can do is to compare the shaft work with the energy available for conversion by the turbine —in other words, the energy available in the water at the dam head.

In our water turbine, then, the efficiency is given by the expression:

$$\frac{H - H_2}{H}$$

Obviously, the smaller the value of H_2, the nearer does the efficiency approach unity, or 100 per cent. In our turbine, the value of H_2 can be very small indeed. It

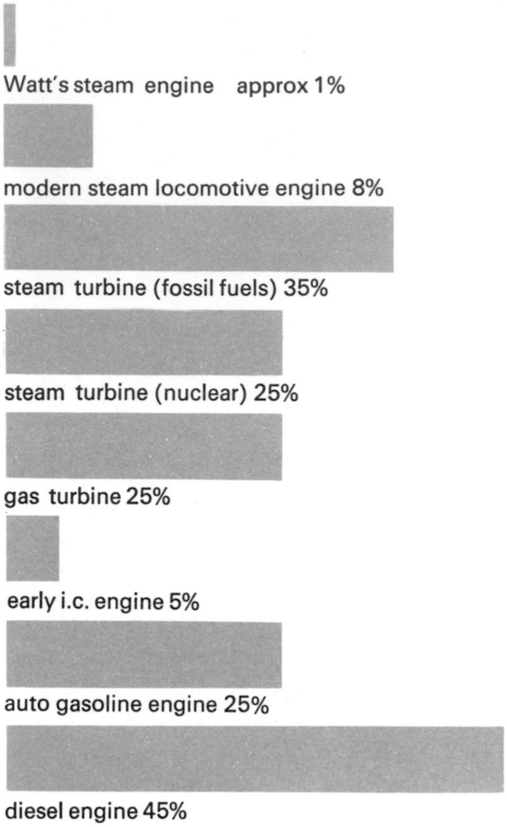

Watt's steam engine approx 1%

modern steam locomotive engine 8%

steam turbine (fossil fuels) 35%

steam turbine (nuclear) 25%

gas turbine 25%

early i.c. engine 5%

auto gasoline engine 25%

diesel engine 45%

Diagram shows approximate efficiencies for a number of engines. Efficiencies have to be evaluated according to the engine's cost, size, and so on. Thus, although the diesel engine is the most efficient, it is not necessarily the most suitable for a particular task. Right: Four of the engines listed above. Top: Watt beam engine, preserved in the Science Museum, London. Second: Locomotive with a steam engine, now being replaced by diesel locomotives. Third: An automobile gasoline engine, particularly efficient for medium-size vehicles. Bottom: Diesel engine in a large truck; although more costly than gasoline engines, diesel engines are more economical to run.

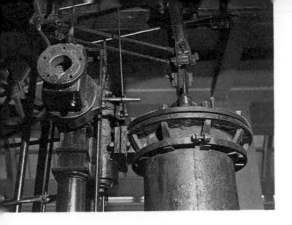

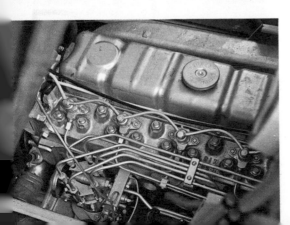

represents the amount by which the pressure of water at the outlet exceeds its normal, atmospheric pressure. If the outlet duct discharges the water into the open air, H_2 will be almost zero. Theoretically, there is no reason why the efficiency of a water turbine should not approach 100 per cent. In practice, efficiencies of well above 90 per cent are attained. The elusive few per cent are lost through friction.

Unfortunately, it is impossible to achieve comparable efficiencies in a heat-power plant. As we saw on page 109, the working fluid must be cooled between the engine outlet and the compressor inlet. Let us suppose a quantity of heat energy (E) is supplied to the engine. Shaft work W (the energy difference between the total work output and the energy input to the compressor) is done. Heat energy (E_1) is removed in the condenser. By the Law of Conservation of Energy, $E = W + E_1$; or, to put it another way, $W = E - E_1$. The efficiency of the power plant is expressed by dividing the work output by the energy input. Thus,

$$\frac{W}{E} = \frac{E - E_1}{E}.$$

If the efficiency of the plant is to be high, E_1 must be as small as possible. For 100 per cent efficiency, E_1 would have to be zero. Now, we know that internal, or heat, energy is kinetic energy due to the random motion of the molecules of the working fluid. The value of this kinetic energy depends on the temperature of the fluid. As the fluid's temperature falls, the value of the kinetic energy dwindles. In order to reduce the value of heat energy E_1 to zero, however, we should have to lower the temperature of the fluid to *absolute zero*—the lowest temperature that can possibly be obtained. Absolute zero is −460°F. (or −273°C.), a very long way below the normal temperature of the atmosphere. Unfortunately, a power plant must depend on natural supplies of water or air as the cooling agent because they are the only coolants freely available. Thus, the lowest value for E_1 is the value for normal atmospheric temperature. This severely limits the efficiency attainable with a heat-power plant.

Thermodynamic theory shows that under ideal conditions, with no energy losses due to friction or other causes, the maximum efficiency that can be attained in a heat-power plant is expressed as:

$$\frac{T_1 - T_2}{T_1}$$

T_1 is the absolute temperature at inlet to the engine, and T_2 is the absolute temperature at outlet. We may be able to improve the efficiency, not by lowering T_2 but by raising T_1. But the amount of improvement is limited by the maximum temperature that the engine's materials of construction can withstand.

The table on the right shows the efficiencies of five heat-power plants with different values for T_1. In each case, the value for T_2 is 60°F., a reasonable average for atmospheric temperature. Since the highest temperatures that normal heat-engine materials can withstand is about 1,500 to 2,000°F., we can see that the maximum efficiency attainable in theory is about 75 per cent. In practice, however, friction, heat, and other losses cut the efficiency to about half this figure, even in the most advanced power plants.

The efficiency of a heat-power plant, then, is less than

$T_1°$ F	$T_1°$ F Abs.	Efficiency $\dfrac{T_1 - T_2}{T_1} \times 100\%$
200	660	21.2
500	960	45.8
1000	1460	64.4
1500	1960	73.5
2000	2460	78.9

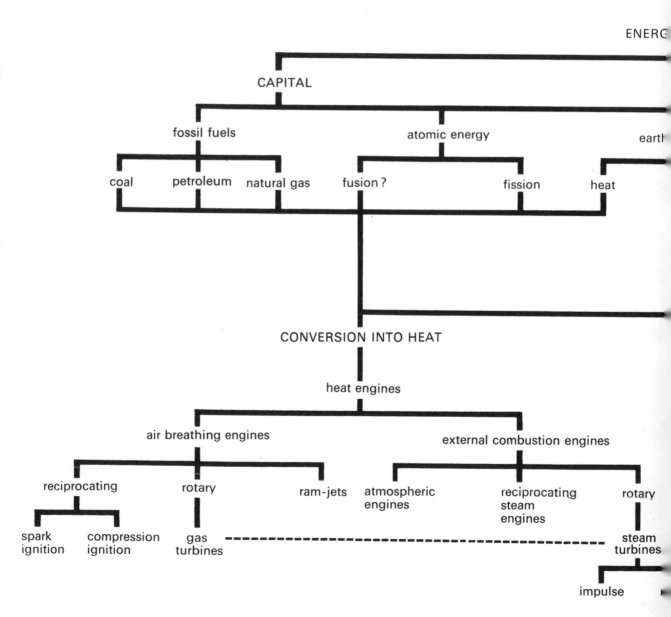

half that of a waterpower plant. This does not mean that heat-power plant designers are inefficient. It merely emphasizes the fact that, in trying to harness the energy of heat, engineers are limited by the properties of the materials with which they have to work. Moreover, efficiency is not the only yardstick of usefulness. Size and portability may be equally important factors in the choice of a power plant. There would be little point in using a bulky water turbine to propel a small family car. Each type of plant lends itself to particular uses, and each application involves at least some compromise between efficiency and other factors. In later chapters we shall see how the needs of power-users determine the design and performance of different kinds of plants.

Chart below gives a "family tree" of energy sources and of ways of converting the energy into power. The dotted line shows a link between energy capital and energy income through the various types of turbines.

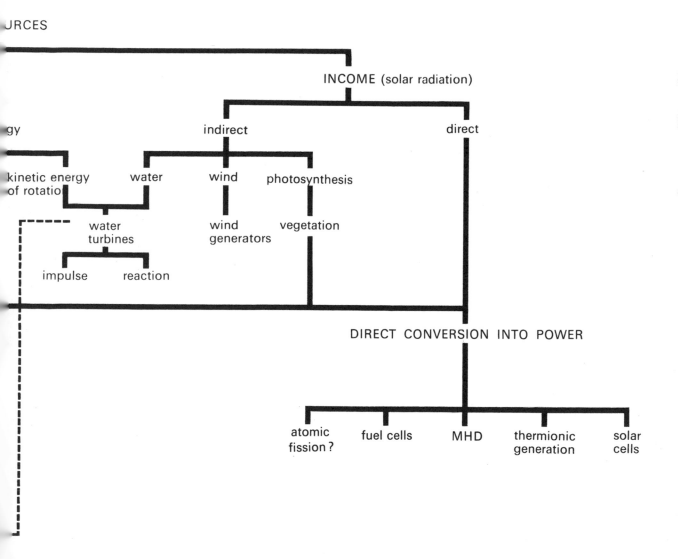

6 Kinetic Energy in Fluids

In the previous chapter we saw how all prime movers that use either water or heat energy work in a cyclic way. We saw, too, that the raw energy must first be converted into a form that the engine can use. In this chapter we shall consider how this initial energy-converting process is carried out in practice. It will be convenient to look first at prime movers that make use of purely rotary motion. In these, the various elements of the cycle are carried out in separate parts of the mechanism, and the flow of working fluid is continuous. The other major kind of prime movers includes the reciprocating engines. In these, the flow of fluid is discontinuous, and the same mechanical parts may deal with each of the elements of the cycle in turn. (These engines will be considered in Chapter 8.)

Let us begin with the waterpower plant, usually part of a *hydroelectric* project (from *hydro*, the Greek for "water"). We have no control over one part of its process —that in which solar energy evaporates water from the sea or from low-lying ground. Neither have we any control over the precipitation (that is, rain or snow), which deposits this water on high ground. From there on, however, man can and does control the process.

Imagine a broad, quietly-flowing river passing through meadows on its way to the sea. We usually think of the surface of a body of water as being dead level. But if we carry out careful measurements of even the most gently-flowing river, we find that the height of water above sea level decreases continuously as we move downstream. Indeed, if this were not so, the water would not flow. As we trace the river back to its source, we find it flows more and more swiftly. Finally, near the source, the water is a rushing mountain stream, dashing wildly down the hillside over boulders and rocks. Suppose we made a journey upstream at a time of heavy rainfall or after the winter snows have melted. Then we might find a raging torrent that in places has burst its banks, flooding low-lying areas. If we went after a prolonged drought, we are likely to see only a trickle of water near the source. Further down, the river would be a turbid stream instead of a pleasant waterway. How is man to

Right: Dam at Watts Bar, on the Tennessee River. The turbulent area at center is caused by the tail-race of water that has passed through the hydroelectric generators. At the top is the lock that enables shipping to pass the dam. Above: An early steam boiler, an indirect way of using water to provide power.

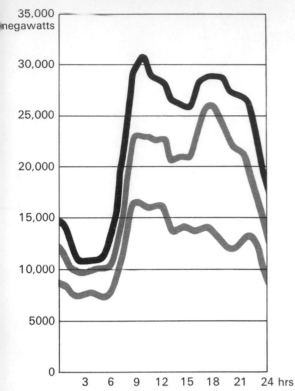

typical 1963 winter day
23 December 1963
typical 1963 summer day

Above: Demand curves, compiled from records of British Central Electricity Generating Board, illustrate daily and seasonal variations in electricity demand that can be anticipated. But sudden surges can take the supplier by surprise. Below: Such a demand occurred in Britain on November 7, 1963, immediately after the televising of the Miss World contest.

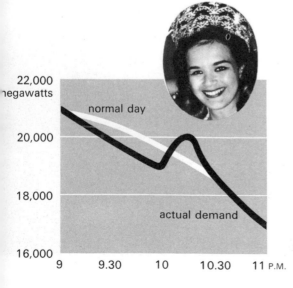

extract from this water a reliable, continuous source of useful power?

The first step is to make a complete survey of the whole of the river and of the land from which water drains into it. This land is known as the catchment area, or drainage basin, or watershed. We need to know the probable average rainfall on this area at every season of the year. Then we can estimate how much water will flow along the river at any given time. In some cases, meteorological records may exist. Of course, allowance must be made for that proportion of the rainfall that is retained in the soil and eventually re-evaporated without ever reaching the river. All calculations must then be checked by actual measurements of the flow of the river at various points along its length. The initial survey will already have revealed the differences in level between the points we choose. Thus an estimate can now be made of the energy available between any two points. From all this, we can work out how much power can be derived from the flowing river.

By its very nature, waterpower is available mainly in mountainous areas. Such regions are usually some distance from large centers of population where the power is needed, so men must also consider the problem of transmitting the electricity produced. The nature of the demand for electricity must also be examined. This demand varies considerably over the twenty-four hours of the day. A typical winter day, for instance, shows a very light demand during the night. The demand rises sharply in the morning as factories begin their operations and housewives start cooking. Then there is a slight fall-off during the early afternoon, followed by another peak towards evening. Demand drops again when factories close down for the night, and a further steady decline follows as people switch off lights and appliances as they go to bed. Since electricity cannot be stored, the output must be controlled to match the demand.

To handle the variations in demand, and also variations in the flow of the river, water is stored in a reservoir. From there, enough water will be allowed to flow down to the power station to produce the quantity of electricity required at any particular hour. The reservoir is made by building a dam across the river, and the choice of the best place to build it is very important. There will inevitably be a rise in the river level upstream of the dam. This backing-up of water will flood part of the valley and create an artificial lake. Obviously, the dam-builder will do his utmost to flood an area that is uninhabited and not very fertile. The ground where the dam is to be built must provide a good foundation to support the great weight of the dam. The earth must not

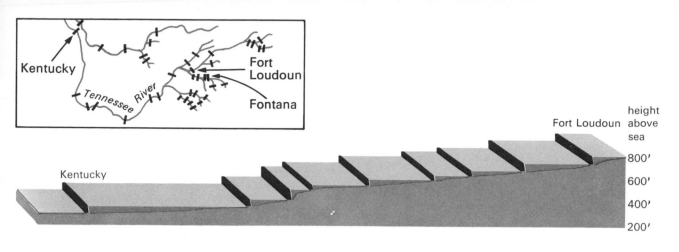

Fort Loudoun

height above sea

800'
600'
400'
200'

Kentucky

Profile of the Tennessee River (above) shows a 650-mile stretch that includes nine dams. Between the Fort Loudoun and Kentucky dams the river falls 515 feet in a series of steps. Photo (below left) shows the Fontana dam, situated on the Little Tennessee River (see map at top of page of complete Tennessee Valley project). The narrowness of the valley and the large head of water contrast with conditions lower downstream, such as found at the Kentucky dam (below right).

be porous, otherwise there may be a serious loss of water by seepage. Finally, the dam must be placed in as convenient a place as possible for the turbine that it is to serve.

In a complete hydroelectric project, it is often necessary to place a number of power stations at various points along the river. If we exaggerate the natural contour of a river from its source to its mouth, we find a steep slope, at the source, that gradually flattens out towards the mouth. The effect of constructing a number of dams is to change this sloping contour into a series of steps. The horizontal distance between each step and the next increases as we approach the mouth of the river. The height of the dam—and hence the available *head* (see p. 117) of water for the turbine—decreases. However, the nearer the mouth of the river, the greater will be the water's flow. This increase is due to the num-

ber of tributaries that have joined the river and the larger areas of land drained.

Flowing water offers a source of energy that is literally free. The aim of those responsible for such hydroelectric projects must be to keep their initial costs as low as possible. This usually means reducing the number of power stations to be built to a minimum. That is where it becomes so important to be skillful in selecting a site. Here is an example. The cost of a dam increases considerably as the height is increased. Yet all the available facts about flow of water and demand for power may indicate that a very high dam is required if we are to prevent wastage of water when the river is in full flood. On the other hand, when the flow of the river is normal, the reservoir will be only partly full. The extra height of the dam will then be serving no purpose. Here the wisest decision might be to build a dam that is not quite high enough to trap *all* the water under flood conditions. This decision would mean that the total amount of power produced in a year would be reduced. But the lower cost of the dam would reduce the initial cost of the scheme and so provide cheaper electricity.

In actual practice, a number of different arrangements of dam and power station are used. The choice depends on the geography of the area. Occasionally it is possible to build the dam on the edge of a plateau and then to convey the water by pipeline to the power station in the valley below. Heads of several thousand feet may sometimes be obtained in this way. At Reisseck, Austria, the head is 5,800 feet. Such large heads are very advantageous because of the great amount of power produced per pound of water. But the lower part of the pipeline must be designed to withstand extremely high pressures. For a head of 5,800 feet, the pressure would be over a ton per square inch. Some projects involve tunneling through a mountain, so that water from a high valley may be conveyed to a lower, adjacent valley.

Most hydroelectric projects cannot employ extremely high heads, however, because the land-forms do not permit it. A typical medium-to-low head project might have a dam and a short connecting pipeline between the reservoir and the power station. Or the power station may be located at the bottom of the dam itself. Without doubt, the most magnificent project of this type is the huge Kariba dam across the Zambesi River, in Rhodesia, Africa. This tremendous structure towers 400 feet above the river bed. The turbines are placed in cavities hollowed out of the rock on either bank. The reservoir forms the largest artificial lake in the world, with an area of 2,000 square miles. The enormous storage capacity provided enables a steady output of power sufficient to supply 7,000,000 one-kilowatt electric

Above: Penstocks leading to the McKee Creek power station, Victoria, Australia. Below: Diagram of a typical high-head hydroelectric project. Shaft on side of dam opposite to the reservoir is a safety valve, which relieves what could be a dangerous surge in the down-pipe if the power station is suddenly shut down.

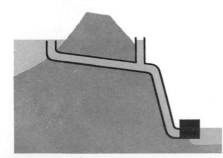

Above: The great Kariba dam, across the Zambesi River in Rhodesia, holds back the world's largest artificial lake—175 miles long and up to 20 miles wide.

Below: Diagram of a typical medium-to-low-head hydroelectric project.

appliances throughout the year. This vast project is, of course, not typical. Many much smaller, but equally satisfactory, projects exist in countries that do not have such large rivers. If the flow of water is sufficient, even heads as low as 30 or 40 feet may be enough to justify an economic hydroelectric project.

With tidal power projects, heads of that size are the most that can be expected. The energy of a river originates, of course, from solar energy. The source of tidal energy is the kinetic energy of the earth's rotation. But we can employ the same kind of engines, namely turbines, to convert both river and tidal energy into useful work. However, the problems involved in the first stage of the power-producing process—getting the energy into a form suitable for use in the turbine—are very different in the two cases. We saw in Chapter 3 that only a few sites appear to be suitable for a tidal power scheme. Such sites are invariably river estuaries or other such tapering inlets. There the great volume of sea-water flowing into the wide opening reaches a much higher level when it is suddenly restricted by the narrower parts further up.

The alternating nature of the tidal flow creates a special problem in harnessing this form of energy. The simplest method is to build a dam (or a *barrage*, as it is usually called in a tidal project) right across the estuary. This barrage will have sluice-gates that are opened to allow the water to enter on the flood tide. When the water is at its highest level, the sluices are closed. When the water level downstream of the barrage has fallen on the ebb tide to a low-enough level, the stored water is allowed to flow out through the turbines. These turbines are housed in the barrage itself. Power generation can continue to be generated until the difference in water level above and below the barrage (the head available for the turbines) has dropped to a level that makes the operation uneconomic.

This discontinuous nature of the power output is the biggest problem in developing tidal power projects. A single-basin system of the kind described above is by far the cheapest method of utilizing tidal energy. Only one side of the basin has to be built—namely the barrage. The other sides are provided by the estuary banks. However, the best that can be hoped for from a single-basin system is power generation for about seven hours in each tidal cycle of approximately twelve hours and twenty-five minutes. Thus, if generation began at noon on a particular day, it would end at 7:00 p.m., begin again at about 25 minutes after midnight the next day, end at about 7:25 a.m. and begin again at about 12:50 p.m. The times during which power is produced, therefore, advance by 50 minutes each day. Obviously, such varying times of generation will not always coincide with the peak periods of demand for power.

There are ways of dealing with this problem, but all of them involve a considerable increase in the initial costs. One way is to use some of the electricity to drive pumps. These will pump sea-water into a storage reservoir, from which it can be taken to produce power during the peak periods. Here some loss of energy is involved because the electric motors and pumps, although very efficient, cannot have 100 per cent efficiency.

Another alternative—again, involving heavy additional expense—is the two-basin system (illustrated on

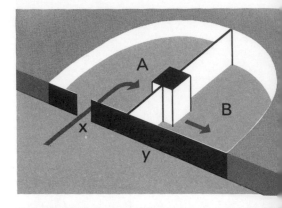

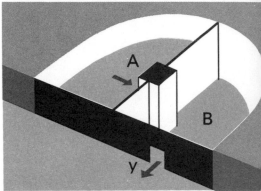

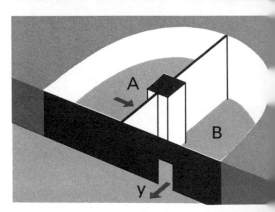

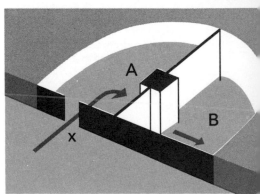

Diagrams show how the use of two basins can permit continuous generation of electricity by a turbine placed between them. In the first diagram, the tide is rising, and basin A is receiving water through sluice x. Basin B has been shut off from the sea (by sluice y) since the previous low tide. Water from A can thus pass through the turbine into B to generate electricity. The size of the basins and the quantities of water involved have been carefully determined to ensure that A fills more quickly from the sea than B gets filled from A.

At the end of high tide, sluice x is shut. Then, as the tide falls, sluice y is opened, letting water out from B. All the time, water from A is passing Into B through the turbine.

As the tide continues to fall, the water level in B falls quicker than the level in A, from which water is passing through the turbine into B. At the end of low tide, y is closed.

As the tide rises, x is opened and A fills, giving a progressively greater head between A and B; x remains open until the end of high tide.

page 128). The turbines thus produce power for the whole of the twenty-four hours of the day. Unfortunately, the enormous cost of building a completely artificial barrier to separate the two basins would quite outweigh the value of the additional power that would be produced.

To make such a project economic, we must therefore look for a place where there are two inlets side by side. The inlets should be separated by a neck of land, or at least by a group of islands that can be joined together by dams. Two such possible places are Passamaquoddy, along the northern coast of Maine, and the Bay of Fundy, on Canada's eastern coast. Passamaquoddy Bay has numerous islands from which either a single-basin or a two-basin scheme could be created. The Bay of Fundy has the highest tidal range in the world. Two estuaries, the Petitcodiac and the Memramcook, both flow into the Bay of Fundy. They are separated by a narrow tongue of rock and form an ideal location for a two-basin scheme. Both the Passamaquoddy and Fundy areas have been fully investigated. Work was actually started in 1935 at Passamaquoddy, but was abandoned in the following year. Nevertheless, there is still some interest in this project today. And various Canadians hope someday to harness the powerful tides of the Bay of Fundy.

So far, only one tidal power plant has actually been constructed. This is on the estuary of the River Rance in Brittany, in northern France, where the maximum tidal range is 38 feet. This is a single-basin system, but it is unique in that the turbines are designed to work on both *rising* and *falling* tides. French engineers have achieved this by a completely new design of turbine and generator. The water can flow equally in either direction past the alternators and expend its force on the turbine blades. Thus, if we imagine the basin to be empty at low water, the incoming tide fills the basin only after it has passed inward through the turbines. When the tide is falling, the same water—having been stored behind the barrage—flows outward. Again the water passes through the turbines. In this way, every rise and fall of tide produces twice as much power as would have been obtained from a simple single-basin system.

But that is not all. We said that electricity cannot be stored, but water can. Furthermore, an alternator that is driven by an outside force (the turbine) generates electricity. But the same alternator, when fed with electric current, acts as a motor. Lastly, a turbine rotated by flowing water can equally well act as a pump if it is driven by an external force. The Rance engineers have arranged matters so that, when the basin is only partly filled by the incoming tide, it can be pumped up to full

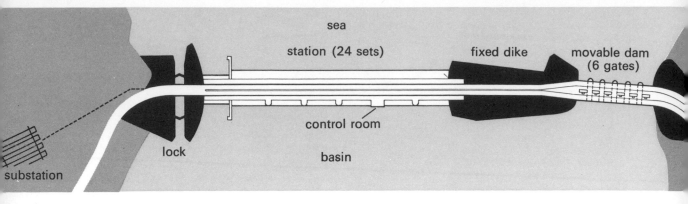

sea

station (24 sets)

fixed dike

movable dam
(6 gates)

control room

lock

basin

substation

Plan of the installation at Rance, France.
Since the basin's capacity is very large,
not all the water impounded behind it at
high tide will pass through the
generators. The movable dam (right)
with six large sluice gates is used to
ensure complete emptying; it also,
on a rising tide, ensures complete
filling of the basin.

Below: Diagram of one of the
turbo-alternators installed in the Rance
barrage. Since the turbine is mounted
horizontally, it can be driven by water
flowing either way—from the sea into
the reservoir during rising tide, and
from the reservoir to the sea during
falling tide. The alternator can also
be fed with electricity, from outside
sources, to drive the turbine and so
pump water into the basin at times when
demand for electricity is small.

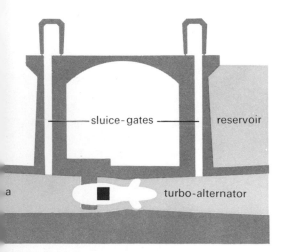

sluice-gates   reservoir

a

turbo-alternator

height by using electricity generated elsewhere in the
national electric system. This may seem to be a round-
about method of storing energy, but it pays to do it at
certain times. For instance, suppose that the tide reaches
its full height late at night when the overall demand for
electricity is at its smallest. The Rance motors can now
draw on spare generator capacity elsewhere in order to
pump up the basin during the early hours of the morning. The project is then ready for generating electricity
at full capacity around the time of low water. This coin-
cides with the heavy demand that comes with the beginning of another working day.

The Rance project ranks among the world's great
power stations, producing electricity at a rate that,
judged as a steady output, is equal to 85,000 horsepower. Here at least is one successful tidal scheme. But
in general we can say that tidal energy is probably the
most tantalizing form of energy ever considered for
power-producing purposes. The energy is there in
plenty, but the form it takes is difficult to manage and
the financial investment would be enormous. Probably
no other source of energy has provoked so much careful
investigation and so many painstaking reports for so
few actual results.

Very different problems are encountered in the first
stage of the heat-engine cycle. The heat is produced by
the combustion of a fossil fuel, or by the fission of a
nuclear fuel. Basically, the problem consists of trans-

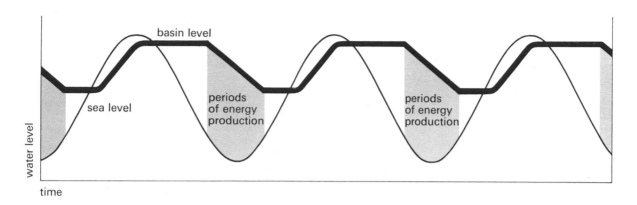

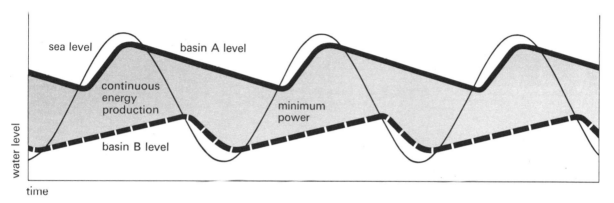

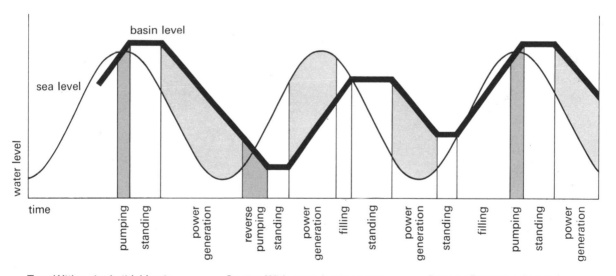

Top: With a single tidal basin and ordinary turbines, only intermittent energy production is possible—during ebb tide. (In all these diagrams, blue areas represent periods of energy production.)

Center: With a two-basin system such as described on pages 128-129, continuous energy production is possible, although available power does vary.

Bottom: Power on demand can be provided by pump turbines, such as used in the Rance barrage (opposite). They use off-peak power from outside sources to pump water in either direction, and they also act as turbines. Diagram shows some of the ways in which they may provide power at any time.

ferring this heat to the working fluid of the engine. The apparatus in which this is done consists essentially of a tube or series of tubes, through which flows the working fluid. The hot material produced by the combustion process is often on the outside of the tubes. In the nuclear reactor, however, it is more convenient for the fissionable material to be inside the tubes. The working fluid then passes over them. This principle is also used in a few types of steam generator—notably, the steam locomotive boiler.

Such devices belong to a class of apparatus called "heat exchangers." Their function is to transfer heat from one medium to another while keeping the two media physically separate. In heat engines used for power-production, the working fluid must enter the engine of the power plant at a high pressure. The combustion or fission process takes place at atmospheric pressure. So it is clear that the tubes of the heat exchanger must be designed to withstand a large pressure difference across them. The tubes must also withstand high temperature.

The steam engine, the first kind of heat engine to be built, has a history going back about 275 years. In the very early engines, the steam pressure was low—indeed, only just above atmospheric pressure. The boiler consisted of nothing but a more-or-less spherical vessel

Modern Lancashire boilers. The fundamental design of this type of boiler has changed little since its introduction over a century ago.

Below: The Lancashire boiler is internally fired and has two central flues within the boiler shell. The products of combustion pass along these flues and are then directed back along the lower flue, from which they pass through the side flues to the rear exit and chimney. This arrangement of flues inside the boiler's brickwork setting increases the available heating surface.

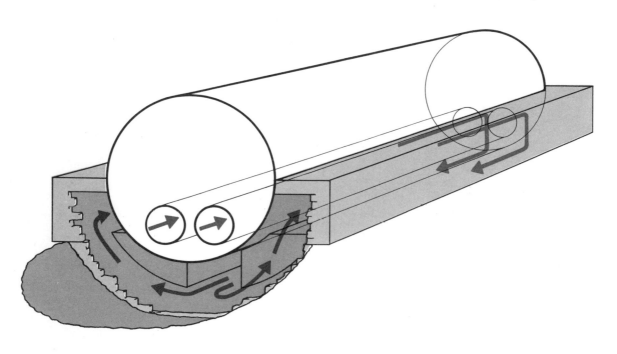

Above: In Stephenson's
Rocket (1829) many tubes
about three inches in diameter ran
from a large firebox through the
boiler shell. They were mounted at an
angle, and not vertically as in
previous locomotives.

In an externally fired boiler, the
furnace is situated outside the
boiler, and usually below it. Compare
with the Lancashire boiler (diagram
opposite), where the furnace is within
the boiler shell.

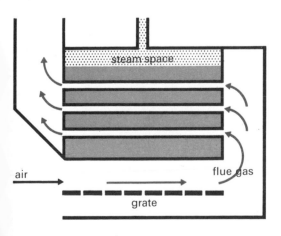

filled with water, with a coal fire burning below it. The pressure difference needed to set steam flowing through the engine was obtained by condensing the steam after it left the engine. This reduced the pressure to 12 or 13 pounds-force per square inch below atmospheric pressure (about 14.7 pounds-force per square inch at sea level). Such low-pressure steam engines continued to be made throughout the eighteenth century, although there were improvements in other directions. In the nineteenth century, however, the advantages of using a higher steam pressure began to be realized, and suitable boilers were designed.

Typical of these was the Lancashire boiler, in which the coal is burnt at one end of a wide tube. The tube passed horizontally through the cylindrical boiler shell containing water. The hot gases leaving the burning mass of coal passed along the remainder of the fire tube, giving up some of their heat to the water. A similar boiler was designed by George Stephenson for his famous steam locomotive, the "Rocket." This had a large firebox, from which came a number of tubes about three inches in diameter. These tubes conveyed the hot gases through the boiler shell containing the water before the gases escaped from the chimney. The advantage of using a number of tubes was that a greater surface area is available for heat flow. This meant that the temperature of the gases that left the flue was reduced, less heat was wasted, and the efficiency of the boiler was increased. Both the Lancashire boiler and Stephenson's boiler showed a recognition that *conduction* of heat by direct contact of the hot coals with the metal of the firebox was not sufficient to ensure high efficiency. It was also necessary to extract heat by *convection* from the hot flue gases.

The use of steam as a working fluid for a power plant was well established by the middle of the nineteenth century. Steam certainly has a number of very considerable advantages over other possible fluids. Steam is cheap, it can be obtained almost anywhere in the world, and it does not attack the metals from which the engine is made. However, it was now time to examine its properties under various conditions of temperature and pressure.

It is common knowledge that in an open vessel, such as a kettle, water boils at 212°F. It is also fairly well known that at a great altitude—for instance, on a high mountain top—the boiling point of water is considerably lower than this. The reason is that, on the mountain top, the atmospheric pressure is lower than at sea-level. The water molecules therefore require a smaller addition of kinetic energy in order to exist as a gas. We find that this is a general rule: The lower the pressure, the

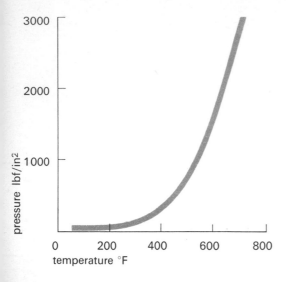

Graph plots boiling point of water against pressure. As pressure is increased, the boiling point rises sharply.

Below: A water-tube boiler. In such boilers the products of combustion pass over tubes carrying the water. This is in contrast to fire-tube boilers (previous pages), in which the combustion products pass through tubes immersed in the water. The flue gas makes several passes over the tubes, being directed by baffles. The tubes are connected to the boiler drum, where steam and water are separated.

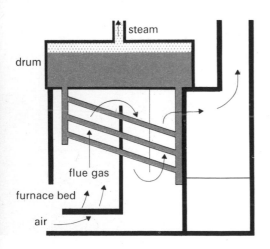

lower the boiling point; the higher the pressure, the higher the boiling point. A graph of pressure plotted against boiling point shows a steeper and steeper slope as the pressure is increased. Thus, if we wished to use a temperature of 500°F. in an engine, we should require 700 lbf/in². To use a temperature of 700°F., we should have to accept a pressure of 3,000 lbf/in².

Materials have long been available that can be satisfactorily used at temperatures of between 700° and 800°F. Modern steam turbines are designed for 1,000° to 1,100°F. The use of very high pressures, however, is extremely inconvenient because they put excessive stresses on the boiler tubes. The solution is to use what is called *superheated steam*. This is steam heated to a temperature above boiling point, as distinct from steam that is just at boiling point (known as *saturated steam*). The use of superheated steam enables us to take advantage of a higher temperature, thus improving engine efficiency. At the same time, it allows a lower pressure so as to avoid difficulties in boiler design. Superheated steam has other advantages in the turbine itself, and these will be outlined in the next chapter.

The types of boiler so far described can be used only to produce saturated steam, because the tubes containing the hot gases of combustion are completely immersed in water. To superheat the steam, we must heat it further after evaporation. This is more easily done if the water and steam pass through the tubes, and the hot gases over them. All power station boilers now work on this principle. Such *water-tube* boilers have other advantages, too. First, there is a much smaller quantity of water present in the boiler. This enables the boiler to respond more rapidly to changes in demands. Next, the tubes can be smaller in diameter, because they are not liable to become clogged with ash. This gives a greater surface area for heat-flow, thus allowing the whole boiler to be smaller for a given output of steam.

With the rapid development of electricity generation in the last thirty years, considerable attention has been given to the science of heat transfer. As a result, engineers have become increasingly aware of the importance of radiant heat as a mode of heat transfer in boilers. It was found that a high proportion of the heat released in the combustion process appeared first in the form of radiation from the flame and hot particles of fuel. Modern boilers make use of this fact. They have a large combustion chamber whose walls are cooled with tubes through which the water flows. The combustion chamber of a typical power station boiler may be 25 feet square and 50 or 60 feet high.

To the untrained eye, a drawing of such a boiler seems

Looking upward inside the furnace of
the High Marnham power station in
England (see next two pages). The
furnace is over 100 feet high.

so complicated as to be quite incomprehensible. Fortunately the main features are relatively simple. One guiding principle is that, as far as possible, the pipes where the steam is coolest are placed in that part of the boiler where the highest gas temperature is expected. This ensures that there is the maximum possible temperature difference across the walls of the tubes. In this way a high rate of heat flow is obtained.

Let us first consider the combustion process and the flow of hot gases resulting from it. The fuel is either oil or coal. If coal is used, it is usually pulverized into small particles, which are sprayed into the combustion chamber. If oil is used, it is sprayed into the combustion chamber in the form of droplets. The air for combustion is fed in by a fan, called the *forced draft* fan. The combustion chamber becomes filled with a mass of glowing hot particles of fuel and flame. The hot products of combustion pass upward and leave at the top of the boiler. The hottest gases will be found at the top of the combustion chamber, because by the time they have reached that position combustion will be complete. All the energy of the fuel will then have converted into heat. From here upward, the temperature will fall as heat is transferred from the gases through the walls of the tubes and into the water or steam. Every effort must be made to lower the temperature of the gases as much as possible before they leave the boiler. The aim is to reduce the amount of heat being carried away up the chimney. The tubes carrying the coldest water are therefore placed near the exit, since the temperature of the gases cannot be reduced below that of the water in the tubes. To assist the flow of gases through the boiler, another fan (called the *induced draft* fan) is placed near the exit to suck out the exhaust gases.

The flow of water and steam is by natural circulation, just as it is in a home's hot water system. The density of hot water is lower than that of cold, so the hot water rises up the tubes. The lowest water temperature is found immediately on leaving the condenser, and at this point might be around 100°F. However, the water does not re-enter the boiler at this temperature. It is found more economical—for reasons that will be explained in the next chapter—to raise its temperature with the help of steam "bled off" from suitable points part way through the turbine. This process, called *feed-heating*, may raise the water temperature to between 200° and 250°F. This water now goes through the *economizer*, a heat exchanger consisting of tubes through which the water passes. After they have left the boiler proper, the flue gases pass over these tubes. Since the flue gases are hotter than the water, the temperature of the water is raised to about 400°F.

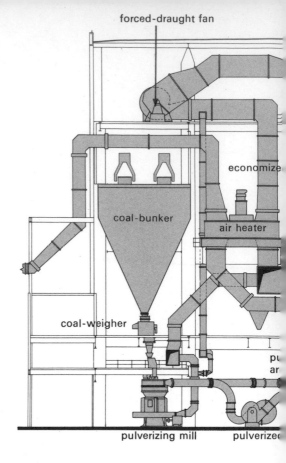

Above: Diagram of the High Marnham power station, Nottinghamshire, England, which has a capacity of 1,350,000 lbs. of steam per hour. Note the superheaters at the top of the furnace, and the economizer on the left side. The furnace uses tangential firing, illustrated below; the burners direct streams of coal and air into the furnace, obtaining a cyclonic movement within it. Right, upper: The huge condensers at High Marnham, used to convert spent steam back into water. Lower: The grinding mills that pulverize the coal into a fine powder.

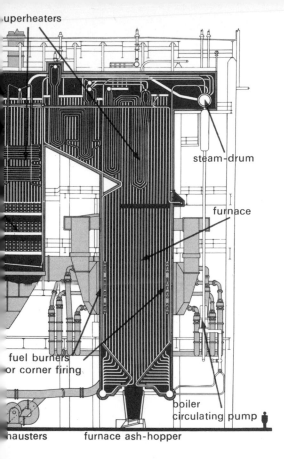

superheaters

steam-drum

furnace

fuel burners
or corner firing

boiler
circulating pump

hausters   furnace ash-hopper

On leaving the economizer, the water passes through the boiler feed pump. There the water's pressure is raised to the full pressure required by the turbine, and then enters the water-cooled walls of the combustion chamber. Here it receives heat by radiation, and its temperature is raised to somewhat below the boiling point corresponding to the increased pressure. The water now moves on through the evaporator tubes (a bank of tubes set across the flow of gases) where it receives heat by convection from the gases and is converted into steam. The steam is collected in a drum to which the tubes are connected. The steam is then conveyed by pipes from the top of this drum to the superheater. This consists of a separate bank of tubes placed near the top of the combustion chamber, where the gas temperature is highest. From the superheater, the steam is now ready to enter the turbine.

There is one further device to reduce the temperature of the flue gases. Because of the feed-heating, the water that leaves the condenser at a temperature of 100°F. enters the economizer at a temperature of between 200° and 250°F. A further heat exchanger is attached and used to heat air before it enters the combustion chamber. This air-preheater, as it is called, is the last part of the boiler through which the gases pass. Because the air enters it at a temperature comparable to that of the water leaving the condenser, the flue gas temperature is correspondingly reduced.

In Chapter 5 we met the steady flow energy equation, $E_1 = W + Q + E_2$. If we apply this to a boiler, we can see how it helps in understanding the ways in which the performance can be improved. We can imagine the boiler as a box into which flows water, air for combustion, and fuel. Out of this box flows steam and exhaust gases. There is no work done, so the term W is zero. The inlet and outlet velocities are sufficiently low for the kinetic energy terms to be ignored. Potential energy terms may also be ignored. We can also neglect the heat loss due to radiation. The term Q in the steady flow equation will therefore represent the heat given out by the combustion of one pound of fuel. Suppose that, for each pound of fuel, m_1 pounds of air are required and m_2 pounds of steam are produced. Ignoring the mass of ash, the mass of exhaust gases must be $1 + m_1$, produced by 1 lb. fuel + m_1 lb. air. The steady flow equation can now be written as follows:

$Q = m_2$ multiplied by the increase in enthalpy in changing 1 lb. water to 1 lb. steam + $(1 + m_1)$ multiplied by the enthalpy per lb. exhaust gases $- m_1$ multiplied by the enthalpy of air.

137

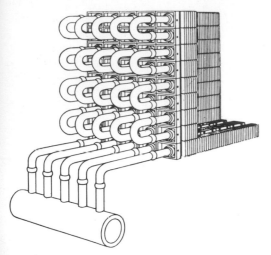

Diagram of an economizer unit shows the tubes through which the water passes, and over which the flue gases pass after leaving the boiler.

Below: Over-all efficiencies of various boilers, all coal-fired. Oil-firing increases these figures. Oil offers further advantages in that it is more easily stored and fired, and leaves very little solid residue.

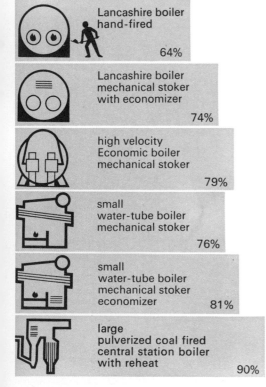

Lancashire boiler hand-fired
64%

Lancashire boiler mechanical stoker with economizer
74%

high velocity Economic boiler mechanical stoker
79%

small water-tube boiler mechanical stoker
76%

small water-tube boiler mechanical stoker economizer
81%

large pulverized coal fired central station boiler with reheat
90%

Since the object of the boiler is to produce steam, the efficiency of the boiler is defined like this:

Boiler efficiency $= m_2$ multiplied by the increase in enthalpy in changing 1 lb. of water to 1 lb. steam and divided by Q.

It is clear that the smaller the enthalpy of the exhaust gases, the greater will be the efficiency. Because enthalpy depends largely on temperature (p. 116), every effort must be made to keep the exhaust gas temperature to a minimum.

One point worth noting is that the expression for boiler efficiency is quite different from the expression for complete heat-engine efficiency. The latter was given near the end of Chapter 5 (p. 119), where we saw that the maximum theoretical efficiency of a complete heat engine is about 75 per cent. Present-day steam boilers, on the other hand, can show efficiencies of over 90 per cent. The problems that have had to be solved in order to achieve such a high efficiency fall into three main categories—heat transfer, metallurgy, and production. The field of heat transfer is one where physicists, mathematicians, and engineering scientists have labored, both by experiment and theoretical analysis. The metallurgical and production problems are very closely connected, since the temperature and the pressure that a boiler can withstand are largely determined by the materials and the method of construction of the drums used to collect the steam from the evaporator. In the earlier boilers, riveted drums were used. Then an increase in temperature and pressure was found possible if a welded construction was adopted. For very high pressures and temperatures, forged drums are essential.

Steel is virtually the only material used in boiler construction. Basically, steel is iron with a small percentage of carbon added. But even what may appear to be tiny changes in the carbon content, ranging from 0.3 to 1.5 per cent, can make a great difference to its properties. To produce improved properties at high temperatures, a small percentage of various other elements may be added. These include, among others, nickel, chromium, cobalt, tungsten, and vanadium.

The metallurgical problems of the boiler designer, however, seem insignificant beside those of the designer of a nuclear reactor. So far, nuclear reactors have been used merely as an alternative to a boiler in a steam power plant. Apart from the method of heating the working fluid, the nuclear plant is in principle exactly the same as one in which traditional fuels are used.

The design of the reactor itself, however, poses some very difficult problems, which have had to be solved in

In these boilers at Warrington, Lancashire, England, pulverized coal is fed from hoppers onto a slow-moving perforated chain, which carries it inside the boiler and forms the actual grate on which it burns.

Below: A boiler drum being installed in a power station at Himeji, Japan.

only the few years that have elapsed since scientists first released atomic energy. The basic principles of nuclear fission were described in Chapter 4. It was seen that there are two main types of nuclear reactor, distinguished by the speed at which the neutrons move when colliding with the uranium nucleus. All the early atomic power stations, and most of those at present under construction, have "slow" reactors. In this type, the neutron speed is deliberately reduced by means of a moderator. There are three essential parts of such a reactor. First, there must be rods of uranium fuel, encased in a leak-proof container so as to prevent the radioactive fission products from escaping into the rest of the reactor. Next comes the moderator through which the neutrons pass. Its function is to slow them down between one collision and the next (p. 95). Finally, there must be some means of extracting the heat from the reactor and transferring it to the working fluid of the engine. The best way of extracting the heat is to pass some coolant—either a liquid or a gas—through a ring-like space between the fuel rods and the moderator.

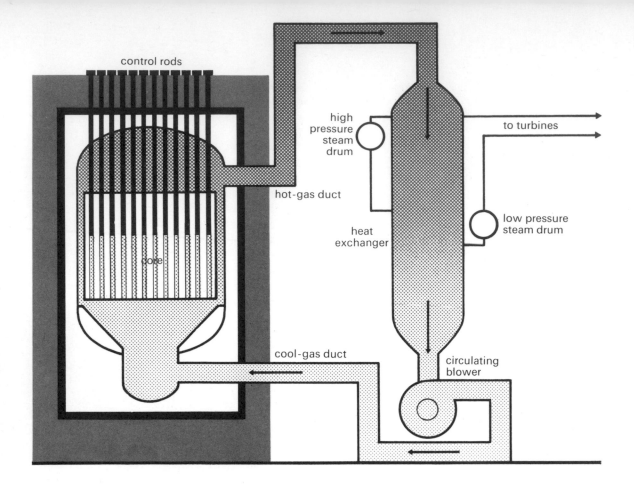

control rods

high pressure steam drum

to turbines

hot-gas duct

heat exchanger

low pressure steam drum

core

cool-gas duct

circulating blower

Engineers thus face the choice of suitable materials for the fuel rod containers, the moderator, and the coolant. All these materials must share one property in common: They must not absorb too many neutrons. Otherwise the neutron level in the atomic pile will fall below the level necessary to maintain a chain reaction, and the reactor will not work at all. The material for the fuel rod containers must be capable of withstanding the internal pressure caused by the fission products. The material must also be capable of being accurately machined, to enable the fuel rod to make good thermal contact so as to facilitate heat flow. These factors suggest the need to use a metal, but suitable metals are few. Only beryllium, zirconium, aluminum, and magnesium have all these desirable properties and—equally important—do not react at high temperatures with uranium. Beryllium is the most suitable of the four, but it is very expensive and not readily obtainable in the quantity needed. After considerable research, an alloy of magnesium with one per cent of aluminum has been developed for this purpose. This alloy, which is less expensive than beryllium, has still other advantages. It is stronger than either of the pure metals, and it can easily be drawn or pressed into tubes.

The Calder Hall (England) type of reactor uses natural uranium as its fuel. The heat given out during fission raises the temperature of the coolant, carbon dioxide. In the heat exchanger, this heat is used to raise steam for driving turbines in the normal way.

Below: Keyed rods of graphite for a reactor core. The fuel elements (opposite) are inserted in the holes.

The Windscale and Calder Works on the west coast of Cumberland, England. Huge quantities of cooling water are needed to condense used steam. Large power stations are therefore located close to the sea—as in this case— or on the banks of a large river.

Below: Fuel-rod containers made of magnox. The fins provide a large surface for heat exchange.

The choice of material for the moderator is perhaps less difficult. The moderator's sole function is to slow down the neutron speed without absorbing too many neutrons in the process. There are three materials in use: graphite; heavy water (water in which the hydrogen is in its isotopic form of deuterium); and ordinary water. Heavy water is expensive in Britain, but is more readily available in the United States and Canada. Plants for its manufacture were set up there for atomic bomb production during the Second World War. Heavy water is a good moderator—better than graphite, in fact. But ordinary water, although also a good moderator, absorbs far more neutrons. It can only be employed if specially treated, or enriched, uranium fuel is used.

The selection of a suitable coolant involves a number of complex considerations. If the reactor employs the enriched uranium fuel, as in the American designs, water-cooled, water-moderated reactors can be used. In these, the same fluid performs both functions. But if the reactor employs natural uranium, as in the British designs, then water is ruled out because of its high rate of absorption of neutrons. There is no other suitable liquid, so consideration must then be given to a gas. There are a number of possible gases, including hydrogen, helium,

and carbon dioxide. Of these, carbon dioxide was selected for the British reactors for three reasons. It is cheap; it has a higher specific heat than the other gases; and it also has a higher density. The second point means that a given mass of gas will remove more heat from the reactor. The third point means that less work per pound has to be put into pumping the gas through the reactor. (This work must, of course, be subtracted from the total power output of the whole plant.) What is more, carbon dioxide offers no explosion hazard, as hydrogen does. And finally, carbon dioxide has no undesirable chemical reaction either with graphite or with the metallic fuel containers.

The water-cooled, water-moderated reactor has a number of advantages over the graphite-moderated, gas-cooled design. Since two inches of water are as effective a moderator as seven inches of graphite, the reactor is considerably smaller and therefore cheaper. The water-cooled reactor can also be made in the factory. The gas-cooled type is so large that it must be taken to the site in pieces and assembled there. Such a procedure is much more costly. Furthermore, the water-coolant requires far less power for pumping than does the gas coolant. On the other hand, the water-cooled

The experimental reactor at Windscale in England (above) uses uranium oxide, and heats the cooling gas (carbon dioxide) to a higher temperature than the Calder Hall types. Operation is otherwise similar. Below: Gas enters at the bottom of the pressure vessel (1), passes up between the fuel elements and graphite, then onto the heat exchangers (2), and back through the circulator (3). Fuel elements can be unloaded by machine (4) and stored in a pit (5). The apparatus is contained in a steel sphere in case of accidents.

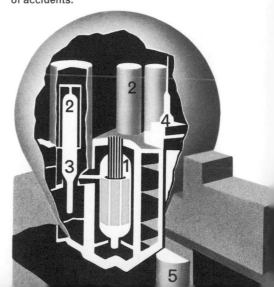

Looking down onto the pile-cap of the Windscale reactor. The four heat exchangers are at the sides of the photograph.

Below: Sketches compare sizes of (left) a conventional coal-fired power station and (right) the Windscale reactor station. The Windscale reactor needs about two tons of fuel a week; it yields about the same amount for reprocessing, and nothing else. The coal-fired station needs 140,000 tons of coal a week, and produces 17,000 tons of ash.

reactor must use the enriched uranium fuel that is so much more expensive than the natural uranium used in the gas-cooled design.

In the gas-cooled reactor, all of the fuel elements are contained in a steel pressure vessel. The carbon dioxide is circulated at a high pressure. It is pumped in at the bottom, passes over the fuel rods, and leaves at the top. The purpose of the high pressure is to increase the density of the gas, so that more heat can be taken away per unit volume of gas circulated. The pressure is limited only by the thickness of steel plate that can be satisfactorily welded to form the pressure vessel. In the early designs, this thickness was two inches, permitting a pressure of 100 pound-force per square inch. Recent developments in welding technology have increased this thickness to 3 or $3\frac{1}{2}$ inches, allowing a corresponding increase in the pressure used.

The hot carbon dioxide is conveyed by pipes from the top of the reactor to one or more heat exchangers. In the heat exchangers, the carbon dioxide passes over tubes containing the water from the steam turbine. The gas converts the water into superheated steam in readiness for re-entering the turbine. These heat exchangers really correspond to the boiler of the traditionally-

This swimming pool reactor at Grenoble,
France, was commissioned in 1963. In
common with other water-cooled,
water-moderated reactors, it uses
enriched uranium.

fueled steam power plant. Separate banks of tubes are provided to perform similar functions to the economizer, evaporator, and superheater sections of the steam boiler. Similar heat transfer problems are met, and they are solved in a similar way.

We saw earlier that in a steam boiler the flue gas temperature must be kept as low as possible for maximum efficiency. In the heat exchanger of an atomic power plant, it is also desirable to reduce the carbon dioxide temperature as much as possible. This is not, however, for the same reason. The carbon dioxide is, after all, returned to the reactor. No heat would be lost, in any case. The reason, rather, is that the lower the temperature of the carbon dioxide, the smaller will be the amount of work required to pump it around the circuit. In the steam boiler the minimum available water temperature, due to feed-heating, is about 200° to 250°F. The final reduction in temperature of the flue gases is brought about by pre-heating the air for combustion. This device is obviously not possible in the atomic plant because there is no combustion.

Atomic reactors have solved this problem in a very ingenious way, by employing what is called a "dual cycle." The steam turbine is made in two separate sections. Each section consists of a casing and a rotor, the two rotors being mechanically joined together. In the dual cycle, only about 70 per cent of the total steam produced enters the high-pressure section. The remainder of the steam is fed at a lower pressure into the pipes joining the high- and low-pressure sections. This low-pressure steam is produced in a separate set of tubes in the heat exchanger. Because its pressure is lower, its boiling temperature is lower. The heat required for its evaporation can thus be obtained from lower-temperature carbon dioxide. The heat needed for this purpose is taken from the carbon dioxide just before it leaves the heat exchanger. This process reduces the gas's temperature below what it would be if a simple cycle were used.

In most modern traditionally-fueled steam plants, high-pressure steam is produced at temperatures up to about 1,100°F. In the gas-cooled atomic reactor, the temperature is normally limited to about 600°F. If a much higher temperature were developed, the metallic uranium fuel would undergo a change in its crystalline form. Such a change would lead to serious distortion and possible fracture of the fuel rod containers. If this happened, the radioactive fission products would mix with the carbon dioxide and contaminate the whole plant. An atomic reactor operates at a lower temperature than a steam plant. This means that the reactor converts heat energy into electricity less efficiently than traditional steam plants do. Higher temperatures may,

Top: The charging face of a reactor at Marcoule, France, designed primarily to produce plutonium for use in breeder reactors. The reactor core consists of graphite piles crossed by horizontal channels into which the fuel elements are loaded. Lower picture: Part of the control panel in the reactor's control room.

however, be possible with a new type of reactor called the "advanced gas-cooled reactor." This differs from the one described in that its fuel is in the form of uranium oxide, a chemical compound instead of the pure metal. The uranium oxide is subjected to a process called "sintering." During this process, fine grains of the oxide are compressed and then held for a considerable period at a temperature somewhat below the melting point. This produces a rod of oxide that is strong but porous. It has spaces that will contain the fission products without distortion. Furthermore, the sintered oxide is a much more stable material than the pure metal, having a melting point of 4,500°F. instead of 2,100°F. Rods of pure uranium metal can heat the carbon dioxide to 750°F. at the very most. Rods of uranium oxide can heat it to just over 1,000°F. Unfortunately, this temperature is too great for the magnesium alloy containers, and either beryllium, zirconium, or stainless steel must be used. The first two metals are very expensive, and stainless steel is a much worse material from the point of view of neutron absorption.

Let us turn, now, from the gas-cooled, graphite-moderated reactors used in Britain to the water-cooled, water-moderated reactors developed in America. We find that there are two types of water-cooled reactors. The difference depends on whether or not the water is allowed to boil in the reactor. In the nuclear power station at Shippingport, Pennsylvania, on the Ohio River, the water is not allowed to boil. It is prevented from doing so because the pressure is maintained above the level at which water would boil at the maximum temperature produced. The pressure employed is 2,000 pounds-force per square inch, corresponding to a maximum temperature of 635°F. The water is circulated through a heat exchanger in exactly the same way as carbon dioxide is in the gas-cooled reactor. Uranium oxide fuel is used, in containers made of a zirconium alloy. Because water is a better moderator than graphite, the rods can therefore be placed much closer together than in the graphite-moderated reactor. The whole reactor is much smaller. Its volume is, in fact, less than one-tenth of that of England's Calder Hall reactor.

Originally engineers were somewhat nervous about allowing the water in the reactor to boil. But experimental plants appear to have done away with this fear. There are certainly many advantages in allowing the water to boil. When it does, there is no need to maintain such a high pressure. It is actually possible to take the steam directly from the reactor to the turbine, eliminating entirely the heat exchangers. At first it was feared that if a leak occurred in one of the fuel rod containers the steam would attack the fuel and carry radioactive

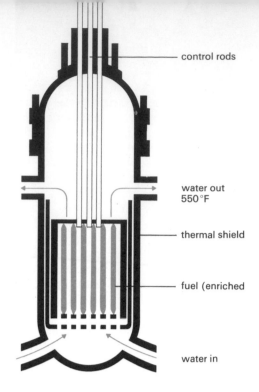

control rods

water out 550°F

thermal shield

fuel (enriched

water in

Above: Diagram of the water-cooled, water-moderated reactor at Shippingport, Pennsylvania. The water is not allowed to boil. Pressure within the vessel is high—2,000 pounds-force per square inch—allowing a temperature of over 600°F.

Below: A water-cooled, water-moderated reactor in which the water is allowed to boil. The steam may be taken directly to the turbine.

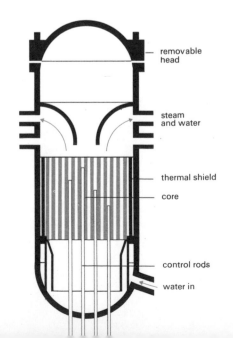

removable head

steam and water

thermal shield

core

control rods

water in

Left: The core of the Shippingport
reactor being lowered into place.
Below: Top view showing grid through
which the fuel elements and control
rods are inserted.

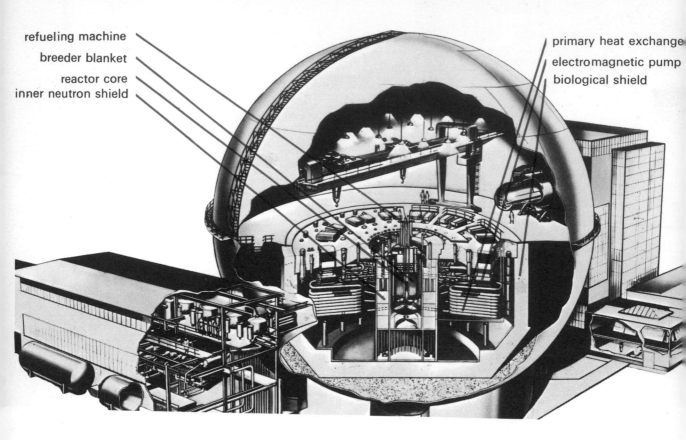

refueling machine
breeder blanket
reactor core
inner neutron shield

primary heat exchange
electromagnetic pump
biological shield

material into other parts of the plant. However, the uranium oxide is so stable that such attack does not occur. The danger of radioactive contamination is therefore much less than was feared.

It is possible that the nuclear reactor of the future will be the fast-neutron breeder reactor. In this type, the neutrons will not have to be slowed down. (The possibility of such a reactor is clear, as was seen in Chapter 4.) Such a reactor is still in the experimental stage although a prototype reactor is now being built at Dounreay, Scotland. A fast reactor has the advantage of not needing any moderator. This means that it can be smaller than any of the slow-neutron reactors. Its very smallness, however, introduces another problem—finding a coolant that will carry the heat away fast enough. To circulate a gas through a small reactor fast enough to carry away all the heat produced would require a great deal of pumping work. This is because the rate of heat transfer from a tube to a gas is much less than the rate from a tube to a liquid. But the use of a liquid raises another problem: Most liquids absorb neutrons, a property that is undesirable in this type of reactor. The answer appears to be that a liquid metal must be used— and preferably one that absorbs very few neutrons. Because metals are good conductors of heat, the rate of

Above right: The experimental reactor at Dounreay, Scotland, is the fast-breeder type—possibly the reactor of the future. Diagram above shows main features of reactor. Its fuel is enriched uranium, and the coolant is liquid sodium potassium alloy. The reactor reached its power level in July 1963, at which time it was the most powerful fast-reactor in the world.

Right: A recent development in nuclear reactors—pioneered by Euratom, a European six-country alliance— is the use of fuel in the form of pebbles. The pebbles, about 2.3 inches in diameter, are hollow graphite balls containing a mixture of coated particles (diagram below right) and graphite. Control rods are unnecessary, adjustments being made by removing or adding pebbles. The pebble bed is replenished from the top, while used-up pebbles are taken from the bottom of the heap.

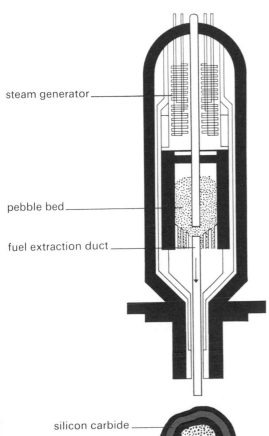

steam generator

pebble bed

fuel extraction duct

silicon carbide
fuel particle
graphite

heat transfer would be better than for non-metallic liquids, such as water. The most suitable metal appears to be a mixture of sodium and potassium. This mixture has a melting point of 40°F. and is therefore liquid at all conditions likely to be encountered.

All nuclear power plants are at present much more expensive than traditionally-fueled plants of a similar size. There are many reasons for this. Some of the materials used in their construction are very expensive. Great care has to be taken in assembling a nuclear plant to keep everything perfectly clear. Considerable research into new materials has had to be done, together with much experimentation to find ways of construction and new techniques of manufacture. All this research and development work has to be paid for, and it is reflected in the costs.

However, as more atomic power stations are built, the lessons learned in the earlier ones are applied. The cost of future nuclear power stations, therefore, is certain to be less than that of the earlier ones. The great advantage they offer, of course, is very much lower fuel costs. Even now, electricity from atomic energy can be produced at a price comparable to that from fossil fuels. As development proceeds, this electricity will eventually become cheaper.

7 Rotary Energy Converters

We have just seen how energy from a variety of sources is converted into kinetic energy in a fluid. We have seen, too, that the same basic rules apply whether the fluid is a liquid or a gas. Now we can examine the methods by which the energy in a fluid is converted into *rotary* kinetic energy. We shall concentrate on the simplest rotary converter, the turbine.

The turbine is both the oldest and the youngest rotary converter. Modern water turbines are the descendants of the water mill—improved beyond recognition, but still located where generous water supplies can be relied on. Primitive water wheels were invented probably a few thousand years ago. And, as we saw (p. 13), the water mill was the mainstay of the Industrial Revolution until it was supplanted by steam.

Turbines using fluids in the gaseous state came later. The earliest, the windmill, is only about 1,000 years old. As a practical energy converter, the steam turbine is no more than 75 years old. But we should pay our respects to Hero of Alexandria, for he invented a toy steam turbine as far back as 1,900 years ago.

But coming between the very old and the very new were the reciprocating steam engines of the late-eighteenth and nineteenth centuries. ("Reciprocating" refers to the fact that the piston goes back-and-forth.) These were the greatest of all prime movers in their day, both for propelling ships and for generating power for industry. They reached their zenith at the end of the nineteenth century. There were some magnificent specimens, beautifully constructed and of gigantic proportions, running at speeds of 500 to 600 revolutions per minute (rpm). These huge engines were built in an attempt to cope with an ever-increasing demand for electricity, but they were doomed for two reasons. One was their limited power. The other was their limited speed, due to the sheer weight of the reciprocating parts. Also, the electrical generators to which they were coupled demanded higher speeds of rotation or they, too, would have to become enormously heavy and complicated.

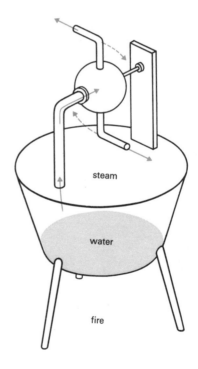

In the turbine devised by Hero of Alexandria over 1,900 years ago, the thrust of the steam escaping from the two outlets turned the sphere in the opposite direction. Right: A modern steam turbine being assembled for testing. The top half of the casing has still to be fitted.

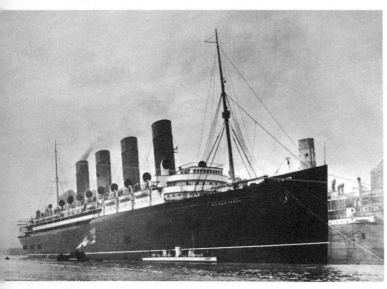

Above: Scale model in the Science Museum, London, of one of the engines of the steamship *Britannic* (1874). Each engine had two high-pressure cylinders 48 inches in diameter, and two low-pressure cylinders 83 inches in diameter. Left: In 1894 the first turbine-driven ship—the *Turbinia* (seen here alongside the *Mauretania*)—was built. It incorporated the turbine as developed by Charles Parsons, which produced more horsepower for its weight than any previous engine.

The steam turbine is superior to the reciprocating engine in several ways. A turbine is designed to produce rotary motion and does so directly, without using reciprocating parts. This eliminates the need for heavy counterpoise weights to balance the forces due to the linear motion of the pistons. The turbine is mechanically economical—that is, it delivers more power for its size and weight, both because it is simple and because the fluid passes continuously through it. This is in contrast to a reciprocating engine, in which the steam is admitted intermittently.

A turbine's advantages add up to the fact that the steam turbine can run at far higher speeds than the steam engine. Indeed, one of the first turbines, made by the Englishman Charles Parsons in 1884 ran at 18,000 rpm. It was only a small experimental machine, but it showed what could be done and it opened the way to a continuous period of turbine development.

Today's stationary turbines are standardized at much lower speeds—3,000 rpm in Europe and 3,600 rpm in North America. This standardization depends on the fact that such turbines are almost entirely used for generating electricity. In this book we do not deal with electricity and the methods of generating it except on the simplest level. All that need be said here is that electricity is an invisible form of energy. Electricity forms a convenient and instantaneous link between the power-*producing* machinery and power-*consuming* appliances, which may be at a considerable distance from each other. Generators convert kinetic energy into electricity, and electric motors convert electricity back into kinetic energy.

There are two main types of turbine—the *impulse* turbine and the *reaction* turbine. Of the two types, the impulse turbine is perhaps the easiest to understand. The potential energy of the fluid is first converted into kinetic energy by making it flow through a specially shaped passage called a nozzle. This kinetic energy is then converted into useful work by directing the high speed jet of fluid onto blades attached to a rotating wheel, or rotor. A simple example of this mechanism is a toy windmill, which can be made to rotate by blowing at it.

The impulse type of water turbine is the simplest of all turbines. We use this type of machine for very high heads of water. The turbine is usually placed in a valley, and the water is brought to it in strong pipes running down the mountainside. Each pipe ends in a nozzle. The nozzle has a circular cross-section that is tapered so that the cross-sectional area steadily decreases as the water flows along it. Now, the quantity of water flowing past every point along the taper must be the same. Thus, the

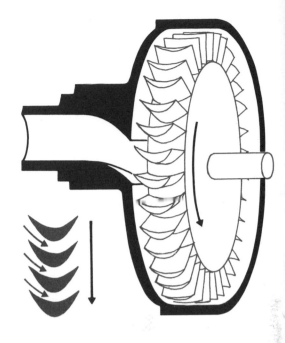

Above: An impulse turbine. Steam passes through the nozzle and hits the ring of blades on the rotor, causing it to revolve (see inset diagram).

Below: In a reaction turbine, rings of fixed stator blades alternate with rotor blades. The stator blades are so shaped that the spaces between them act as nozzles. The steam then hits the rotor blades, similarly shaped as nozzles. As the steam leaves the rotor blades, its pressure falls and it expands. Thus the blades receive a continuous thrust from the steam, causing the rotor to revolve.

fixed stator blades   moving rotor blades

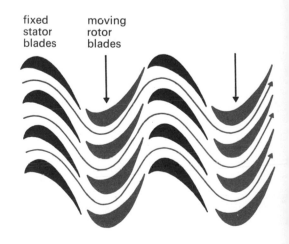

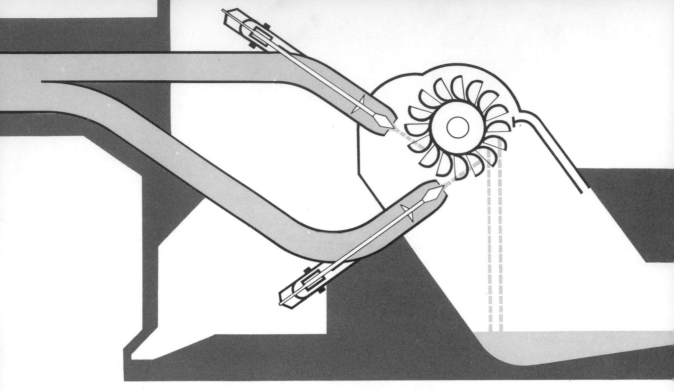

only way the water can flow through the nozzle is with ever-increasing speed. The final discharge diameter of the nozzle is calculated so as to pass the required quantity of water at the speed c. This process can be expressed by an equation, $\dfrac{c^2}{2 \times 32} = h$, where h is the pressure head of water available. Everything is designed to ensure that all the potential energy is converted into kinetic energy.

The jet of water is now directed onto the blades—or buckets, as they are usually called in this type of machine. The cross-section of these buckets is a double-U-shape, so that the water-jet is split in two parts. Each part of the water then follows the curved shape of the bucket, and changes its direction by approximately 180 degrees. Suppose that the bucket remained stationary, and the effect of the slowing-down of the water due to friction were neglected. Then the velocity of the two streams of water leaving the bucket would be the same as at entry. The sole effect would thus be to reverse the water-jet, so that the water would be flowing at its original speed but in the opposite direction. The bucket, however, moves in the same direction as the water. Let us call its velocity u. This velocity must obviously be less than the jet speed c, otherwise the water would never reach the bucket at all. The velocity of the water *relative* to the bucket at inlet will be the *absolute* velocity of the jet ("absolute" here means relative only to the earth) minus the velocity of the bucket. This is expressed as $c - u$. The two streams of water will now flow around the curved shape of the bucket with this relative velocity.

An impulse water-turbine is called a Pelton wheel. A two-jet version is shown in the above diagram. The pear-shaped needle within each nozzle can be moved back and forth to control the amount of water leaving the nozzle and hitting the runner.

The buckets of a Pelton wheel are in the shape of a double U. The water is directed at the center of the buckets and splits into two streams, changing its direction by about 180°.

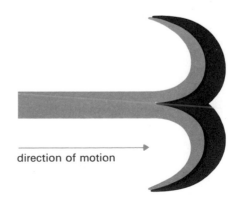

direction of motion

Close-up of the nozzles and runner of a Pelton wheel. The two nozzles are set at an angle of 180° to one another. The jet deflectors, used to divert the water in case of emergency, can be clearly seen on the left jet.

The absolute velocity of the water leaving the bucket will be given by the relative velocity minus the bucket velocity, or $c - u - u = c - 2u$.

The work done per pound of water is found by calculating the difference between the kinetic energy at inlet and that at outlet. This is expressed in the equation:

$$W = \frac{c^2}{2 \times 32} - \frac{(c - 2u)^2}{2 \times 32}$$

For maximum work to be produced, the second and negative term must be as small as possible. That is, $\frac{(c - 2u)^2}{2 \times 32}$ should be, if possible, zero. Expressed another way, $c - 2u = 0$, or $c = 2u$. The condition for maximum work is therefore that the bucket speed must be *one-half* the speed of the water-jet. Of course, this cannot be exactly achieved in practice. But the equation $u = \frac{c}{2}$ is a good guide to establishing the best conditions for maximum efficiency.

This type of turbine (called the Pelton wheel, after its inventor, the American, Lester A. Pelton) is capable of very smooth running and has a high efficiency—well over 90 per cent. In water turbine practice, the assembly of axle, wheel, and blades (or buckets) is called the *runner*. If the flow of water available is too much for one nozzle, two or even four may be used. These nozzles are arranged so as to deliver the jets of water at different points around the periphery of the runner. It is important to be able to restrict the flow of water through the nozzles so that the power output can be controlled if

If the absolute velocity of the water jet is c, and the velocity of the bucket is u, then the absolute velocity of the water leaving the bucket will be $c-2u$. Ideally this should be zero.

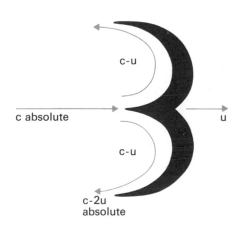

c-u

c absolute

u

c-u

c-2u
absolute

the demand for electric power drops. This is done by mounting a pear-shaped "spear" centrally in each nozzle. If less power is required, the spear is pushed further towards the nozzle outlet.

The centrifugal force of the buckets due to rotation is quite large. On a large machine, each bucket will exert a pull of several hundred tons on the hub. One important practical point in the design of these machines concerns the "runaway speed." This is the speed that the runner could reach if the electrical load were suddenly removed. This can and does occasionally happen in the event of a break in the transmission line. We have seen that the runner is designed so that its peripheral speed is one-half the speed of the water-jet. If the load is suddenly removed, the runner speed will increase until it is equal to the water-jet speed. That is, its speed will double. Now the centrifugal force depends upon the runner speed—but that speed is mathematically squared. If the speed is doubled, the centrifugal force is quadrupled. If this were allowed to happen, the enormous forces exerted on the runner would cause it to fly to pieces. To avoid this, jet deflectors are fitted. These are hinged flaps that can be quickly swung in front of the water jets so as to deflect all the water away from the runner. This is done automatically if the speed rises more than about 10 per cent above normal. It is much quicker than closing the water inlet valve.

What are the factors involved in the design of a Pelton wheel that is intended to drive an electrical generator? We must know the quantity of water available—usually measured in cubic feet per second (abbreviated to cusec)—and the head of water. Let us take an example. Suppose we have a head of 1,000 feet. The velocity of the jet will be given by $\dfrac{c^2}{2 \times 32} = 1,000$, or $c^2 = 64,000$. (In actual practice, there would be some friction loss in the pipe from the reservoir to the nozzle, but for simplicity we shall neglect this.) From this equation, $c = 250$ ft. approximately. The bucket speed is, as we said, half the jet velocity—125 ft/sec.

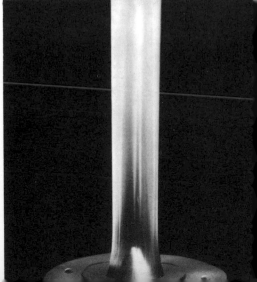

Models of turbines can be tested in laboratories, but much information can also be gained by tests on site. Top photo shows a huge waterspout formed as a jet nozzle is tested at a power station under construction. Lower photo shows a nozzle emitting a smooth jet of water—necessary for the efficient working and long life of a turbine.

Now, the bucket speed depends on two factors—the mean diameter of the runner (D feet) and the rotational speed (N in rpm). In one revolution, each bucket travels a distance equal to the circumference of a circle D feet in diameter. That is πD feet. In one minute, it will therefore travel $\pi D N$ feet; and in one second, $\dfrac{\pi D N}{60}$ feet. Thus:

$$u = 125 = \frac{\pi D N}{60}, \text{ or } DN = \frac{125 \times 60}{\pi} = 2{,}400$$

(Note that DN is only a number; it is the runner's diameter multiplied by rpm.)

We now have to choose a value for either D or N. Here, too, we have to link the turbine's performance with that of the generator to which it is coupled. This has an effect on the possible values for N. The principle of the electric generator is based on the discovery made by Michael Faraday in 1831: If a conductor is moved across the lines of force of a magnet, an electric current will flow in the wire. If we consider a very simple form of generator—consisting of a magnet pivoted at its center, and surrounded by a single loop of wire—we shall see how this discovery is applied. The coil of wire is fixed in the vertical plane. The magnet can be rotated by means of a spindle. First, let us imagine that the magnet is horizontal, with its north pole to the left of the coil and its south pole to the right. The lines of force between the two poles of the magnet are exactly at right angles to the top and bottom horizontal parts of the coil. In this position, the lines of force do not cross the conductor, and no current is produced. But when the magnet turns through a right-angle and is vertical, the lines of force are also vertical and cut across the conductor. This causes a current to flow from right to left in the top of the coil, and from left to right in the bottom. As the magnet continues to rotate, the current will gradually decrease to zero when the magnet becomes horizontal again. The current will then increase to a maximum value when the magnet is again vertical. However, when the magnet becomes vertical the south pole will be at the top. This means that the direction of the current in the top part of the coil will be from left to right; in the bottom part, the direction will be from right to left. If we made a graph that plotted current against time for one revolution of the magnet, it would show a gradual increase up to a maximum, followed by a decrease to zero. Then these events are repeated, but with the direction reversed. Such a current is called an *alternating current*. Large power station generators invariably produce current of this nature; for this reason, these generators are called alternators.

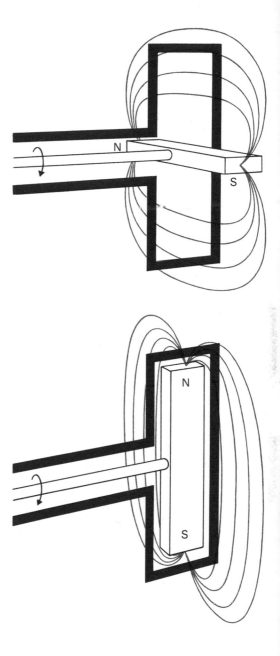

A simple electric generator, consisting of a magnet that rotates within a loop of wire. When the magnet is at right angles to the loop (top), no current is produced in the wire. But as the magnet rotates, an increasingly stronger current flows in the wire. The current is strongest when the magnet is in the same plane as the loop (lower diagram).

The complete process (as described above) is called a *cycle*, and the number of cycles per second (cps) is called the *frequency* of the current. It is important for the proper working of electrical appliances that the frequency (f) of current generated should be standardized. The standard frequency in Europe is 50 cycles per second; it is 60 cycles per second in North America. Now, the simple alternator produced one cycle per revolution of the magnet. To produce at 50 cycles per second it would have to revolve at 50 revolutions per second, or 3,000 rev/min. But if we arranged two magnets at right-angles to each other, one complete revolution would produce two cycles. Then the appropriate speed for 50 cycles per second would be 1,500 revolutions per minute.

In actual practice, complete magnets are not used. Instead, pieces of iron called "pole-pieces," or just "poles," are used. Each pole has a coil of wire wound around it. When a direct current is passed through the coil, the pole is magnetized and becomes a powerful electromagnet. The poles are fixed to the rotor, and arranged in pairs. The direction of the currents in the coils is such that one pole becomes a north pole, and the next a south pole. We can now state a general rule for relating the number of poles (p), the speed of the alternator (N rpm), and the frequency (f):

$$N = \frac{120f}{p} \text{, or, if } f \text{ is taken as 50, } N = \frac{6,000}{p}$$

We can now see that the value of N for a turbine cannot be chosen at random. The number of poles p must be an even number, so we can write down what values of N are possible.

p	2	4	6	8	10	12	14	16	18	20	22	24
N	3000	1500	1000	750	600	500	428	375	333	300	273	250

Let us now return to our impulse turbine. We had worked out an equation connecting speed of rotation (N revolutions per minute) and diameter (D ft.) which was $DN = 2,400$. Now that we know the permitted values for N, we can solve this equation for D. Trying the various values of N in the table, we find the following possible values for the diameter (D) of the runner:

N	3000	1500	1000	750	600	500	428	375	333	300	273	250
D ft	0.8	1.6	2.4	3.2	4.0	4.8	5.6	6.4	7.2	8.0	8.8	9.6

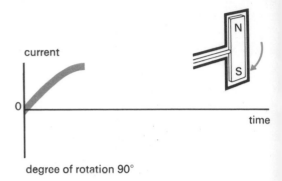

current

time

degree of rotation 90°

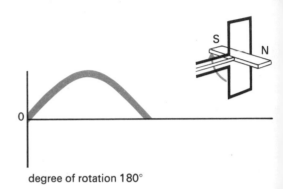

degree of rotation 180°

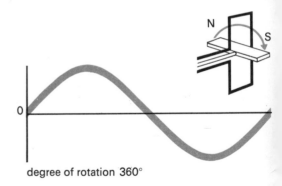

degree of rotation 360°

Alternating current produced by a magnet rotating within a vertical loop of wire. Top: The magnet rotates a quarter-turn from a horizontal position (no current) to a vertical position (maximum current). Center: Another quarter-turn and current drops to zero as the magnet returns to horizontal. Bottom: To complete one revolution the magnet makes a half-turn, during which current changes from zero to maximum and back to zero. This time, however, current flows in reverse direction through the loop—hence curve lies below zero line.

Engineers working on the stator windings of a large generator. The rotor, which revolves inside the stator, creates a rotating magnetic field that generates current.

We now have to decide on one of these values. It begins to look as if the higher speeds will be unsuitable, because 0.8 ft, or even 1.6 ft, appears to be a very small runner indeed. At this point, we also have to pay attention to the quantity of water available. From this quantity we can calculate what diameter of the nozzle is likely to be needed. Suppose that we have 100 cusecs of water available. This flows through the nozzle at 250 feet per second. If we imagine the water jetting out like a solid bar, in one second we would have a cylinder 250 feet long occupying a volume of 100 cubic feet. If the diameter of the nozzle is d feet, we can calculate as follows:

$$\frac{\pi d^2}{4} \times 250 = 100$$

or, $d^2 = \dfrac{100 \times 4}{250\pi} = 0.507$, or $d = 0.71$ feet, or 8.5 inches

We could, of course, decide to have two nozzles. In that case, each nozzle would have one-half the *area* of the single one, with a diameter of about 6 inches. This area determines the size of the bucket, which must be about twice the diameter of the nozzle in order that the water may flow satisfactorily around the curved shapes. If we decide on two nozzles, our buckets would be about 12 inches across. Such buckets could not possibly be fitted to a hub less than about 3 feet in diameter. The diameter of the complete runner would then be about 4 feet, so a speed of 600 rev/min would appear to be suitable, with a 10-pole alternator. In actual practice, we would now make a trial layout of the runner and calculate the centrifugal stresses in the hub. If the stresses were too high for the available materials, we would have to choose the next lowest speed and try again.

Having got this far in our design study, we might find it interesting to estimate how much power this machine could produce. The maximum possible power would be given if all the potential energy were fully utilized. The flow of water is 100 cusecs, and 1 cubic foot of water weighs 62.5 pounds. We therefore have 62.5×100, or 6,250 pounds of water per second falling through a height of 1,000 ft. The work done per second is therefore $6,250 \times 1,000 = 6,250,000$ ft.lbf/s. Since one horsepower equals 550 ft.lbf/s, the maximum possible horsepower is $\dfrac{6,250,000}{550} = 11,300$. There will, of course, be friction losses in the pipes and in the turbine. But the usable power produced would not be far short of 10,000 horsepower. This is quite a remarkable power output for such a relatively small machine.

We have dealt with the principles of design of an impulse water turbine in some detail, because the main ideas are applicable to all types of turbines. The steam impulse will be considered next. In the steam turbine it is heat energy that is converted into kinetic energy. We present our steam nozzle with hot, high-pressure steam. The steam is allowed to pass through a carefully shaped passage from which it emerges at high velocity, but with a lower pressure and temperature. The principle is exactly the same as the water nozzle, but with one added

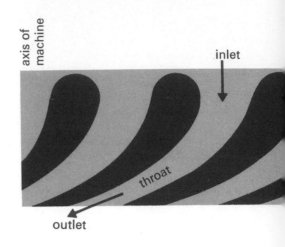

Impulse steam-turbine inlets. The converging passages force the steam to increase its velocity as it passes through, so that steam emerges from the nozzles at very high speed. Below: Section of a ring of nozzles, showing the rectangular shape of the outlets.

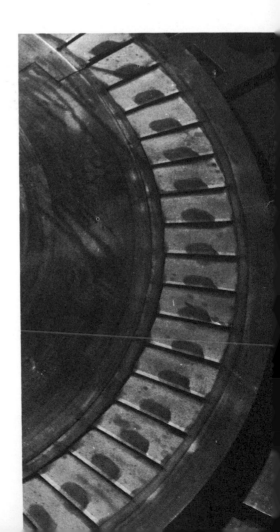

complication. The specific volume of the steam increases as the pressure falls; but with water there is no change in its density as it passes through the nozzle. We saw that, for the water nozzle, a converging passage was required to make the water proceed through it with ever-increasing speed. The continuous increase in specific volume of the steam as it passes through the nozzle would seem to demand a greater area for flow. But for moderate ratios of inlet to outlet pressure, the increase in velocity outweighs the increase in specific volume. Thus, a converging passage is also required for steam.

We can apply our basic energy equation to this nozzle. There is no work output, so $W = 0$; and any heat loss can be neglected, so $Q = 0$. There is no question of potential energy. And in most practical cases, the inlet velocity is small enough to make the initial kinetic energy zero. The energy equation therefore becomes, for one pound of steam:

$$h_1 = h_2 + \frac{c_2^2}{2g}$$

where h_1 and h_2 are the inlet and outlet enthalpies, and c_2 is the outlet velocity.

In an actual situation, we know h_1, because we know the pressure and temperature of the steam delivered from the boiler. Our unknown quantities are h_2 and c_2. Let us suppose that the outlet pressure from the nozzle has been decided upon. We now have a situation somewhat similar to the water turbine. But in the steam turbine nozzle, we have to find the difference in enthalpy, and enthalpy depends upon both pressure and temperature (p. 116). We can find h_1 because we know both the inlet temperature and pressure. But we cannot find h_2 because, although we have found the pressure, we have so far no means of finding the temperature. Our objective will be to arrive at a condition where h_2 is as small as possible, so that c_2 can be as large as possible. What we need is some process similar to measuring water height vertically.

To do this, we have to introduce a new and rather difficult concept, *entropy*. The theory behind this is dealt with more fully in the Appendix (p. 245). Entropy is a property whose value depends upon pressure and temperature. It is possible to assign a value to the entropy of steam if the pressure and temperature are known. Entropy is defined as follows: If during a perfectly reversible process, a small quantity of heat (q) is added to a system—the temperature of the system being $T°$ absolute—the change in entropy of the system is given by $\frac{q}{T}$. The term *reversible* is important. It suggests that if the process is reversed, by removing the heat (q),

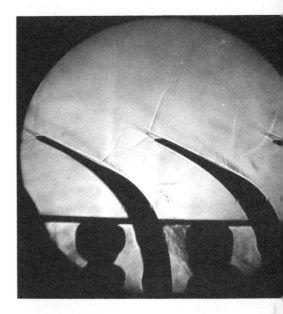

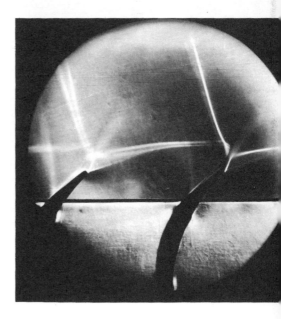

It is important to know how steam will behave when passing through nozzles or blade passages. To find out, the blades are put in wind tunnels where special lighting and photography render the flow of air visible. Top picture shows the flow lines clearly; lower photo shows shock waves produced by air flowing at supersonic speed.

no change can be detected in the system or its surroundings. This means that there must be no friction involved in the process, so we come back to our first measure for maximum release of energy. The definition given above is in terms of a small addition of heat. If a large quantity of heat is involved, the temperature of the system will increase. We would then have to imagine that the process is broken down into a number of small processes. The total change of entropy is then found by adding up all the terms $\frac{q}{T}$. Expressed mathematically, we say that the change of entropy is given by $\sum \frac{q}{T}$ (the symbol $\sum$ means "the sum of all the terms like"). The symbol normally used for entropy is s.

Now, in our nozzle, we said that there was no transfer of heat. We have also been discussing an ideal case, where there is no friction—that is, a reversible process. From the definition of entropy, therefore, the change of entropy is zero. That is because if $q = 0$, then $q/T = 0$. This is the other way of measuring, similar to measuring the height vertically. Fortunately, we have available an extremely useful tool for dealing with constant entropy processes for steam. This is the Mollier diagram (see p. 163); it is a graph of enthalpy plotted against entropy. On it are drawn lines of constant pressure and lines of constant temperature. There is also a thicker, curved line, running from left to right, called the saturation line. Above this level the steam is superheated. Below it the steam is only partially evaporated and is a mixture of steam and water, called wet steam.

Let us suppose that the inlet pressure to our nozzle is 100 lbf/in², and that the temperature is 500°F. We can locate the point (A on the Mollier chart) where the 100 lbf/in² pressure line intersects the 500°F. temperature line. This point represents the condition of the inlet steam. We can now read off the enthalpy at that point and find that its value is 1,279 Btu. Suppose that the outlet pressure from the nozzle is 70 lbf/in². We have said that the maximum possible energy release is obtained when the process is performed at constant entropy. On the Mollier chart, a constant entropy process is represented by a vertical line. We can thus draw a vertical line from our first point until it intersects the 70 lbf/in² line, at (B). This point represents the condition of the steam at outlet from this ideal nozzle. We can read off the value of the enthalpy at this point, and find it to be 1,244 Btu. Notice that we are not concerned with the numerical value of the entropy—we care only that it remains constant. We can now apply the equation $h_1 = h_2 + \frac{c^2}{2 \times 32}$. At the same time we introduce the mechanical equiva-

Right: A simplified Mollier diagram showing constant pressure lines (red) and constant temperature lines (black; scale in °F). The enthalpy scale is in Btu. A full Mollier chart has many more intermediate lines on it, as well as other information. The lines shown here are selected to complement the text, where points A, B, and C are fully discussed.

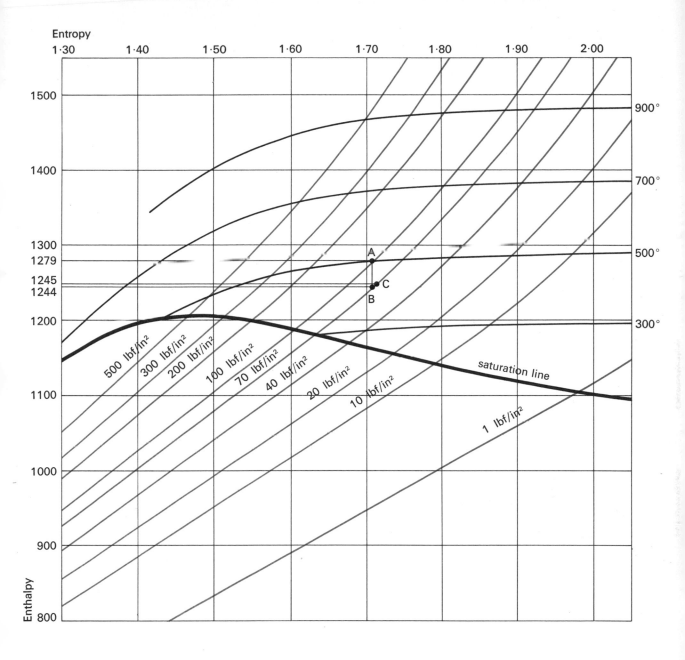

lent of heat (p. 110) to bring the kinetic energy terms to heat units. Then:

$$\frac{c^2}{778 \times 2 \times 32} = 1{,}279 - 1{,}244 = 35$$

Thus, $c^2 = 1{,}730{,}000$, or $c = 1{,}320$ ft/s

In actual practice there will be some friction in the nozzle, but this is easily allowed for. The effect of friction is to increase the value of h_2, thus reducing c. Suppose that friction increases h_2 to a value h_3. We define the nozzle efficiency as $\dfrac{h_1 - h_3}{h_1 - h_2}$. We can establish typical values for various kinds of nozzle by experiment. The actual value is usually very high. If we assume that the efficiency is 0.97, then

$$h_1 - h_3 = 0.97\,(h_1 - h_2) = 0.97 \times 35 = 34 \text{ Btu.}$$
$$\text{Thus, } h_3 = 1{,}279 - 34 = 1{,}245 \text{ Btu.}$$

We can now plot on the 70 lbf/in² line the point (*c*) at which the enthalpy has the value 1,245. This represents the actual condition of the steam at outlet. The diagram also has lines of constant specific volume. We can also estimate the value of this, and find that it is 7.2 ft³/lb. The actual value of *c* will now be given by

$$\frac{c^2}{778 \times 2 \times 32} = h_1 - h_3 = 34 \text{ Btu.}$$
$$\text{Thus, } c = 1{,}305 \text{ ft/s}$$

Now that we have arrived at the jet speed, we can go on to examine just how the jet is applied to the turbine blades.

In the case of the impulse water turbine, we established that the bucket speed must be one-half the water-jet speed. This is also approximately true for the steam impulse turbine. In actual practice, the ratio used is less than 0.5 and in this example we shall use 0.45. For the steam speed we have just calculated, therefore, we should require a blade speed of $1{,}305 \times 0.45 = 587.5$ ft/s. Note how much higher this is than that for the water turbine example. Suppose we calculate what the steam speed would be if the pressure dropped from 1,000 lbf/in² (a normal starting pressure in steam turbines) to 1 lbf/in², the approximate pressure at the outlet. The answer would be a speed of about 5,000 ft/s, and therefore a blade speed of about 2,000 ft/s. Such a speed would be quite impossible, because the centrifugal stresses would be much too high. It is therefore necessary to break down the expansion of the steam into stages. Each stage consists of fixed nozzles followed by rotating blades, and a steam turbine may have 40 or 50 such stages. The function of each stage is exactly the same as that of a complete Pelton wheel. We can visualize the multi-stage steam turbine as being a series of such runners all mounted on one long axle. Each runner is designed to make use of steam at a different velocity.

The construction of the steam turbine, however, is very different from that of the water turbine. Because the blade speed is so much higher, the turbine can revolve at speeds equal to those of their alternators—either 3,000 or 3,600 rpm. Also, because we have a higher speed of rotation, the diameter of the machine is smaller than that of a water turbine. In the example

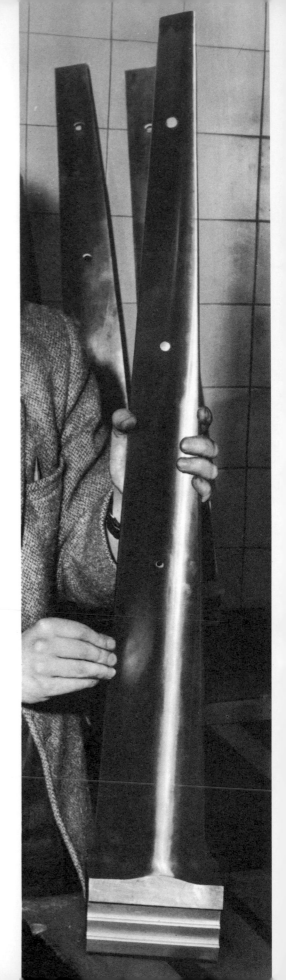

Opposite: A 36-inch blade used in the low-pressure stage of a steam-turbine. The holes are for the lacing wires that brace the completed ring of blades. Above: A high-pressure blade. Compare different fixing devices for attaching blades to rotor, shown here, with those pictured on page 170.

Once one blade has been made, a set of matching blades must be produced. This is done on a profile-cutting machine (below). The profile of the completed blade is "felt" by the machine (section nearest operator) and the cutter (center) is directed to cut an identical blade.

chosen, for instance, the diameter would be given by $\frac{\pi D \times 3000}{60} = 587$. From this equation we find that $D = 3.74$ ft.

Another important difference is that, instead of Pelton wheel buckets, each runner is fitted with curved blades. These blades are specially designed to make the best use of the steam jet. Now, we saw that the Pelton wheel buckets were struck one after another by a water-jet only when they came around to a certain position opposite a nozzle. Moreover, the number of nozzles was limited—from one to perhaps three. But in the steam impulse turbine, there are nearly as many nozzles as there are blades. A blade moves past one nozzle and then it immediately comes in contact with the jet from another. This is entirely logical, because steam has a lower specific volume compared with that of water. This means that a much greater volume of steam than water must pass through a prime mover in a given time to produce the same output of power. This can be achieved by introducing steam onto all blades simultaneously, and by making every blade work all the time.

The nozzles of an impulse steam turbine are arranged in a complete ring. They are formed by arranging steel segments, equally spaced and specially shaped, so as to produce the desired converging passage. The segments have a rounded shape at the entrance. They are arranged so that the steam enters in a direction parallel to the axis of the machine. The segments then curve around so that the steam leaves the nozzle at an acute angle to the plane of the nozzles (usually of about 15° to 20°). The narrowest part of the passage, the throat, is formed between the discharge tip of one segment and the back of the next

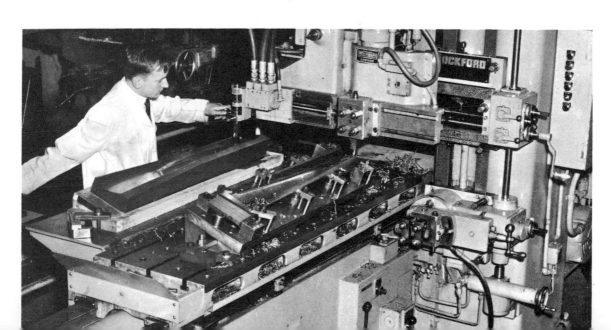

one. The steam now impinges upon the blades. It is important that the blade angles are correctly designed so that the steam enters smoothly and without shock.

If the blades were stationary, the direction of attack of the steam on the blade (or blade inlet angle) would be the same as the nozzle discharge angle. Because they are moving, this angle would not be correct. To calculate the correct angle, we have to draw a velocity diagram for the blade. First we draw a line representing the direction of motion of the blades. We then draw another line inclined to it at an angle equal to the nozzle angle—let us say, 15°. We mark off along this line a distance (to scale) representing the velocity of the steam leaving the nozzle. In the example chosen, this is 1,305 ft/s. This line is called a *vector* and it represents the velocity in direction (as well as magnitude relative to the fixed earth). We now need to find the magnitude and direction of the steam speed relative to the blade. The blade, we decided, is moving from right to left (across the page) at a speed of 587 ft/sec. To do this, we superimpose on the whole system a velocity equal in magnitude but opposite in direction to this blade speed. We represent this by drawing a line at the end of the steam velocity vector. This line is parallel to the direction of motion of the blade, but from left to right—that is, opposite to the direction of blade motion. We now mark off along this line a length (to scale) representing the blade speed. The line completing the triangle now represents the velocity of the steam relative to the blade. We can measure off its value, 752 ft/s, and also the blade inlet angle, 27°.

All that remains is to find the blade outlet angle. Here we must allow for the reduction in relative velocity due to friction over the blade surface. This is done by multiplying the inlet relative velocity by a coefficient, a figure that accounts for various changing conditions. The value of the coefficient is found by experiment. Suppose this coefficient is 0.9. Then the outlet relative velocity is 0.9 multiplied by the inlet relative velocity. That is, $0.9 \times 752 = 677$ ft/s. Now the *absolute* discharge velocity must be along the axis in order that the steam may enter the next set of nozzles without shock. To construct the outlet velocity triangle, therefore, we draw one line representing (to scale) the blade velocity. Another line, at right angles to this, represents the absolute velocity. (We do not yet know the length of this line.) With a pair of dividers set to a length representing the outlet relative velocity, we complete the triangle. We can now measure off the outlet blade angle, and we find it to be 30°.

The blade section can now be designed. This must have the correct angles, as found from the velocity triangles. It must also have a shape such that the passage between adjacent blades is as near parallel as possible.

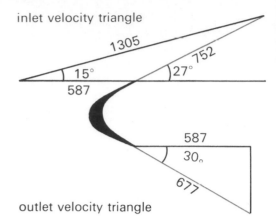

inlet velocity triangle

outlet velocity triangle

Since a turbine blade is moving, its inlet angle will have to be greater than the angle at which the steam leaves the nozzle, if the steam is to do its work properly. Top part of the above diagram shows how to calculate the inlet angle, given the nozzle angle, steam velocity, and blade velocity. The construction of the velocity triangle, as it is called, is described in the text. The triangle also gives us the speed of the steam relative to the blade. During its passage over the blade surface, the steam's speed falls, and tests can determine by what percentage. We can thus work out the speed of the steam relative to the blade at outlet. With this figure and the blade speed, we can construct an outlet velocity triangle (lower part of diagram) that will give us the blade outlet angle. (Two lines are marked in red to aid correlation with diagram below.)

Below: If we superimpose the inlet velocity triangle on the outlet velocity triangle, using the blade velocity line as base, the line (*AB*) joining the apexes represents (to scale) the velocity of the steam leaving the blade.

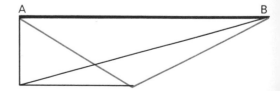

Such a parallel passage allows the steam to flow through with no drop in pressure. This is the essential aim of the impulse turbine.

The velocity triangle can be used for calculating the work done in this stage. To do this, we may refer to Newton's Third Law of Motion. We may state it, not in its usual form—Force = mass × acceleration—but in its original form—Force = rate of change of momentum. By *momentum* is meant mass multiplied by velocity. If we consider one pound of steam, there is obviously no change in mass. Thus, we are concerned only with the change in velocity. Suppose we redraw the velocity triangles, using the lines representing the blade velocity as a common base. Then the line adjoining the apexes of the triangles represents (to scale) the change in velocity of the steam in passing through the blade. The mass multiplied by this velocity gives the force acting on the blade. The direction of this force is also the direction of this line. It will be seen that, in this particular example, it is parallel to the direction of motion of the blade. If we measure the length of this line (to scale), we find it to be 1,256 ft/s. The value of the force, per pound of steam, is therefore:

$$\frac{1{,}256 \times 1}{32} = 39.3 \text{ lbf.}$$

The work done per second is given by this force multiplied by the distance moved per second. Since the blade is moving at 587 ft/s, the distance moved by the force per second is 587 ft. Thus:

$$\text{Work done} = 39.3 \times 587 = 23{,}100 \text{ ft.lbf/s}$$

This is the work done per pound of steam per second. If the mass rate of flow is known—let us say 100 lb/s—then the horsepower produced by this single stage is

$$\frac{23{,}100 \times 100}{550} = 4{,}200 \text{ horsepower.}$$

The completely assembled bottom half of the stator of a large steam turbine. The next stage is the installation of the rotor.

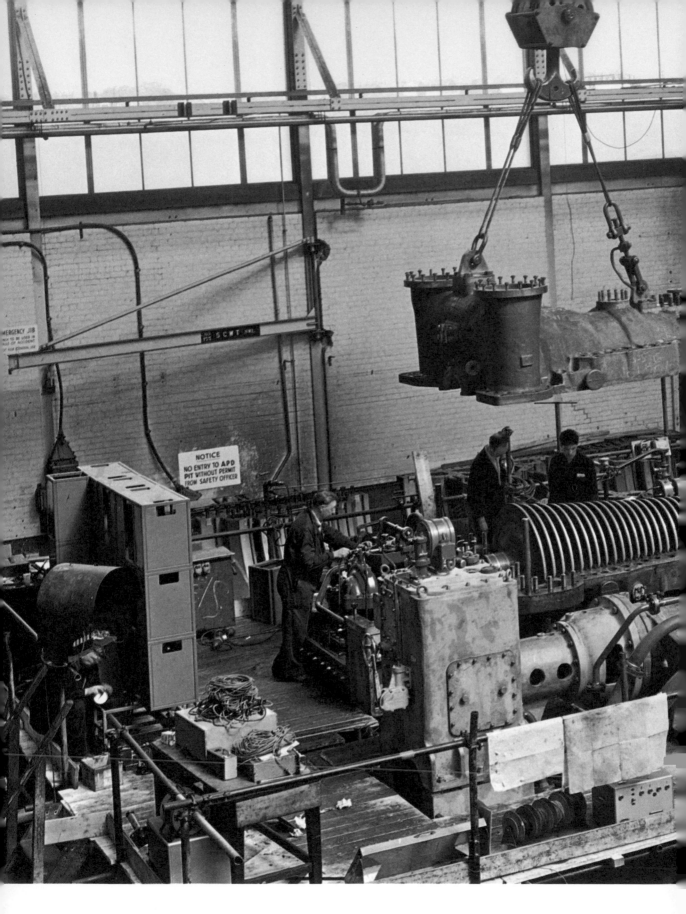

A 40,000 horsepower turbine being assembled for testing in the factory. Part of the upper casing is being lowered into position.

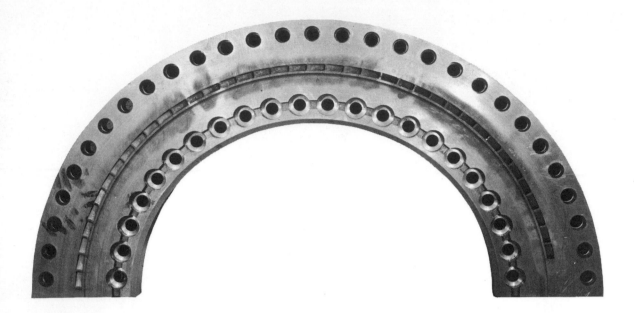

The nozzle segments are attached to a ring, made in two halves so that the rotor can be inserted. The completed assembly of nozzles and ring is called a diaphragm. It is fitted into grooves machined in the casing. The blades are attached to the periphery of discs formed by machining from the solid forged steel rotor. The whole rotor is supported on special bearings, which are lubricated by oil under pressure. Steam leakage from one stage to another—where the rotor passes through the casing—is reduced by providing a *labyrinth gland*. This consists of a number of sharp-edged rings fixed into the casing. These rings reach to within about 0.010 inch of the shaft itself. The diameters of adjacent rings are slightly different, and corresponding grooves are machined in the shaft. The leaking steam therefore has to follow a tortuous, or labyrinthine, path. Similar but smaller labyrinth glands are provided to reduce steam leakage across the diaphragms. One advantage of the

Above: High-pressure nozzle plate, showing steam outlets between upper and lower bolt holes. Two such plates form a diaphragm surrounding the rotor shaft. Above right: A shaft ready for the blades to be fitted onto the discs. Below: Blade ends showing different ways of attaching blades to discs. Below right: A shaft with blades affixed; note the lacing wire running through the blades. The speed of the blade tips is 1,215 mph when this turbine is working at normal speed; centrifugal force on each blade is 110 tons.

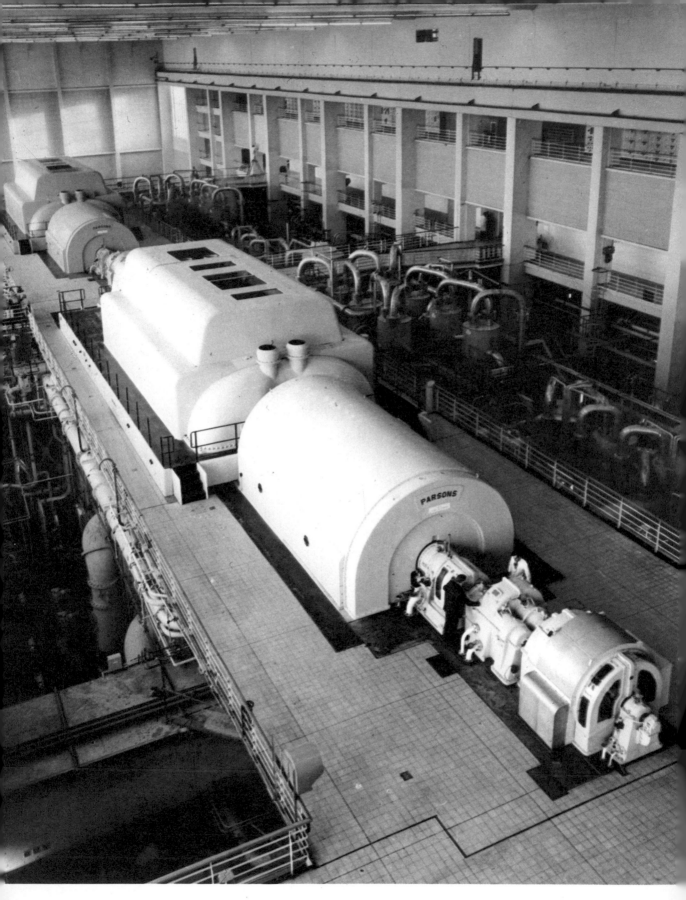

Two generators at a power station in Essex, England. Each has four turbines—one high-pressure, one medium-pressure, and two low-pressure—and produces over 264,000 horsepower. Steam enters the high-pressure turbine at 2,350 lbf/in² and at a temperature of 1,050°F.

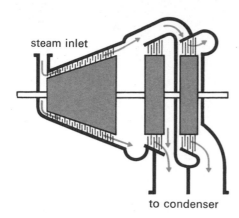

steam inlet

to condenser

Above: A single-cylinder turbine of medium output. The first rotor carries blades of increasing length. The low-pressure stage is duplicated to minimize blade length and hence centrifugal stress; each of these rotors has a separate exhaust outlet.

Below: Cut-away drawing of a 400,000 horsepower multi-stage turbine; this also has duplex low-pressure units.

impulse turbine is that there is no leakage across the tips of the blades. That is because there is no pressure-drop across the blade. There is thus no need to ensure very fine clearances between the blades and the casing.

So much for impulse turbines. The other main type of turbine is the *reaction* turbine. This differs in principle from the impulse type in one way only. Instead of all the pressure-drop taking place at the nozzle and none at the moving blades, some pressure drop takes place in the moving blades also. In the "pure" reaction steam turbine, the enthalpy (p. 114) difference across each element of a stage is the same. In physical terms, this means that the passage formed between adjacent moving blades must also be a converging one, so as to ensure a drop in pressure. In fact, the shape of the passages for a pure reaction stage will be the same for both nozzle and moving blades. Thus the shape of the nozzle segments will be the same as the shape of the moving blades.

The advantage of the reaction machine is that there is a somewhat lower loss of energy by friction and steam turbulence at the moving blade. This advantage can be

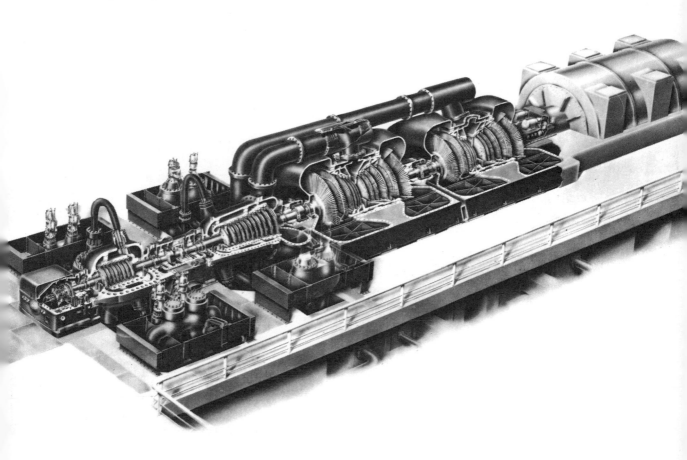

proved by wind-tunnel tests. Such tests show that fluid flow at increasing velocity is more efficient than at constant velocity. The disadvantage of the reaction machine is that very fine clearances have to be used to reduce leakage between the blade tips and the casing. This leakage becomes a much more significant factor with high pressure steam. Inspection of the Mollier chart diagram (p. 163) will show that the specific volume of steam at, let us say, 1,000 lbf/in² is much smaller than at 10 lbf/in². The area for flow through the blade passages at high pressures will therefore be correspondingly smaller than at lower pressures. The flow area, represented by the smallest practical tip clearance, is therefore a much greater percentage of the flow area at high pressures. A good compromise is therefore to use impulse blades for high pressures and reaction blades for lower pressures. The complete turbine is, in fact, often divided into two or sometimes three separate turbines.

When reaction type blading is used in a low pressure turbine, the diaphragm type of construction is abandoned. As we have observed, the shape of the cross-section of the moving blades is the same as that of the nozzle segments. Thus the latter can be made as separate blades, with root fixings of suitable type held in circumferential grooves machined in the casing. There is then a small space between the tips of these fixed blades and the rotor.

It may be shown that, for maximum efficiency of reaction blading, the ratio of blade speed to steam speed leaving the fixed blades should be slightly less than one. For impulse blading, we use a ratio of one-half. For a given blade speed (u), therefore, the steam speed for impulse blading would be $2u$. For reaction blading, the steam speed would be approximately u. Hence the enthalpy difference for impulse blading would be proportional to $(2u)^2 = 4u^2$. For reaction blading, it would be proportional to u^2. There would, of course, be an equal enthalpy difference across the moving blade of the reaction stage—giving a total of $2u^2$ for the stage. Hence an impulse stage of a given blade speed can deal with double the enthalpy difference of a reaction stage having the same blade speed. We could express this another way: For particular inlet and outlet steam conditions, a reaction turbine requires twice as many stages as an impulse turbine.

The calculation of blade angles and work done proceeds in a similar way for reaction blading as for impulse. The enthalpy difference for the fixed blade gives the discharge velocity. Then the velocity triangle is drawn to obtain the moving blade inlet angle. An equal enthalpy difference occurs across the moving blade. Thus, the calculation to find the discharge velocity is

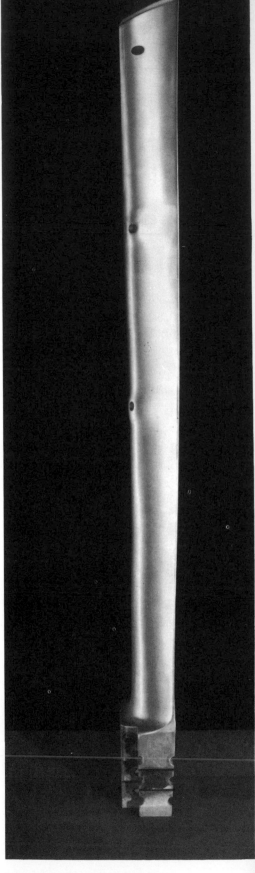

Two views of a typical low-pressure blade. Such blades combine characteristics of both impulse and reaction blades, the degree of reaction increasing from root to tip.

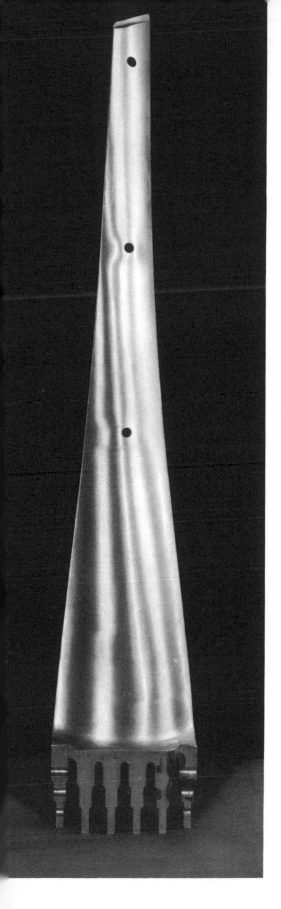

exactly the same as for the fixed blading. The discharge velocity is, however, the velocity *relative* to the moving blade. So another velocity triangle must be drawn to give the absolute discharge velocity.

As the pressure of the steam falls in its passage through the turbine, its specific volume increases. The area for flow must therefore increase, creating a need for larger blades. The elementary theory outlined here is no longer adequate for the design of such long blades. Other factors must also be taken into account. This results in a very complicated blade shape, the cross-section varying a great deal from root to tip. There is a definite twist and quite a bit of tapering. To relieve the problem of accommodating this increased steam flow, the low pressure turbine is made as a double flow machine. The steam enters at the middle and flows outward toward each end. Each half of the rotor takes half of the steam flow. For the very large machines now being built, with outputs of around 650,000 horsepower, two double-flow low pressure turbines are used.

The choice of steam conditions at the turbine inlet is very important. The need to use as high a temperature as possible has already been emphasized. This depends on the material available for the blades in the high temperature region of the machine. These blades are subjected to considerable stresses due to centrifugal force. It is also important, for maximum efficiency, that the steam temperature at exit should be as low as possible. This depends on an abundant supply of cooling water, either from a river or the sea. It is possible to condense the steam using cooling towers. But the temperature obtained is substantially higher than if a natural source of water is available.

The one remaining factor is the steam supply pressure. This must depend upon the boiler design to a large extent. But the turbine itself exerts some influence on the pressure chosen. Earlier in this chapter (p. 162), we showed how the Mollier diagram could be used in the design of a turbine nozzle. We found that the ideal frictionless process could be represented by a vertical line. Friction in the nozzle increases the enthalpy at the nozzle outlet. Thus the condition of the steam at outlet is not a point vertically below the starting point. It is a point on the same pressure line, but farther over to the right. If we allow for friction in the moving blade as well, the final outlet condition is farther over still.

If we now look at the turbine as a whole, we can first plot on the chart the steam condition at inlet. Suppose this is 1,000°F. and 1,200 lbf/in². The enthalpy at this point is 1,498 Btu, (at A on chart, p. 176). We now draw a vertical line to the condenser pressure line, which we will suppose is 0.8 lbf/in². The enthalpy at this point (B)

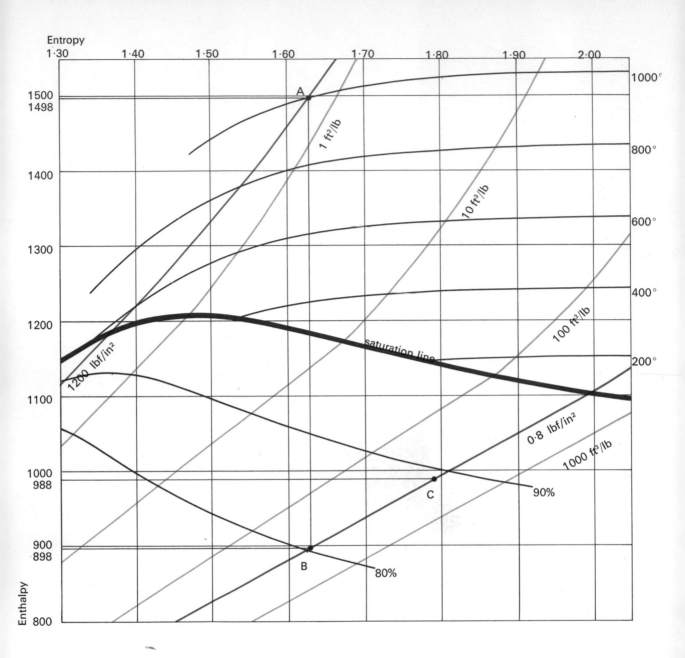

Entropy

1·30 1·40 1·50 1·60 1·70 1·80 1·90 2·00

1000°

1500
1498 A

800°

1400

600°

1300

400°

1200 1 ft³/lb
10 ft³/lb
100 ft³/lb
saturation line 200°
1200 lbf/in²

1100

0·8 lbf/in²
1000 ft³/lb

1000
988 C
90%

900
898 B
80%

Enthalpy 800

For a description of a Mollier chart,
see text and caption on page 162. On
the above chart, constant volume lines
are blue, constant pressure lines are
red, and constant temperature lines
are black. Also marked in black (below
saturation line) are lines of the
percentage dryness of the steam. For
a description of the points marked
on this diagram, see text opposite.

is 898. Thus, the ideal frictionless process would give a difference of $1,498 - 898 = 600$ Btu. From previous designs, engineers know that we can only expect to achieve about 85 per cent of this. (This 85 per cent is called the turbine efficiency.) Thus the actual enthalpy difference is $600 \times 0.85 = 510$ Btu. The actual enthalpy at outlet is $1,498 - 510 = 988$ Btu.

We now find the point on the 0.8 lbf/in² line where the enthalpy is 988 Btu. Note that this point is below the saturation line. Thus the steam is partially condensed, consisting of a mixture of steam and water droplets. There are lines drawn on the chart showing the percentage of steam in the mixture. At this point, the percentage can be read off as 88.8 per cent. The presence of the water droplets in the turbine can be a great nuisance. In such a mixture, the drops of water tend to become slowed by comparison with the steam. The droplets strike the inlet edges of the blades with great force and can quickly cause serious erosion of the blades. In the example chosen, we would have more than 10 per cent of the fluid in this condition. This would be just about the amount of droplets the blades could withstand. But even so the blade inlet edges would have to be reinforced with some very hard material. Furthermore, for the last few stages of the turbines, we have less steam to do work, so there is also a loss of efficiency. It will be seen that the choice of steam pressure influences the percentage of water in the mixture. The farther to the left of the Mollier chart we start, the greater will be the percentage of water. This percentage is a very significant factor in the choice of steam conditions.

In the previous chapter (p. 136), we mentioned feed-heating. This consists of drawing off steam from the low pressure turbine to heat up the water from the condenser. Ring-like passages, called *belts*, are cast into the turbine casing and the steam for feed-heating is extracted at these points. The principle is that, toward the end of the expansion process, the available enthalpy of the steam is progressively nearer to that at outlet. The enthalpy difference between the steam and the condensed water, however, is quite large. It represents the latent heat required to evaporate water to steam. If a little steam is removed from the turbine, therefore, the loss of work will be small. However, the heat transferred to the condensed water will be considerable. The higher the temperature at which the steam enters the boiler, the less heat will have to be supplied by burning fuel, thus improving plant efficiency.

The reaction water turbine is very different in appearance to a reaction steam turbine, but the principle is the same. Reaction turbines are used when the available head is low, below about 1,000 feet. Usually, low heads

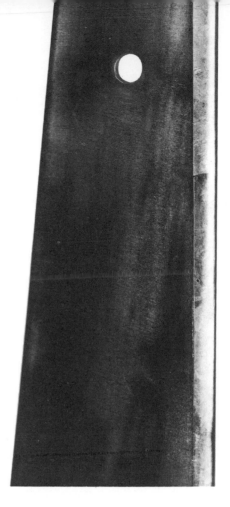

The efficiency of modern turbines increases the degree of wetness at the low-pressure end; this wetness can cause serious erosion of the blades. One way of combating this is to shield the blade edge with a very hard alloy called *Stellite*. Picture above shows part of such a blade. Another method is to drain off some of the water through holes in the casing, as shown in diagram below.

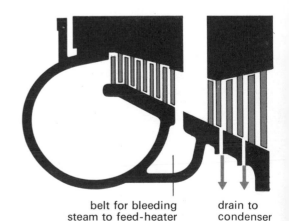

belt for bleeding
steam to feed-heater

drain to
condenser

are accompanied by a large flow of water. Under these conditions, the impulse turbine, with its few separate nozzles, is not suitable. The reaction turbine, however, admits water through a ring-like space, as does a steam turbine. It is thus able to deal with a much greater quantity of water.

There are two types of reaction turbines. The Francis turbine is used for intermediate heads, from 100 feet to 1,000 feet. For heads below about 100 feet, the Kaplan turbine is used. These two types have a number of features in common. Each is arranged with its axis of rotation vertical, whereas the Pelton wheel almost always has a horizontal axis. The water is admitted to the turbine through a casing, which looks a bit like a snailshell, called a *spiral casing*. The water leaves this casing in a radial direction, through a series of adjustable vanes. As the water flows around the spiral casing, the area of cross-section decreases. This decrease allows for the water that has passed through the vanes nearer the entrance. This explains its snailshell shape. The vanes are arranged so as to provide a contracting passage-way. This passage causes the velocity of the water to increase and converts some of the potential energy into kinetic energy. These vanes are mounted on pivots

Above: In reaction water turbines, water is admitted to all sides of the runner through a casing that is in the shape of a snailshell. Below: A runner for a Francis turbine.

and linked together so that, if the demand for power decreases, they can be swivelled around.

The runners of the Francis and Kaplan turbines are quite different. The Francis runner takes the water in radially, as it leaves the adjustable vanes, and discharges it axially. The Kaplan runner, on the other hand, has no radial part. It has blades somewhat like those of a ship's propeller. The Francis runner has between 16 and 24 blades, whereas the Kaplan runner only has from 3 to 8. The special feature of the Kaplan runner is that the angle of the blades is adjustable by means of a mechanism inside the hub. If the demand for power falls off, the angle of the blades to the axis can be increased. This reduces the area for flow in conformity with the reduced quantity of water admitted. This action improves the efficiency under reduced load. It is in this respect that the Kaplan turbine is superior to the Francis turbine.

In both these types of turbines, the principles of design are the same. The blade inlet angles are calculated in much the same way as for a steam turbine—from a consideration of the velocity triangle. Thus the water enters without shock. That part of the head that has not been converted into kinetic energy in the inlet vanes is available for conversion in the runner. It will increase the velocity relative to the runner blades. The angle of the blades at exit is arranged so as to make the absolute velocity as low as possible. This reduces the kinetic energy at outlet to as low a value as possible, giving maximum efficiency.

A feature of turbines of this type is the *draft* tube. This is a tube connecting the outlet of the turbine to the tail-race, or channel, that conveys the water away to the river downstream. The draft tube has a gradually increasing cross-section, so that the water velocity decreases as it passes through. It is thus the opposite of a nozzle, and converts kinetic energy into potential energy. The pressure at outlet from the draft tube, where it joins the tail-race, is atmospheric. The pressure at its inlet must then be less than atmospheric. Thus the available difference of head across the turbine has been increased by the draft tube. This increases the efficiency of the entire plant.

A discussion of rotary energy converters would be incomplete without some mention of windmills. In recent years there has been a revival of interest in these machines. For people living in remote areas, wind-power may be the only way in which they can enjoy the benefits of electricity. Such machines in the under-developed countries of the world could provide a temporary solution until sufficient money is available to provide larger electricity supply systems. Some enthusiastic people imagine that power generation by the

Diagram of a hydroelectric plant using a Kaplan turbine. The cross-section of the casing, through which the water reaches the runner, is different on either side in the diagram, because of its snailshell shape. After turning the runner, the water flows into the tail-race, through the draft tube, which gradually widens. This decreases the water velocity and therefore increases the plant's effective head. The generator is on top of the turbine.

Below: A Francis turbine. Water enters the runner from the sides and leaves the vanes at the bottom. The general arrangement of a hydroelectric plant using a Francis turbine is the same as a plant with a Kaplan turbine (diagram above).

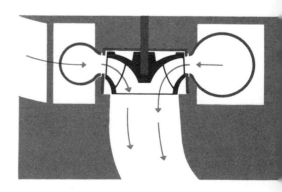

179

wind will form a significant contribution to a nation's electricity supply system. This does not seem likely except under very unusual economic and geographical conditions.

Like water, the wind itself is free. It has been calculated that the cost of wind-generated electricity is roughly comparable with that from coal- or oil-fired power stations. But this holds true only if the average wind-speed over the year is greater than about 20 miles per hour. This requires a situation that is, by normal standards, very windy. Such areas exist—on the northwest shores of the British Isles, for example. These areas are, moreover, remote and sparsely populated. In fact, such an area is very suitable for wind-power generation.

One of the most serious problems of wind for power generation is the fact that the wind is not steady or dependable. Therefore, if a constant supply of electricity is required, some method of storage is essential. The direct storage of electricity requires some type of storage battery, or accumulator. This increases the initial cost of the plant. Such accumulators have a notoriously short life compared with the rest of the plant. Other forms of storage—such as pumped water or thermal storage—also involves additional investment as well as various complications.

As a form of energy, the wind—compared with water

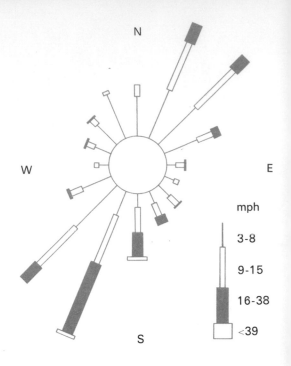

mph

3-8

9-15

16-38

<39

A wind-rose presents in visual form wind data for a location over a certain period. The lengths of the arms indicate the proportion of the period (say, a year) that wind blew from each direction. The divisions of the arms analyze the winds according to velocity.

Below: Histograms based on frequency of occurrence of winds of different speeds at the Butt of Lewis, Outer Hebrides, Scotland. Horizontal scale is wind velocity; shown on the vertical scale is the power potential of 100 square feet of swept air space, expressed in horsepower hours. The total number of horsepower hours is the sum of the vertical lines in each histogram. Note marked difference between power potentials of January and August.

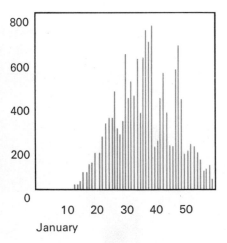

January

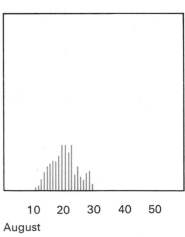

August

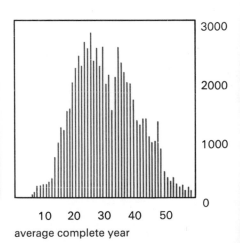

average complete year

Wind has a number of disadvantages as a source of power, but has nevertheless been used for centuries to provide power for many small tasks. Above: Cloth-sailed windmills used for pumping water in Spain.

and heat energy—is low-grade. Air has a low density compared with water. For a given mass of air, a much larger area for flow is required. Compared with steam, air's natural velocities are much lower. A wind of 88 feet per second (or 60 miles per hour) is exceptional. Yet we have seen that, in the calculations on steam turbines, a nozzle outlet velocity of about 1,000 ft/s is quite usual. We should therefore expect that a very large machine would be required to generate an appreciable quantity of electricity. It is clearly important that the design of the blades should be as good as possible to extract the maximum amount of energy from the air.

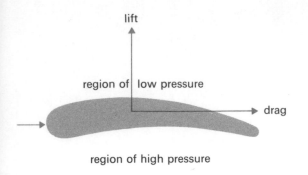

lift

region of low pressure

drag

region of high pressure

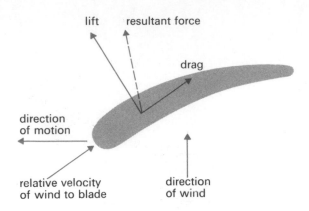

lift   resultant force

drag

direction
of motion

relative velocity
of wind to blade

direction
of wind

The modern wind-generator rotates much faster than the old-fashioned windmill. But the modern device resembles the older one in having only a few blades. We cannot, therefore, apply the same reasoning to a wind generator as to a steam or water turbine. Both turbines have many blades. In the case of the turbines, we focused attention on the shape of the passage between the blades, rather than on the blades themselves. It hardly makes sense to talk about a passage between only two blades on a rotor. It is more profitable to compare the movement of the blade to that of an aircraft wing. This is where modern engineers' experience with aerodynamics becomes useful in designing windmills.

Consider the forces that act upon the wing of an aircraft in flight. The leading edge of the wing strikes the air with a velocity equal to the forward velocity of the aircraft. The shape of the wing causes the air to flow around it in such a way as to cause a region of high pressure on the underside and low pressure on the upper side. The end result is an upward force on the wing. This force is usually divided into two components: The vertical component is called the *lift*, and the horizontal component the *drag*. The lift is the force that supports the aircraft. The drag is the force that impedes the forward motion. A good wing shape gives high lift and low drag. If the wing remained stationary and air was blown at it, the result would be the same. It is the research on wing sections, carried out in wind-tunnels, that is made use of in modern windmill design.

Let us now consider one section of the blade of a windmill. The direction of motion of the blade will be at right-angles to the direction of the wind. Thus we can construct a velocity diagram to find the direction of the wind relative to the blade. Our blade section must now be set at an angle to the direction of motion so as to receive the wind at this relative velocity. The motion of the air will generate lift and drag forces. The end of

Above left: An aircraft wing moving through air creates a region of low pressure above it and high pressure below. The resultant lift supports the aircraft, although drag impedes its forward motion to some extent. Above right: A windmill blade moves at right angles to the wind; a velocity triangle will give the relative velocity of wind to blade, and the blade will be angled accordingly.

Opposite: A 140-foot-high experimental windmill. The hollow propeller throws air out by centrifugal force from the tips of the blades. Air is thus sucked in through an intake near ground-level and drives a turbine (see diagram below).

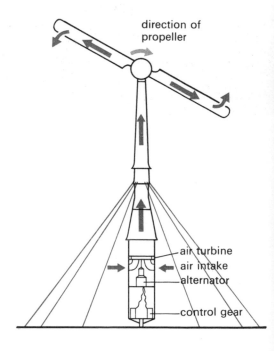

direction of
propeller

air turbine
air intake
alternator

control gear

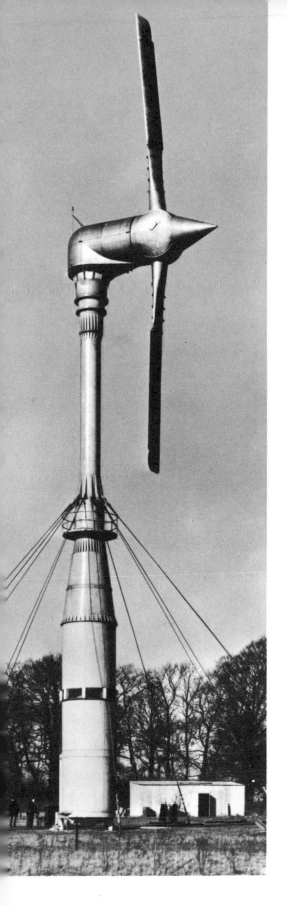

these forces will have a component in the direction of motion. This component is the force that drives the blade around. The other component, at right-angles to the driving force, merely produces a thrust on the rotor and does no work.

Windmills have long blades attached to a small central hub. The blade speed therefore varies a great deal from its root to tip. Since the wind speed itself is the same at all sections, the velocity triangles at the root and at the tip will be quite different. The blades are therefore of complicated shape, twisted shape. They are also tapered to reduce weight and therefore the centrifugal stresses.

Windmills also raise very interesting control problems. The rotor assembly must be pivoted so that it can be turned always to face the wind. In old-fashioned windmills, this was done by a vane, or tail, at right-angles to the plane of the rotor. The vane turned the rotor until it faced into the wind. In modern machines, this vane is much smaller. The force produced on it is hydraulically magnified to produce a force sufficient to turn the rotor into the wind. The electrical problems are also important. If direct current is to be generated, the inevitable variation of rotor speed with wind speed is easily dealt with. A direct current generator can be built that produces almost constant voltage over a wide speed range. If, however, alternating current is required, the frequency must be kept constant. This involves some form of governor, or control device, that will maintain constant rotor speed.

There is also the problem of protecting the apparatus against dangerous overspeeding in case of unusually high wind speeds. Various ingenious devices have been used for this. One method is to provide a second set of blades, adjusted to produce a driving force opposite in direction to the main blades. These secondary blades are hinged to the hub and are normally kept out of action by springs. If excessive speeds are reached, the centrifugal force on the blades overcomes the spring force. The blades rotate on their pivots to provide a braking force. A mechanical brake can also be used. This, too, comes into action when the speed rises to a dangerous level. It is also possible to have small, spring-controlled flaps near the tips of the blades.

The problems to be solved in windpower generation cover a wide range of engineering and scientific knowledge, and there is great scope for ingenuity. Some very ambitious designs have been produced for machines of up to 20,000 kilowatt output. Such machines have not yet been made, however. The limit to power appears to be about 1,300 to 2,000 horsepower. It is unlikely that machines much larger than this will ever prove practicable.

8 Air-Breathing Engines

In the previous chapter we considered several kinds of turbines, all of which form part of power plants of various types. In only one of these plants—the steam plant—does atmospheric air serve any function at all. But in none of these turbines does air enter into the actual working cycle. In air-breathing engines, on the other hand, the air serves a double purpose. Not only does its oxygen provide the means of achieving combustion of fuel. The air also acts as the working fluid for the engine. And because air is free, the exhaust gases are ejected from the engine at the end of the working process, and a new supply of air is taken in. The cooling of the working fluid can be omitted in the air-breathing engines.

The term "air-breathing engines" covers all types of engines that use air for this double purpose. They include the reciprocating gasoline and diesel engines, gas turbines, and various other types. (As mentioned earlier, a reciprocating engine is one in which pistons are moved back-and-forth by the working fluid.) The most familiar air-breathing engine is the internal combustion engine, which forms the prime mover for automobiles, buses, and trucks. If we stand back and examine it scientifically, we must admit that a reciprocating engine is a very complicated piece of machinery compared with a turbine. Both set out to achieve the same result—to make a shaft rotate. The turbine goes straight to its objective. The reciprocating engine first produces motion in a straight line, which then has to be converted into rotary motion. We might well ask why this type of engine has achieved such widespread use for so long a time.

The answer involves largely an historical approach. The first successful heat engine happened to be a reciprocating engine—the steam engine. The internal combustion engine was a later and parallel development from it. Many people have claimed that the invention of the steam engine was a classic example of the interplay of science and engineering. This is only partly true, and then only in a rather indirect way. The beginning of systematically recorded science dates back to the middle of the seventeenth century, when three learned scientific

Over 70 years separate the four-stroke 35 horsepower engine above and the modern gas turbine jet engine shown right. The jet engine is being studied on a special test rig. Its jet outlet, nearest the camera, has louvres that can direct the air stream in different directions. This is called a vectored-thrust jet engine, and is used on vertical-take-off aircraft.

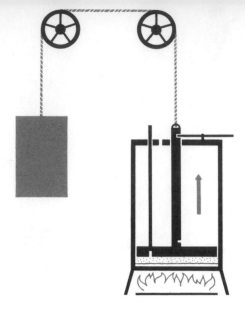

Above: In Papin's engine (1681), the counterweight raised piston to top of cylinder when space below it was filled with steam at atmospheric pressure. When the steam condensed, creating a partial vacuum, external atmospheric pressure forced piston down. Below: Newcomen engine, 1712. Steam entered the cylinder and was condensed by admitting cold water. This created a partial vacuum within the cylinder, so that piston and beam-end were pulled down. When fresh steam was admitted, pressure on both sides of the piston became equal, and weight of pump-rod and equipment pulled other end of beam down. Water was drained from bottom of cylinder.

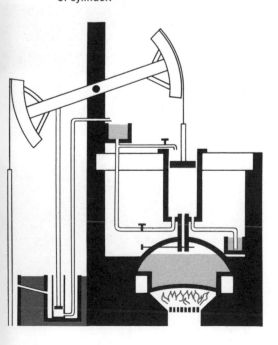

societies were founded—the Accademia del Cimento in Italy, the Académie des Sciences in France, and the Royal Society in England. It was a member of the Royal Society, one Denis Papin, who in 1681 demonstrated an embryo steam engine. It consisted merely of a cylinder with some water in the bottom. Above the water was a piston. When the water was heated, steam was formed. The piston then rose to the top of the cylinder, where the piston was held by a catch while the steam cooled off and condensed. Then, when the catch was released, the atmospheric pressure acted on top of the piston and forced it back to the bottom of the cylinder. The device owed its success to the fact that the atmosphere has weight—a fact first conclusively demonstrated in 1642 by Evangelista Torricelli, a pupil of Galileo.

It was Thomas Newcomen, of Dartmouth in Devon, England, who applied this cylinder of Papin's to a pumping engine. This was the first really practicable steam engine. Newcomen spent some 25 years in developing his engine, which was finally completed in 1712. Essentially it was a village pump on a large scale, with a steam cylinder serving as a substitute for the human hand. The pump lever became a great beam, pivoted on a masonry column, with the pump rod hanging from one end by a chain. The piston of the steam cylinder was attached to the other end of the beam. Steam was admitted to the cylinder at atmospheric pressure, and condensed by injecting cold water. The steam pressure then fell to one or two pounds per square inch. The weight of the atmosphere acting on top of the piston (with a pressure of nearly 15 pounds per square inch) moved it downward, raising the pump rod upward. When fresh steam was admitted to the cylinder, the pressure on both sides of the piston was equalized. The weight of the pump rod on one end of the beam was sufficient to tilt that end downward. This raised the piston, at the opposite end of the beam, to the top of the cylinder again.

Engines of this kind were used for mine drainage for fifty years before anyone became fully aware of their basic flaw. Then James Watt, a young instrument-maker working in Glasgow, realized what this flaw was. The water that condensed the steam also cooled the cylinder, which later had to be heated again by the next charge of steam. He provided a condenser separate from the steam cylinder. This allowed the cylinder to remain hot, thus bringing about a considerable improvement in efficiency. All the engines designed by Watt, including his later rotative engines, had steam supplied at atmospheric pressure. It was only in the early part of the nineteenth century that steam at pressures above atmospheric pressure was introduced.

It is important to realize that neither Papin, New-

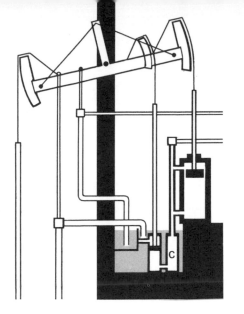

Above: A Watt steam engine (1788), showing one of his important improvements—the separate cylinder for the condensation of the steam (C).

Below: This photo of a beam engine and its housing, being dismantled about 50 years ago, shows the size and massive construction of such engines.

comen, nor Watt were using steam for the sake of the kinetic energy that it might contain. They were exploiting steam's property of existing as a gas: That is, steam occupied a large volume at 212°F., which could shrink drastically into a few drops of water at any lower temperature. In other words, they were introducing a "collapsible atmosphere" into one side of their engines. Furthermore, in the early days of the steam engine these inventors had no concept of the principles of turning heat into work. The laws of thermodynamics were not set forth until the middle of the nineteenth century. Thus, the basic science upon which the working of these engines depended was unknown until 150 years after the first steam engine was built. It is therefore somewhat misleading to describe the steam engine as an example of the cooperation of science and engineering. What *is* true is that, as the science of thermodynamics developed, it led to a fuller understanding of heat engines and to many improvements in their design.

Parallel with the early development of the steam engine, several inventors cherished the idea of an engine in which the combustion would take place inside the cylinder. As far back as the late seventeenth century, the Dutch scientist Christiaan Huygens actually built a gunpowder engine. This engine successfully lifted five men off the ground for the outlay of a thimbleful of explosive.

It worked by displacing cold air with hot gases from the explosion. These gases cooled and contracted so that the weight of the atmosphere pressing on top of the piston did useful work. However, this early attempt was blocked by lack of a suitable fuel. But by the outset of the 1800's, it was already known that if coal is heated in a closed vessel a combustible gas is given off. The first experiment in the public use of coal-gas lighting on a fairly big scale was made in London on June 4, 1805. The use of coal gas for a fuel in an engine came in 1826, with the first successful coal-gas engine, invented by an Englishman named Samuel Brown. It made use of the fact that, when a mixture of coal gas and air is ignited, the products of combustion, *when cooled*, occupy a slightly smaller volume. The gas-and-air mixture was ignited in the cylinder. The contraction in volume after cooling caused a low pressure beneath the piston. The atmospheric pressure could then force down the piston and turn the engine shaft. A four-cylinder version of this engine was made and it was used to propel a launch on the Thames River.

The composition of coal gas at that time probably included approximately 50 per cent hydrogen, 32 per cent methane, and 7 per cent carbon monoxide. All these gases combined with air in the proper way for such an engine. The small component of carbon monoxide would combine with half its volume of atmospheric

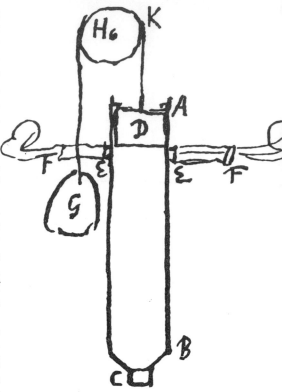

Sketch by Huygens (1673) of his gunpowder engine. The piston (D) was held at the top of the cylinder by a much heavier weight (G). A small charge of gunpowder inserted at C was detonated, driving out cold air through "non-return" valves (EF) of soft, moist leather. When the hot gas remaining in the cylinder cooled, there was a pressure difference that enabled atmospheric air to bear down on the piston top and so lift the weight.

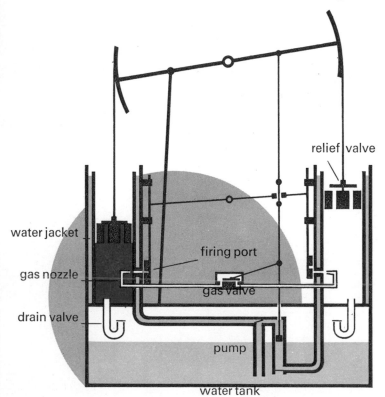

water jacket

gas nozzle

drain valve

relief valve

firing port

gas valve

pump

water tank

Left: Samuel Brown's engine (1826) used a mixture of gas and air that was admitted to each cylinder during the first quarter of the upstroke. The mixture was then ignited; the relief valve on top of each cylinder allowed excess hot gases to escape. As the cylinder was cooled by the circulating water, a partial vacuum was formed under the piston, causing it to fall. In order to obtain uniform motion, it was necessary to have a few pairs of cylinders so that at least one would have a driving vacuum while the others were forming theirs.

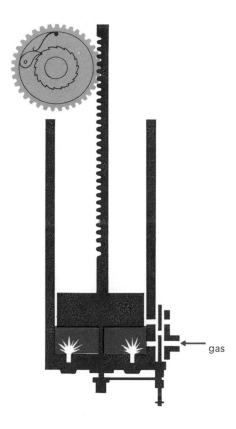

A primitive gas engine was made by Barsanti and Matteucci in 1854. Ignition of a gas-air mixture forced the piston to the top of the cylinder. During this stroke, the ratchet device on the wheel at the top allowed the wheel to be rotated by the piston shaft without doing useful work. But on the downward stroke, the teeth engaged and the central shaft was turned.

Right: Diagram of the Lenoir engine (1860). This engine used the energy of the flywheel, due to the previous power stroke, to draw a gas-air charge into the cylinder. When the piston had covered part of its outward stroke, the mixture was cut off and the charge in the cylinder was ignited by an electric spark, so forcing the piston to the end of its stroke. The momentum of the flywheel carried the piston back again and the burned charge was forced out through a slide-valve.

oxygen to produce two-thirds of their joint volume. The combustion of the methane with its appropriate volume of oxygen would result in a shrinkage of two-thirds. Best of all, the large hydrogen component, combining with half its volume of oxygen, would virtually disappear as the resulting water vapor condensed. Thus the Brown engine was similar to the Newcomen engine. It was an atmospheric engine in which the collapsible atmosphere of water vapor was produced by internal combustion instead of being provided by an external boiler.

The next 20 or 30 years saw a number of designs and patents for gas engines. The most successful one was made in 1854 by two Italians, Eugenio Barsanti and Felice Matteucci. It had a vertical cylinder open at the top, like a gun barrel. The heavy piston was fitted with a long piston rod in which gear teeth were cut. A flywheel was mounted on a horizontal shaft, together with a gear wheel that could engage with the teeth on the rod. There was also a ratchet arrangement, allowing the teeth to engage on the down-stroke of the piston, but not on the up-stroke. A mixture of gas and air was introduced into the cylinder and ignited by a spark when the piston was at its lowest position. The energy released by combustion drove the piston to the top of the cylinder, thus converting the heat-energy into potential energy of the piston and piston rod. A catch then held the piston in this position. When the speed of the flywheel fell below a certain value, the catch was released and the piston dropped to its lowest position. But on the down-stroke, the gear teeth engaged. The potential energy of the piston was thus converted into the kinetic energy of rotation of the flywheel.

Several hundred of these engines were built, and their thermal efficiency was reckoned to be about 5 per cent. This compared quite favorably with the thermal efficiency of early steam engines. It is doubtful if the thermal efficiency of the best engines designed by James Watt exceeded 1 per cent. The Barsanti-Matteucci en-

Three of the key figures in the development of the internal-combustion engine. From the top: Nikolaus Otto (1832-1891), Gottlieb Daimler (1834-1900), Rudolf Diesel (1858-1913).

gine is the first known example of the use of heat as a positive driving force.

The real breakthrough in the design of internal combustion engines came about 1876, with the engine built by the German Nikolaus Otto. Otto was a good practical engineer, and his name has been attached to the working cycle used to estimate the performance of internal combustion engines. Some of the credit for the theory of the internal combustion engine should probably go to the nineteenth-century French engineer, Alphonse Beau de Rochas. He listed the principal factors to which attention must be paid in order to achieve high efficiency.

These early engines all depended on gases. The use of liquid fuels was not introduced until near the end of the nineteenth century. Two main types of engine then emerged. One was the gasoline engine (developed by Gottlieb Daimler), which used a volatile fuel ignited by a spark. The other was the heavy-oil engine (known as a diesel engine, after its chief inventor Rudolf Diesel) in which the fuel was injected into the cylinder and spontaneously ignited by contact with air heated by compression. The modern versions of both engines employ the Otto cycle.

This cycle consists of four distinct processes. In the first one, a charge of air, or a mixture of air and gasoline vapor, is drawn into the cylinder and compressed. This compression process is carried out relatively quickly, so that there is little time for heat losses. In the ideal cycle, therefore, compression can be regarded as *adiabatic*. This term (derived from Greek words meaning "not passable") refers to processes that occur without heat entering or leaving the system. This compression is accompanied by a rise in temperature, similar to the effect obtained when the end of a bicycle pump becomes noticeably hot in use.

At the end of the compression stroke, combustion takes place. This is the second process of the Otto cycle, and in the ideal Otto cycle it occurs at constant-volume. That is, the volume remains the same, and in practice this is very nearly true. With a conventional crank and connecting rod mechanism, there is very little movement of the piston for quite a considerable angular movement of the crankshaft. Since the crankshaft rotates at constant speed, this means that near the end of the stroke the piston will remain almost stationary for an appreciable time interval. During this constant-volume combustion process there is a considerable rise in temperature, and therefore also a rise of pressure.

The third process is the expansion of these hot, high-pressure gases. It is during this stage that the useful work is done by the moving piston and crankshaft. At the end

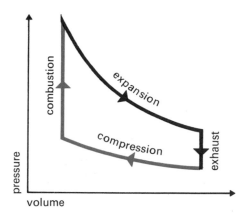

The operations of the Otto cycle shown on a graph of pressure plotted against volume. The area within the curves represents amount of work done.

Otto cycle efficiencies for various compression ratios, according to the formula discussed in the text. Note how the gain in efficiency drops off as the compression ratio is increased beyond about 15. Tests have shown that, in practice, Otto engines have peak efficiencies at a compression ratio of about 17.

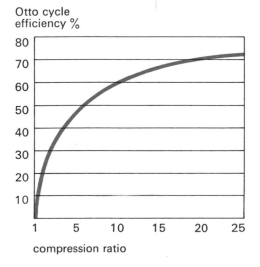

of the expansion stroke, the gas pressure is higher than the atmospheric pressure. The Otto cycle now requires that the gases be cooled at constant volume back to their original condition. In actual practice, the gases are discarded from the cylinder and a fresh charge of air, or air and gasoline vapor, is drawn in. We can show this cycle of operations on a graph that makes it clear that the greater the rise of pressure during combustion, the greater the amount of useful work done.

The thermal efficiency of an engine working on the Otto cycle can be calculated by a formula:

$$\text{Otto cycle efficiency} = 1 - \left(\frac{1}{r}\right) 0.4.$$

In this formula, r is the ratio of the volume of air at the beginning of compression to the volume at the end of compression. This is called the *compression ratio*. This simple formula makes it possible to draw up a table showing efficiencies for various values of r, or compression ratio.

r	1	2	4	7	10	15	20	25
Otto cycle Efficiency (%)	0	24.2	42.6	54.1	60.2	66.1	69.8	72.3

If we plot a graph of these figures, we see that, as the compression ratio increases, efficiency also increases, but in a special way. At first the efficiency increases rapidly. But by the time we reach ratios above ten, the curve flattens out. Thereafter, very little increase in efficiency is achieved by even a large increase in the compression ratio. In actual practice, a high compression ratio also increases the mechanical problems in the design. Very few internal combustion engines have a higher compression ratio than 20, or at most 25. Indeed, in the engines of most passenger vehicles the ratio is between eight and ten. And we must not be misled by the values of the calculated Otto cycle efficiencies. These figures are for an ideal, perfect engine. In practice the actual efficiency attained will only be about 60 per cent of the ideal value, because of friction, heat losses, and other factors.

The Otto cycle is applied in various ways. An engine may be constructed on the four-stroke or the two-stroke principle. A "stroke" is a movement of the piston from one end of the cylinder to the other. In one complete revolution of the crankshaft, the piston will move from its outermost position in the cylinder—called the "outer dead center" (O.D.C.)—to the innermost position—the "inner dead center" (I.D.C.)—and back again. This means there are two piston strokes for each crank revolution. A two-stroke engine is one in which the complete cycle of operations is completed in two strokes of the piston, or one crank revolution. A four-stroke engine is one in which the cycle takes four strokes, or two crank revolutions.

In the cylinder-head of the four-stroke engine, there are valves operated by cams carried on the camshaft. The camshaft is driven through gears by the engine and runs at half the engine's speed. Such an arrangement is necessary because the complete cycle takes two engine revolutions. One of the valves, the inlet valve, admits the fresh charge of fuel. The other, the exhaust valve, opens to allow the spent gases to leave the cylinder. Let us start with the piston at inner dead center. As it moves outward, the inlet valve opens and the piston sucks the charge of fuel into the cylinder. This is called the suction, or induction, stroke. At outer dead center, the inlet valve closes. During the next stroke, the piston compresses the charge. A little before the piston reaches I.D.C., combustion begins. Combustion proceeds at approximately constant volume. The expansion, or firing stroke, now takes place until the piston is at O.D.C. Then the exhaust valve opens. During the next stroke, the exhaust stroke, the piston sweeps the exhaust gases out of the cylinder.

The two-stroke engine is much simpler mechanically. Because it has no valves, there are no separate suction and exhaust strokes. The fuel charge enters through a hole in the cylinder wall called the *inlet port*. The exhaust gases leave at the same time through the *exhaust port*, on the opposite side of the cylinder. These ports are simply uncovered and closed by the movement of the piston. Suction first draws a mixture of gasoline vapor and air into the crankcase and lower part of the cylinder. Then, as the piston moves downwards on the combustion stroke, it compresses the fuel mixture in the crankcase. This assists the mixture's entry into the cylinder as soon as the inlet part is uncovered.

As the piston moves upward on the compression stroke, both ports are at first open. The fuel charge is forced into the cylinder by the compression effect produced in the crankcase. The incoming charge, deflected up to the top of the cylinder by the shaped piston crown, pushes out any remaining exhaust gases through the exhaust port. When the piston has moved far enough to cover the inlet port, no more of the fuel mixture can enter. A little later in the stroke, the exhaust port is also closed by the piston. The remaining part of the stroke is

Top diagrams opposite show the working of a four-stroke diesel engine. (1) The piston has just begun the induction stroke, drawing air into the cylinder through the open inlet valve. Once the piston is at the bottom of the cylinder, inlet valve closes. Piston then rises (2—compression stroke), compressing the air, causing it to heat up. At maximum compression, fuel is injected and ignites, and exploding gas forces piston down (3—firing stroke). When piston is at the bottom of the cylinder, exhaust valve opens, so that as piston rises (4—exhaust stroke) the burned gases are forced out of the cylinder.

Lower diagrams: In the two-stroke engine there are no valves; instead the piston itself covers and uncovers openings (ports) in the cylinder wall. During part of the upward stroke, the piston covers up all three ports, and pressure drops within the crankcase. Eventually the lower port is uncovered (1), and the pressure difference sucks in an air-fuel mixture through this port. As piston descends, ports are covered and the charge in the crankcase is slightly compressed (2). Eventually both upper ports are opened (3) and the charge transfers to the cylinder. Then, as the piston rises, all ports are closed and the charge in the cylinder is compressed (4) until, at the top of the stroke, the charge is fired, so forcing the piston down again. It will be clear from the diagrams that more than one event takes place at the same time. Thus, as the charge transfers from crankcase to cylinder (3—red), the burned charge of the previous explosion (blue) is leaving the exhaust port.

Above: A two-stroke engine as used on a motorcycle. Right: A much larger—and more complicated—four-stroke automobile engine.

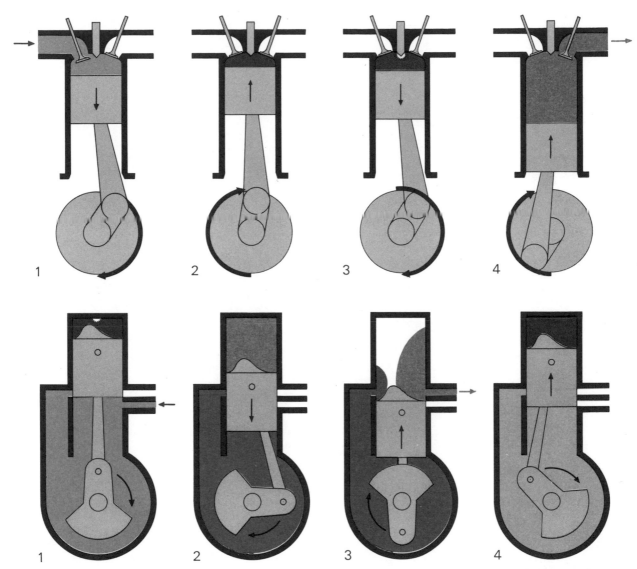

used for compression, followed by combustion when the piston reaches the top of the stroke. The expansion stroke then takes place, and the piston uncovers the exhaust port again, allowing the exhaust gases to escape.

The two-stroke engine has definite advantages because of its simplicity. Not only does it eliminate valves, with their necessary cams and camshafts, but it also simplifies lubrication. Oil is mixed with the gasoline. The gasoline-air mixture that is drawn into the crankcase thus contains oil droplets, which provide adequate lubrication. The two-stroke engine also gives double the number of firing strokes for the same engine speed. Thus the power output for a given size of engine is usually greater. On the other hand, there are certain disadvantages to the two-stroke engine. There is a somewhat lower efficiency because the exhaust gases are not so

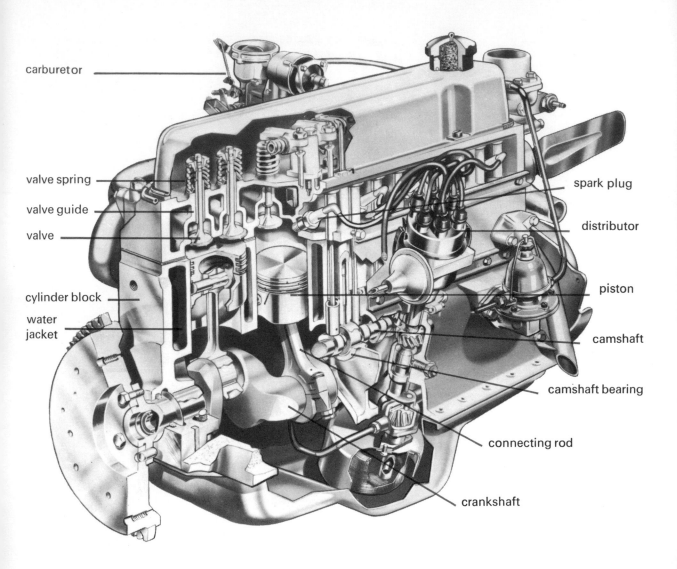

carburetor

valve spring

valve guide

valve

cylinder block

water jacket

spark plug

distributor

piston

camshaft

camshaft bearing

connecting rod

crankshaft

Above: Cut-away view of a six-cylinder automobile engine, using gasoline as fuel. The cylinder block has water jackets, for cooling purposes, which are cast with the block. The overhead valves are operated by rockers and push-rods from the camshaft. At the side of the engine is the distributor that fires each spark plug at the correct instant. The carburetor is fed from a fuel pump driven by the engine.

positively cleared out of the cylinder and because some of the gasoline-and-air mixture must pass straight through the cylinder into the exhaust. Also, it is difficult to construct large two-stroke gasoline engines. But for something like a small, single-cylinder motorcycle engine, the two-stroke principle is excellent.

Curiously, with the diesel engine the two-stroke principle is used at the other end of the scale—for very large marine engines. Such engines are frequently double-acting—that is, the underside of the piston, as well as the upper side, is used for compression and expansion. Effective removal of the exhaust gases is achieved by a small air compressor, called a scavenge **pump**, which blows fresh air through the cylinder. The double-acting two-stroke engine gives two power strokes for every revolution. Thus the power-output for a given size of cylinder is greatly increased.

The main differences between the gasoline engine and the diesel oil engine stem directly from the method of igniting the fuel. In the gasoline engine, the mixture of air and gasoline vapor to be ignited is produced in the *carburetor*. This mechanism consists essentially of two parts. First, there is a device for maintaining a constant level of gasoline, so that the pressure of the gasoline supply remains constant. This is called the float chamber. It consists of a closed vessel, to the top of which gasoline is supplied by a pump from the gas tank. Inside is a hollow metal cylinder that floats in the gasoline. If the level of the gasoline exceeds its proper amount, the metal cylinder rises. This lifts a needle valve in the top of the float chamber, thus pressing the valve against a hole and preventing any more gasoline from entering. Gasoline for combustion in the cylinder is drawn off

Below: A marine two-stroke diesel engine, with six cylinders and a scavenge pump.

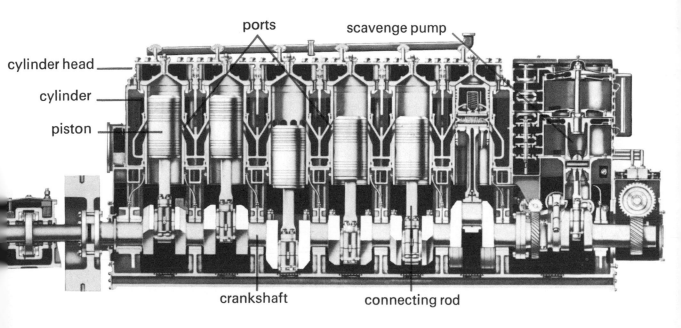

ports

scavenge pump

cylinder head

cylinder

piston

crankshaft

connecting rod

from the bottom of the float chamber. If the gasoline in the chamber falls below its proper level, the hollow metal cylinder sinks slightly, thus opening the needle valve and admitting more gasoline.

The second essential part of the carburetor is its main body. This has a passage, first converging and then diverging, through which the air passes. The gasoline pipe from the float chamber leads to a fine orifice, or jet, placed in the center of the narrowest part of the air passage. (The top of the jet must, of course, be above the level of the gasoline in the float chamber. Otherwise gasoline would flow from the chamber at all times, even when the engine was not running.) The converging passage acts exactly like the nozzle of a turbine. The air velocity is higher at the narrowest part than at the inlet. Thus some potential energy has to be converted into kinetic energy, and the pressure in the narrow part is therefore below atmospheric. This reduction in pressure allows the atmospheric pressure acting on the surface of the gasoline in the float chamber to force gasoline out through the jet. The high-velocity air stream then breaks up the stream of gasoline into small droplets, producing a gasoline-and-air mixture that enters the cylinder.

The carburetor is essentially a very simple device. But modern ones contain a variety of refinements designed to improve the performance and economy of the engine. All types, however, have the float chamber and the converging-diverging air passage.

Inside the cylinder the gasoline-and-air mixture is ignited by a spark passing between the electrodes of the spark plug. What happens after the spark passes is of great importance to the design of gasoline engines. The first gasoline to ignite is that immediately surrounding the spark. Then a flame-front, more-or-less spherical in shape, sweeps through the remaining mixture. As it travels through the combustion space, the flame-front ignites the mixture. This traveling flame-front has the effect of compressing the unburnt part of the mixture and therefore raising its temperature. If the unburnt part of the mixture has its temperature raised too much, it may all suddenly ignite. This happens if the temperature exceeds the self-ignition point of the fuel—that is, the temperature at which it will burn *without* a separate igniter. Such a sudden ignition of all the remaining unburnt mixture brings about a very rapid rise of pressure, which may cause mechanical damage to the engine. It is just this sudden rise in pressure that produces the characteristic "knock." This noise was especially familiar to early motorists, but improvements in engines and fuels have largely eliminated it.

The tendency for an engine to knock is related to the temperature of the unburnt part of the fuel charge.

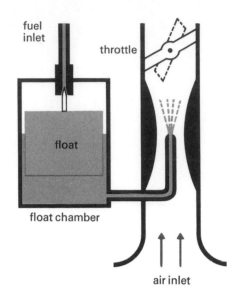

Carburetor diagram. Fuel level in the chamber is regulated by a valve operated by the float. The engine sucks air in through the air inlet; the air pressure decreases in the restricted part of the passage, thus drawing fuel from the chamber. As the fuel leaves the nozzle, it breaks up into droplets. The throttle controls the amount of mixture being fed to the engine. Below: Photos taken during tests on fuel-air mixing efficiency.

Knocking can be reduced by keeping that temperature as low as possible. One way of doing this is to make sure that there are no odd "pockets" in the combustion space where unburnt fuel can be trapped and become highly compressed. A compact combustion chamber with the spark plug placed centrally helps to eliminate this problem. A high compression ratio, however, will increase the tendency to knock. This happens because the higher the compression ratio, the higher will be the temperature at the end of compression. This high temperature will be increased still further by the subsequent compression produced by the traveling flame-front.

There are experimental engines in which the compression ratio can be varied during running. Such engines prove that increasing the compression ratio does eventually result in knocking. They also show that the compression ratio that can be reached before knocking occurs depends upon the fuel. Octane, a hydrocarbon of the methane series, was found to be a particularly good fuel. Other fuels are compared with it on the basis of their "octane rating." A fuel with 100 octane rating is as good as octane itself; one with less than 100 is worse; and one with more than 100 is better. Modern techniques of catalytic cracking in oil refineries have produced greatly improved fuels. These, together with the use of anti-knock additives such as tetra-ethyl lead, have allowed engine designers progressively to raise the compression ratio of automobile engines. As we saw in the table of Otto efficiency values (page 191), this results in higher efficiency. Today, compression ratios of eight and nine are commonplace, and some high-performance engines go up to ten.

It is clear, however, that the problem of knocking sets a practical upper limit to the compression ratio that may be used in a gasoline engine. This is not so with a diesel engine, where the practical limit is actually set by the lower range of limits. In a diesel engine, instead of a mixture of fuel and air being drawn into the cylinder, air alone is taken in and compressed. Near the end of the compression stroke, fuel is injected into the cylinder through a fine orifice, or opening. The fuel is injected by a very high pressure pump, delivering at about 2,000 lbf/in^2. The fine orifice is needed to break up the fuel into tiny droplets, so as to ensure good mixing with the air. At the moment of injection, compression must have raised the air to a temperature exceeding the self-ignition temperature of the fuel, for there is no spark plug. That is why there is a lower limit to the compression ratio that may be used. There is no upper limit, except that which it is not worth exceeding. As we have seen, in practice this ratio is about twenty. The diesel engine is thus able to use a much higher compression ratio than the gaso-

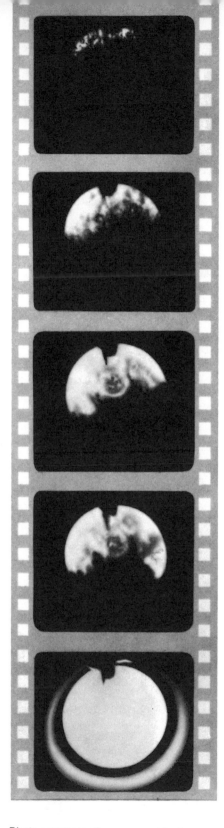

Photo sequence shows normal fuel burning in a cylinder, ending in rapid knock combustion. The top three photos (covering 8 milliseconds after ignition) show the flame-front advancing normally across the cylinder. In the fourth photo—0.1 milliseconds later—knock combustion has started along the right-hand wall. After another 0.15 milliseconds, the remaining fuel has abruptly ignited, causing knock.

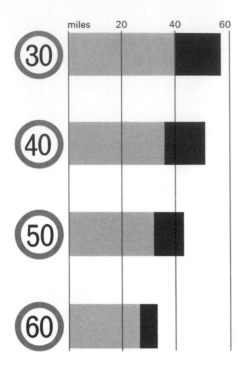

miles 20 40 60

30

40

50

60

Diagram compares fuel consumption (miles per gallon at constant speed) of similar cars driven by a gasoline engine (gray) and a diesel engine (black). The diesel engine is 30% more efficient than the gasoline engine at 30 mph, but its advantage diminishes as speeds increase, and it is only 19% more efficient at 60 mph.

Below: Close-up view of the top part of a diesel engine showing the strong metal tubes necessary to convey fuel at very high pressure from the fuel pump to the cylinders.

line engine and is therefore inherently more efficient.

If that is so, one may ask why the diesel engine has not completely replaced the gasoline engine. There are three main reasons. First, the diesel engine must be built to withstand higher pressures, and it is therefore heavier and more expensive. Second, the combustion process requires high temperatures, so it is harder to start a diesel engine. Third, the high pressure pump and injection equipment are very expensive. For the ordinary automobile, therefore, the additional cost of the diesel engine outweighs its advantage of efficiency. But for vehicles expected to do a very high annual mileage, such as buses, taxis, and trucks, the extra capital cost is soon recovered in lower fuel costs.

The diesel engine is the most efficient heat engine yet produced. It attains an overall thermal efficiency of 40 to 45 per cent, compared with 30 to 35 per cent for a steam turbine plant. The reason for this high efficiency lies in the high maximum temperature reached in the engine cylinder. This temperature may be as much as 5,000°F. The higher temperature in the diesel engine can be withstood only because it is a peak temperature, reached at one brief moment at the end of combustion. The temperature of the working parts usually reaches only some intermediate value. In the turbine, on the other hand, the blades are continuously exposed to the hot fluid. Therefore the blades remain at the temperature of that fluid.

Air-breathing engines are subject to a particular natural limitation—the condition of the atmospheric air they use. This does not affect their thermal efficiency, but it does have a considerable influence on the amount of power a given engine can produce. To appreciate why this is so, we have to remember that the maximum power-output of an engine depends upon the quantity of fuel it can use in a given time. This, in turn, depends upon the mass of air, containing roughly 20 per cent oxygen, that the engine can breathe in during the same

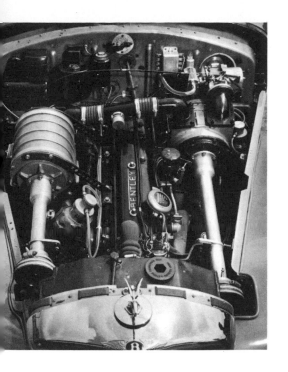

Top: Two-stage belt-driven supercharger fitted to an automobile engine to improve its power output. The larger drum on the left (shown in lower photo) partly compresses the air, which then passes to the smaller drum on the right, where compression is completed.

time. For a particular engine running at constant speed, a constant volume of air is taken in per minute. This volume is equal to the number of suction strokes per minute multiplied by the volume of the cylinder. The mass of air drawn in per minute is equal to this volume multiplied by the density of the air. If we know the chemical composition of the fuel the engine uses, we can calculate how much air per pound of fuel is needed for combustion. Then, if we also know the mass of air consumed per minute, we can work out the mass of fuel that can be burnt. This would tell us the maximum power that can be obtained. It is clear that if we could somehow increase the density of the atmospheric air, more fuel could be burnt in a given time. This would result in a bigger power-output from the same size of engine.

This problem first presented itself in the reverse form. Once airplanes became a practical proposition, something soon became obvious. At high altitudes, where the air density is greatly reduced, engine power falls off considerably. The solution was a simple one: Provide an air compressor, driven by the engine, which forces a greater mass of air into the cylinder. Naturally, however, there was a disadvantage. Part of the engine's power-output had to be used to drive the compressor, or *supercharger*, as such a device is called. Fortunately the increase in power due to supercharging exceeds the amount required to drive the compressor. For reciprocating airplane engines, the supercharger is essential. Superchargers are also commonly fitted to racing cars, which demand the utmost power-output from a limited size of engine.

An interesting variation of the engine-driven supercharger is the supercharger driven by exhaust gas. In this device the compressor is driven by a small, high-speed single-stage turbine, through which the exhaust gases pass. These gases, when released from the cylinder, are at a pressure and temperature above those of the atmosphere. Thus they have some energy, which can be used to drive a turbine. Such exhaust-gas-driven superchargers, or *turbochargers*, have been applied with success to airplane engines and also to large diesel engines.

It is interesting to speculate about the development of a combination of turbine-compressor and piston engine. Suppose the size of the turbocharger is increased relative to the engine. Eventually a stage would be reached where power could be taken from the turbocharger shaft as well as from the engine. The logical development of such thinking might be to take no power from the engine at all. The whole of the power-output would come from the turbine. The engine could then be simplified mechanically, for it would no longer require a

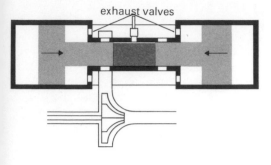

exhaust valves

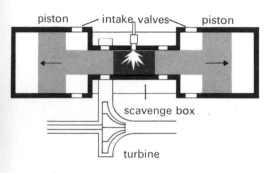

piston — intake valves — piston

scavenge box

turbine

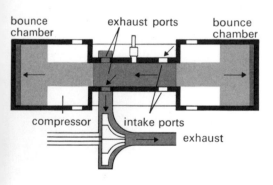

bounce chamber — exhaust ports — bounce chamber

compressor — intake ports

exhaust

The operation of a free-piston engine. Top: Air (blue) has been highly compressed by the coming together of two opposed pistons. Middle: Injection of fuel into compressed air causes an explosion (red): the pistons are now moving outwards. Bottom: Hot gases, still at high pressure, escape into the turbine casing, driving turbine before exhausting to air. Pistons meanwhile compress air (blue) in bounce chambers, prior to recoiling and compressing fresh air in combustion chamber as in top diagram. This fresh air is forced in by a scavenge pump, replacing the remnants of exhaust gas, and preparing the engine for a fresh cycle.

crankshaft. The whole machine would then become what is called a *free-piston* engine.

The free-piston engine consists of two opposed pistons working in a single cylinder. Combustion takes place in the space between them. Each piston has a piston rod, at the end of which is a larger piston that compresses air in a separate cylinder. The engine works on the two-stroke principle. Diesel fuel is injected into a supercharged combustion space, and the exhaust gases are scavenged. Two cushion cylinders, which act as pneumatic springs, return the pistons to their firing position. All the gases leaving the cylinder pass into a turbine, from which the useful power is taken.

The free-piston engine first appeared on the scene when the gas turbine proper was still in its infancy. It seemed to have a number of interesting possibilities. As we shall see later, the two most difficult problems in gas-turbine development were to construct a rotary compressor of high efficiency and to find materials to withstand high temperatures. The free-piston engine avoided both problems. The method it employs for compressing air—the use of a reciprocating piston—is already a very efficient one. Furthermore, the really high temperatures occur only in the engine cylinder, just as in any internal combustion engine. In addition, a free-piston engine is practically vibrationless, since there are no out-of-balance forces. However, severe mechanical problems were encountered in trying to develop this engine. Its attractiveness as a prime mover gradually declined as the gas turbine proper was improved.

As a means of obtaining a high power-output from a small, light engine, the gas turbine stands supreme. It is no exaggeration to say that recent advances in aircraft design, in terms of both speed and size, would have been quite impossible without the gas turbine. Basically the gas turbine is simple. It consists essentially of an air compressor; a combustion chamber in which fuel is burnt at constant pressure; and a turbine driven by the hot, high-pressure gases from the combustion chamber. The turbine and the compressor are mechanically coupled together, so that the compressor is driven by the turbine.

This arrangement can be used in two ways. If we want to produce rotative power—to drive, for example, a propellor or an electric generator—the gases are allowed to expand right down to atmospheric pressure in the turbine. This expansion produces much more power than is needed to drive the compressor, so that an excess of power is available. If, however, we want to propel an airplane, the gases in the turbine are allowed to expand only part-way to atmospheric pressure—just enough to provide power to drive the compressor. The exhaust

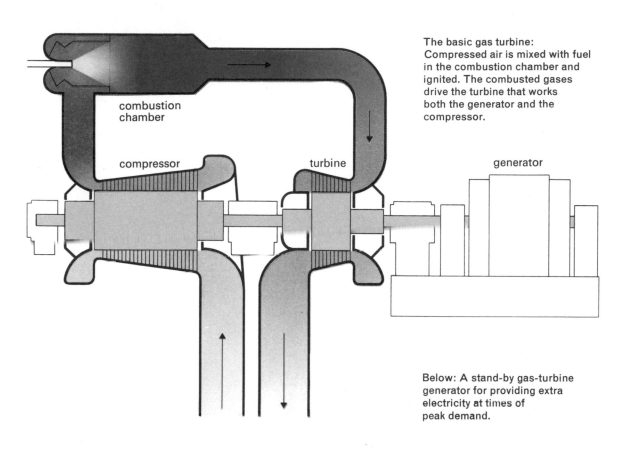

combustion chamber

compressor

turbine

generator

The basic gas turbine: Compressed air is mixed with fuel in the combustion chamber and ignited. The combusted gases drive the turbine that works both the generator and the compressor.

Below: A stand-by gas-turbine generator for providing extra electricity at times of peak demand.

A radial piston engine from about 1920,
developing 500 horsepower, alongside
a modern jet engine of similar size
that develops about 5,000 horsepower.

Wind-tunnel photo of the v-shaped shock wave that occurs in intake air at supersonic speeds.

gases from the turbines are then at a pressure above atmospheric. These gases expand through a nozzle and emerge at high velocity. If we now think of the engine as a unit, air has entered at a velocity, relative to the engine, equal to the forward speed of the airplane. The exhaust gases have left at a much higher speed. There has thus been an increase in *momentum* of the air in passing through the engine. According to Newton's Third Law of Motion, to every action there is an equal and opposite reaction. Here the action is the force of the gases rushing out the back of the airplane. The reaction is the force that propels the airplane forward. This is precisely similar to what happens in a propeller-driven airplane. There it is the propeller that accelerates the air passing through it, so increasing its momentum.

For aircraft propulsion, the advantage of the gas turbine over the piston engine and propeller is that it produces far more power from a single unit. The gas turbine does so, moreover, with a much better power-weight ratio. Furthermore, the propeller becomes less and less efficient at increasing air speeds. A propeller-driven airplane is limited to a maximum speed of about 450 miles per hour. The gas turbine, on the contrary, becomes more efficient at higher speeds. The propulsive efficiency of a gas turbine engine depends on the ratio of the forward speed of the aircraft to the speed of the gases leaving the nozzle. For maximum propulsive efficiency, this ratio is one-to-two, or 0.5. Since the gas speed is at least 2,000 feet per second, the aircraft speed for maximum propulsive efficiency is at least 1,000 feet per second (nearly 700 m.p.h.). In order to calculate the thermal efficiency of a gas turbine, we divide the net work done by the heat supplied in the combustion chamber. In the power-producing engine, the useful work is the difference between the work done by the turbine and the work required to drive the compressor. In the jet engine, an equivalent figure can be obtained by considering the kinetic energy of the gases leaving the nozzle.

Right: Diagram shows regions of efficient operation of three types of aircraft. The speed of sound varies with altitude; it is called Mach 1, in honor of the Austrian physicist Ernst Mach (1838-1916).

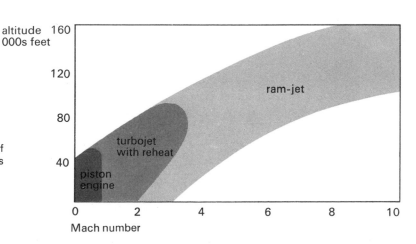

Unfortunately, the work required to drive the compressor is a fairly high proportion—between one-half and three-quarters—of that produced in the turbine. If, therefore, the compressor were somewhat inefficient, the useful work might be reduced almost to vanishing point, resulting in almost zero efficiency. This was one of the difficulties facing the early designers of gas turbines. The nature of aerodynamics makes it far more difficult to design an efficient rotary air compressor than to design an efficient turbine. The reason for this is that the compressor acts in the opposite way to a turbine. A turbine has blades and nozzles in which the gas is always flowing through *converging* passages with increasing speed and decreasing pressure. But in a compressor the air is flowing through *diverging* passages with decreasing speed and increasing pressure. Now the awkward aerodynamic fact is that, while air works well in the former arrangement, it takes very badly to the latter. Indeed, if the diverging conical passage has an included angle of more than about 8°, air simply will not pass through smoothly. Instead, the air will leave the sides of the passage altogether. This is known as "breakaway," and it results in turbulence and loss of efficiency.

Designing an efficient compressor became a key problem in producing an efficient gas-turbine engine. The solution depended on applying the results of aerodynamic research. The result is that the shape of the blades of an axial-flow air compressor, the type eventually developed, closely resembles the shape of an aircraft wing. Because of the "breakaway" problem, the air has to be taken much more gradually through the compressor than through the turbine. This means that the compressor has many more stages than the turbine.

The work required to drive the compressor is directly proportional to the absolute air temperature at inlet. For an earth-bound engine, the variations of atmospheric temperature are not likely to have any considerable effect, except in extremely hot or cold conditions. For the airplane engine, however, this fact amounts to a very real bonus. Atmospheric temperature decreases rapidly with increasing altitude. The blades of the airplane's turbine are similar in design to those of the steam turbine, and the basic principles of the two engines are identical. Just as in every other heat engine, the work output is directly proportional to the absolute temperature at inlet. This temperature should be made as high as possible. Indeed, in the jet engine remarkably high temperatures are used—up to 1,650°F. Compare this with the maximum temperature—just over 1,000°F. —in the most recent steam plant.

One reason why a jet engine can work at high temperatures lies in a peculiar property that metals exhibit

Above, left and right: Two views of a gas-turbine jet engine. Note how the components are compactly arranged so as to reduce as far as possible the frontal area of the engine, thus reducing air resistance.

Right: Exploded view of the above engine. The compressor has many more stages than the turbine, because the air has to be compressed gradually; otherwise air turbulence is created, resulting in lower efficiency.

Right: The multi-stage compressor rotor. Air is drawn from left to right, with decreasing speed and increasing pressure, between diverging blade passages. Thus, the arrangement of the blades is just the opposite of that found in steam turbines (see page 171).

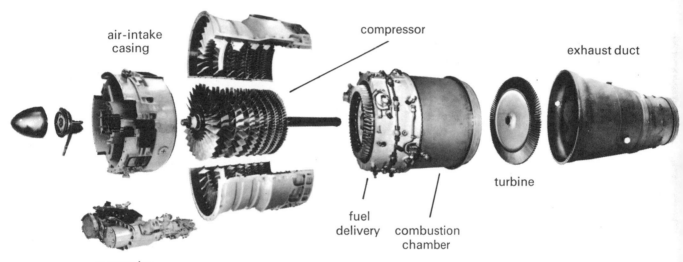

compressor casing

air-intake
casing

compressor

exhaust duct

fuel
delivery

combustion
chamber

turbine

accessories
gearbox assembly

Investigating the properties of gas-turbine blades. The blade is mounted on a stand, and a powerful jet of air is directed onto it from the right. The observer is measuring the extent and direction of the blade's vibration at the top.

at high temperatures. If a piece of metal is subjected to a constant force at room temperature, the metal will extend slightly. However long the force is applied, this extension will remain constant. If, however, the metal is at the same time subjected to a high temperature, the extension will continuously increase. (This explains the term "creep" used to describe this property.) Eventually the metal breaks, possibly after only a few days. The longer the metal is required to withstand a particular temperature, the smaller must be the force applied to minimize "creep." Similarly, the longer the metal is required to withstand a particular force, the lower must be the temperature to minimize "creep."

It is on this question—how long they are expected to operate without risk of failure—that the steam plant and the jet engine differ so considerably. A steam plant installed in a power station is expected to run continuously, night and day, for at least ten years, with stops only for annual overhaul. That means about 9,000 hours a year for 10 years, or a total of about 90,000 hours. An airplane engine, on the other hand, is acceptable to an airline operator even if it has to be completely overhauled every 2,000 hours. Indeed, many jet engines have a much shorter period than this between overhauls. Thus, in spite of the creep phenomenon, a jet engine can be designed with a much higher inlet temperature than a steam turbine.

The gas-turbine combustion chamber is a most elegant piece of mechanical engineering. Simple in principle, it turns what might be regarded as a difficult problem to advantage. Getting the fuel to burn is easy. The fuel is merely sprayed into a cylindrical chamber, or flame tube, through one or more fine jets and ignited by an electrically heated glow plug. Once combustion is started in this way, it continues as long as fuel and air are supplied. The problem is that there must be a very much greater intake of air than is needed to burn the necessary quantity of fuel. The maximum temperature the turbine blades can withstand is far lower than the temperature that would be reached if the fuel were burnt with only the chemically necessary quantity of air. This problem is solved by providing the combustion chamber with an outer casing. This casing is concentric with, but of greater diameter than, the cylinder in which combustion takes place. Some of the air delivered by the compressor enters the inner chamber through holes in the wall of this cylinder, or flame tube. The remainder passes along the *annular space* between the flame tube and the outer casing. The quantity of air admitted to the flame tube is enough for satisfactory combustion. The very hot gases produced by combustion then mix at the end of the combustion chamber with the cooler gases

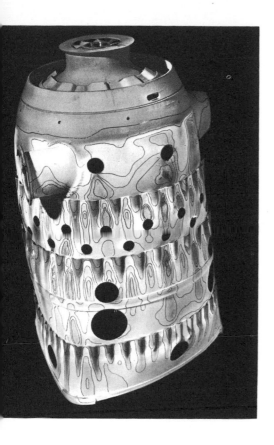

Dangerously hot spots in a jet-engine combustion chamber can be detected by applying a special paint that changes color in proportion to the heat of the metal. The lightest parts of the combustion chamber above are those that have been subjected to the greatest heat. The continuous lines outline areas of similar paint color.

Red curves relate thermal efficiency to pressure ratio for various turbine inlet temperatures; arrow shows increasing inlet temperature.

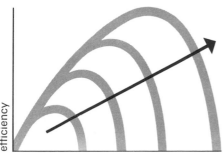

efficiency

pressure ratio

flowing through the annular space. The hot gases and the cooler gases together produce a mixture of the right temperature for the turbine.

This arrangement has three main advantages. The cooler gases flowing through the annular space provide an insulating layer around the very hot combustion zone. This reduces heat losses and avoids a dangerously hot exposed surface, which could become a fire hazard. The layer of cool gases also cools the outside of the flame tube itself and prolongs its life. Finally, the flame tube is relieved of stresses due to gas pressure, since the pressures inside and outside the tube are the same. The pressure stresses are taken instead by the cool outer casing, which can withstand them better. Here is an example of really good design. The engine not only does the job expected of it, but does it in the best possible way.

When considering the reciprocating internal combustion engine, we referred to the Otto cycle as the ideal cycle of operations (p. 191). We found that the ideal efficiency for this cycle could be expressed by a very simple formula. Unfortunately, no such simple formula can be found for the gas turbine. An equation can, of course, be worked out, but it is much more complicated. In the gas turbine we have two variables—the turbine inlet temperature and the pressure ratio. We can show graphically the effect of these two variables on the thermal efficiency. This is done by plotting a number of curves relating thermal efficiency to pressure ratio for various values of the turbine inlet temperature. These curves show that, for any particular temperature, the efficiency first increases with increasing pressure ratio. Eventually the efficiency reaches a maximum, and then it decreases. It is also noticeable that the higher the turbine inlet temperature, the higher the optimum pressure ratio becomes. In practice, the exact shape of these curves varies with the values of compressor and turbine efficiency. The curves also vary with the pressure losses in the combustion chamber and ducts. Each design must thus be studied individually before the choice of optimum pressure ratio is made.

There are several possible variants of the basic gas turbine, which consists merely of compressor, combustion chamber, and turbine. One important arrangement has two turbines. The hot gases pass first through a turbine that drives the compressor, and then through a second one, which provides useful power. Such arrangements have been successfully applied to very high-speed ships. There the gas turbine's ability to provide a high power output from a small size of power unit is extremely desirable. This type of turbine was also used in Sir Donald Campbell's car "Bluebird," which broke the land speed record in 1964. This type has found a further

single-spool turbojet

The basic gas-turbine aircraft engine— the single-spool turbojet—consists of compressor, combustion chamber, and turbine. The two-spool turbojet has two compressor-turbine units, each mechanically separate. It is used in planes flying at speeds in excess of Mach 1.

two-spool turbojet

turbofan

In the turbofan the second compressor-turbine unit directs air through passages outside the combustion chamber. This air thus goes straight to the jet nozzle, where it mixes with the hot exhaust gases from the turbine. The engine is used in planes flying just below the speed of sound.

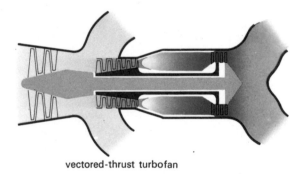

vectored-thrust turbofan

The vectored-thrust turbofan. The jet nozzles can be directed downwards, to permit the plane to take off and land vertically, as well as horizontally for normal forward flight.

turboprop

In the turboprop engine—used in planes flying at about 400 mph—a second turbine unit drives a propeller. In the variation of this engine—called the turboshaft—the second turbine is used to turn a shaft behind the engine. Such an engine is suitable for ships, where the shaft is coupled to the ship's propeller.

turboshaft

successful application in the generation of electricity.

For this latter purpose, the gas turbine is particularly useful as a stand-by power plant. It can be started up quickly when the normal power generation system is unable to meet a peak demand. A stand-by gas turbine generator offers three further advantages. It can be installed virtually anywhere, since it needs no supply of cooling water. It can, if desired, be started up and stopped by remote control. Furthermore, when a gas turbine is used as a stand-by power plant, its comparatively short working life between overhauls is unimportant. The gas turbine is put into service for only an hour or two a day, at times of peak demand.

In the air, this type of turbine has been applied to propeller-driven planes flying at speeds of about 400 miles per hour. (At these speeds, pure jet propulsion would not be so efficient, because the speed of the gases leaving the jet would be much more than twice the aircraft speed.) In this arrangement, the separate turbine drives the propeller. A variant of this arrangement is to incorporate the propeller within the engine itself. Such an engine is called a *turbofan*, or fan-jet engine. It consists of a simple gas turbine with compressor, turbine, and combustion chamber. Part of this engine's useful work-output drives a second compressor or fan, corresponding to the propeller. The air delivered by the fan does not pass through the combustion chamber. It goes direct to the jet nozzle, where it mixes with the hot exhaust gases from the turbine. This arrangement gives the most efficient engine for aircraft speeds just below the speed of sound in air—about 700 miles per hour. For supersonic speeds, the so-called "two-spool" engine has been developed. This has two turbines and two compressors, each compressor-turbine unit being mechanically separate. The use of two compressors enables a higher jet speed to match the higher forward speed of the aircraft.

As the aircraft speed is increased, the "ram-effect" becomes more and more important. Ram-effect refers to the kinetic energy of the intake air due to the forward speed of the engine. At really high speeds—let us say, twice the speed of sound or more—it becomes possible to use a ram-jet engine. In the ram-jet engine, the kinetic energy of the intake air is converted into potential energy in a carefully designed entry duct. Instead of a high velocity, the engine gets air at high pressure. This air is then used for the combustion of fuel in a combustion chamber, and the high-pressure hot gases expand in a nozzle. Because of their high temperature, the velocity of the exhaust gases is greater than the inlet velocity. The change of momentum produces a force that propels the aircraft forward.

A transportable power unit. Enclosed within this trailer is a 4,500 horsepower gas turbine and generator.

Below: A patrol boat belonging to the Royal Danish Navy, which is driven by a turboshaft engine. The boat is capable of speeds of over 50 knots.

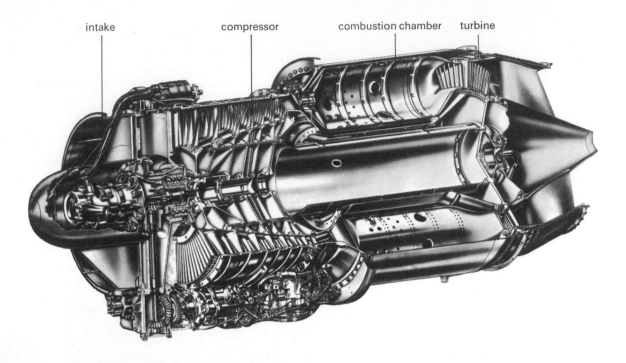

intake compressor combustion chamber turbine

The ram-jet is a model of simplicity, having no moving parts whatsoever. Unfortunately, it has one very big disadvantage. Because it relies on a very high forward velocity for compressing the air, it cannot produce any thrust when stationary. Either conventional engines or rockets must first be used to accelerate the vehicle up to a satisfactory speed before the ram-jet can start to work. At present, ram-jets are used as a power unit for some types of guided missile. The initial acceleration for these is provided by booster rockets. The very high-speed aircraft of the future will be flying at 1,500 m.p.h. and more. Such aircraft may well have a ram-jet to take over from conventional jet engines when the cruising speed has been reached.

In the varieties of gas turbines that we have described, the problem of thermal efficiency has been solved sufficiently for each purpose. The pure jet engine, for example, effectively converts heat into the kinetic energy of exhaust gases. The turboprop engine makes good use of the residual energy in its exhaust gases by directing them backwards so as to increase the thrust. Some

Left: Exploded diagram of a single-spool turbojet. It has a seven-stage compressor driven by a single-stage turbine. The engine develops a thrust of 5,000 pounds. Use of alloys for such engines makes them suitable for small strike aircraft. Below left: A two-spool engine, of 35,000 pound thrust, on test in the factory.

Above: A ram-jet engine, used at twice the speed of sound and above. Below: There are no moving parts on a ram-jet; air is compressed in the entry duct by virtue of the engine's forward motion. Fuel is burned in the combustion chamber, and the exhaust gases leave the engine at a higher velocity than the intake air entering—thus the forward thrust.

intake   fuel jets   combustion zone   propelling nozzle

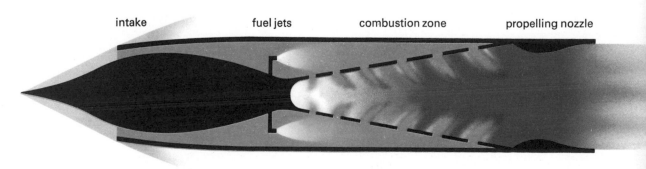

stationary gas turbine generators use a heat exchanger. This device enables the intake air, after compression, to be pre-heated prior to entering the combustion chamber. Such a heat exchanger is, however, bulky. Although suitable for a stationary power plant, it seemed unsuitable for a gas turbine intended to drive a vehicle. However, in 1965 a gas-turbine car was successfully raced in competition with conventional cars at Le Mans, France. Its heat exchanger, compact and ingenious, was composed of rotating ceramic discs containing thousands of thin-walled, parallel holes. Each disc is heated during one half of its rotation by exhaust gases flowing through the holes. During the other half of its rotation, the compressed intake air passes through the holes. This air takes up the heat in the disc and passes to the combustion chamber at a temperature of 1,100°F. For the first time, man has a prospect that cars of the future may be powered by gas turbines.

Below: Diagram of the layout of a gas-turbine engine, which has been successfully used to drive an automobile. Also shown is the temperature of the air and gases at various stages. Note the heat-exchanging device between the exhaust and the entry to the combustion chamber. Intake air that reached a temperature of 360°F. by compression is heated to 1,100°F. before reaching the combustion chamber. In this way heat of combustion is not wasted, and engine can compete with other forms of prime mover for automobiles.

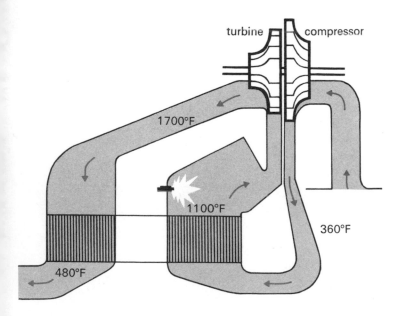

turbine   compressor

1700°F

1100°F

480°F   360°F

Top: Transport aircraft powered by two piston engines, with a jet engine on top of the fuselage. This increases load-carrying capacity and general performance when operating from high-altitude airfields in hot climates. Photo shows aircraft flying with the two piston engines stopped. Above: Bloodhound surface-to-air guided missiles, powered by ram-jet engines, with solid-fuel booster rockets to accelerate the missiles to about 700 mph. At this speed, the rockets are jettisoned and the ram-jets take over.

Right: Vertical-take-off-and-landing aircraft, powered by vectored-thrust turbofan engines. The jets are here directed downwards for vertical movement; for normal flight they are directed horizontally.

Section 3: Looking Ahead

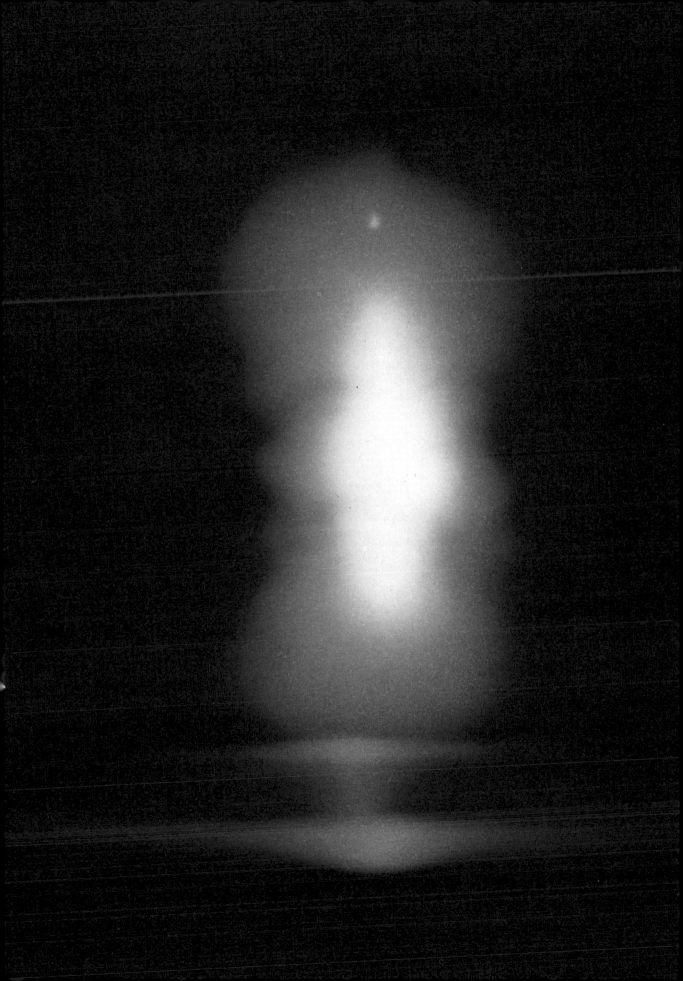

9 Problems and Possibilities

By now we have made a reasonably thorough survey of the sources of energy available to mankind and the main types of engine used to convert energy into useful power. This final chapter will review some of the problems connected with existing engines and to look at a few of the problems that may arise in the future.

We have seen that, at present, most of our power is derived from fossil fuels. Their stored solar energy is converted into heat energy by combustion. The heat energy is then turned into useful power by a heat engine. Meanwhile, man turns more and more to the energy of the atom. Of course, this energy is also turned into heat energy and converted into power by means of a heat engine. So it is clear that, for many years to come, the heat engine will be our most important prime mover.

Unfortunately, the efficiency with which a heat engine turns heat into work is not very high. In the language of physics, T_1 and T_2 represent the highest and lowest temperatures in the conversion cycle. The laws of thermodynamics impose a limitation of $\dfrac{T_1 - T_2}{T_1}$ on the maximum efficiency obtainable (p. 119). In actual practice, the imperfections of the engine itself reduce efficiency considerably further. Thus even the best thermal power stations are able to convert only about one-third of the heat energy they consume into useful power.

The simple formula above indicates how the problem of increasing heat engine efficiencies must be approached. There is little engineers can do about decreasing the low temperature, T_2. For all practical purposes, it is limited by the atmospheric temperature. So the only roads to improvement lie in increasing T_1 and in reducing the imperfections of the engine. First, what can be done about increasing T_1? In turbine plants, both steam and gas, this involves finding better materials for the blades and rotors. Or it might also mean cooling the hot parts so that they do not reach the full temperature of the working fluid. Gas turbines blades already run at a bright red heat. It may be possible to cool the blades with cool air drawn off from the compressor. But the

Two lines of research into new power sources. Top: Equipment used in the thetatron coil project attempting to reproduce and control on earth the fusion of atoms that goes on in the sun. Photo on previous page shows a plasma, produced by heating air to over 100,000°C. Controlled thermonuclear fusion will be possible only when much hotter plasmas can be sustained; if this is achieved, an unlimited power source would be available. Lower: Testing a methanol-air fuel cell. Fuel cells convert chemical energy directly into electricity; they are still in the development stage, but they may prove to be an efficient power source in the very near future.

design and manufacture of suitable hollow blades has so far proved very difficult. An alternative that looks more promising is to use non-metallic blades, possibly of some ceramic material. Unfortunately, ceramics tend to crack if heated or cooled rapidly. Nevertheless, research is being undertaken on ceramics and also on composite materials called *cermets*, or *ceramals*—partly ceramic and partly metallic.

Meanwhile much thought and work go into the effort to reduce the imperfections of the engine. Turbine blades are examined and tested in wind-tunnels, in the hope of devising more efficient shapes. Careful attention is given to the detailed design of bearings, seals, and other components. In steam power plants, the recent tendency has been to design much bigger machines than formerly. This has two advantages. The first is that the cost (per kilowatt output) is lower for a large machine than for a smaller one. The second advantage depends on the fact that many of the losses in a steam turbine plant are more or less constant, no matter what the size of the machine. This means that the larger the machine, the smaller in proportion are these losses. Hence the greater is the efficiency. The problem of cooling is one of the major factors in limiting the size of a steam turbine plant. Early machines—small by today's standards —were air-cooled. Hydrogen, a better coolant than air because of its higher specific heat, was later used instead. This made it possible to increase the size. The most recent machines, however, are even more effectively cooled with water. This has permitted the building of plants with an output of 500 megawatts, and plans are now being made to build even larger machines. If we consider all these improvements, both existing and prospective, it seems probable that heat engines of the future may waste only half the heat supplied to them instead of two-thirds.

Even so, it does seem that existing forms of heat engines have almost reached their ultimate in efficiency. Substantial improvements will probably be brought about only by using some completely new device, most likely based on a new principle. One such device is the Wankel engine, named after its German inventor. This is considered to be a competitor to the reciprocating gasoline engine. It has no reciprocating parts or valves, and its only moving part is a three-lobed rotor turning on an internal gear. This rotor revolves in a specially shaped casing. The casing has an inlet port for admitting the charge and an exhaust port for releasing the spent gases—just as in the two-stroke engine. These ports are opened and closed by the lobes of the rotor. As the diagram shows, the freshly drawn-in fuel mixture occupies a relatively large space between the rotor and the

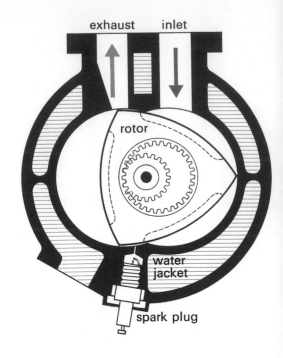

Diagram shows the general arrangement of the Wankel engine. As the rotor rotates about the central gear (the output gear) its three apexes always remain in contact with the inner sides of the casing. Opposite are shown the various stages of the engine's cycle.

Below: Photograph showing the interior of a Wankel engine.

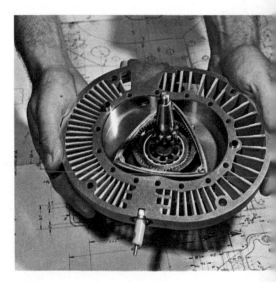

The sequence of events in one of the three chambers of the Wankel engine.
1: The air-fuel mixture is drawn in through the inlet port. 2: Induction is complete and as the rotor continues to revolve, the area that the mixture occupies decreases; this is the compression stage.
3: Compression is complete and the mixture is ignited by the spark plug.
4: The mixture expands; this is the power stroke. 5: The exhaust outlet is uncovered, and the spent charge escapes. 6: Exhaust continues and induction is about to begin again. In the other two chambers the exact sequence of events occurs, although differently phased.

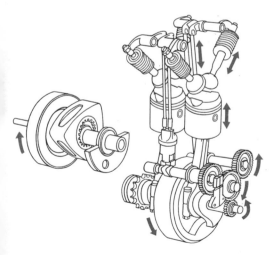

Below: These drawings—approximately to scale—compare the NSU Wankel engine and a conventional reciprocating engine. Note the great reduction of moving parts.

casing. But by the time the rotor has turned one-third of a revolution, the fuel charge is compressed into a much smaller space. The spark is then given off, and combustion takes place with a consequent rise in pressure. The high pressure, acting on the rotor, provides the driving force for the next one-third of a revolution. Finally, the exhaust port is uncovered and the exhaust gases leave the engine. The advantages of this engine are threefold: Simplicity and cheapness; smooth running due to the absence of reciprocating parts; and a good power-to-weight ratio, because there are three firing "strokes" for every revolution of the rotor. The major problem is to provide an adequate seal to prevent leakage between the lobes of the rotor and the casing.

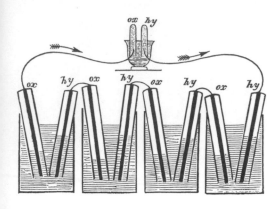

The first fuel cell was described by Sir William Grove in 1839. The above drawing accompanied an article by him published in 1842. The electrolyte was sulphuric acid, and the electrodes were blacked platinum. Each cell generated about one volt, but only tiny currents could be drawn because of the small area of contact between the reacting gases (hydrogen and oxygen), the electrolyte, and the electrodes.

The modern hydrogen-oxygen fuel cell uses electrodes of porous nickel; the electrolyte is a potassium hydroxide solution. The text discusses the working of the cell.

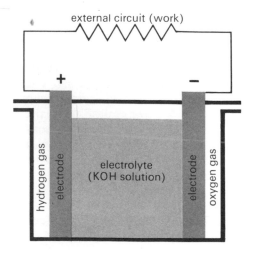

external circuit (work)

+   −

hydrogen gas | electrode | electrolyte (KOH solution) | electrode | oxygen gas

The Wankel engine is most attractive for its simplicity and ingenuity. The engine is therefore subject to the same limitations of maximum attainable efficiency as are all other heat engines. To be free from these limitations, we must get away from the idea of combustion. We should consider, for instance, a new way of converting the potential energy of a hydrocarbon fuel into some more readily usable form such as electricity. In the last few years considerable attention has been paid to the *fuel cell*. The fuel cell is really an adaptation of the simple electrolytic cell. In the traditional electrolytic cell, two electrodes of dissimilar materials are placed in an electrolyte, or conducting fluid. An electromotive force is then produced between them. An example of this is the simple Daniell cell, consisting of electrodes of zinc and copper in dilute sulphuric acid. When the two electrodes are connected across a resistance, a current flows and a small quantity of electrical power is produced. If such a device were allowed to function continuously, the zinc electrode would eventually be consumed. If the electrodes could be continuously replaced, power could be produced indefinitely.

It is just this problem of continuous replacement that the fuel cell has succeeded in solving. The fuel cell does this by reversing the process of electrolysis. In the fuel cell, the two electrodes of the regular electrolytic cell are replaced by oxygen and a gaseous or liquid fuel. Both the oxygen and the fuel are continuously supplied. An example of a fuel cell that has been successfully operated is the hydrogen-oxygen cell. This has two porous nickel plates, which act as electrodes. The electrolyte that circulates between them is potassium hydroxide solution. The hydrogen and oxygen are supplied to the cavities between the outer faces of the electrodes and the outer casing. The porous nature of the electrodes allows the charged atoms *(ions)* of oxygen to pass through them. The oxygen then unites with the hydrogen to form water. At the same time, the plates provide an adequate barrier to prevent the ordinary chemical combustion of the two elements.

When hydrogen and oxygen combine by normal combustion, the energy of the electrons in the uncombined atoms is greater than that of the electrons in the final water molecule. The difference appears as heat. In the fuel cell, the rearrangement of the electrons still occurs, but the energy difference appears directly as electricity. The fuel cell thus avoids all the complicated and inefficient machinery necessary to convert heat into electricity. It is therefore not surprising that the energy-conversion efficiency of the fuel cell is much higher than that of a heat engine plant. There is still some limitation on efficiency imposed by the laws of thermodynamics.

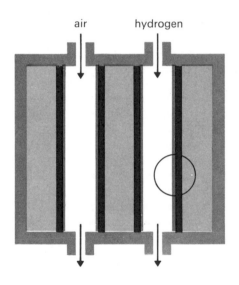

hydrogen

silver and catalyst

electrolyte

pore in PVC bringing fuel, electrolyte, and catalyst into contact

air   hydrogen

But the maximum theoretical efficiency is close to 99 per cent. In actual practice, such a high efficiency cannot be achieved. As soon as a current is taken from a fuel cell, some heat is generated within the cell due to its own internal resistance. Nevertheless, efficiencies of 60 to 70 per cent are still attainable.

The use of hydrogen and oxygen turns out to be somewhat expensive, but it is possible to use a gaseous fuel and air instead. In this case the electrodes are made of zinc oxide alloyed with a small percentage of silver. The electrolyte is a fused mixture of sodium and lithium carbonates. Such a cell will work only at a high temperature—about 1,100°F,—but a wide range of gaseous and vaporized hydrocarbon fuels can be used. The *electromotive force* produced by a fuel cell is small—only one or two volts. To produce a workable voltage, a large number must be connected together in series. To produce a substantial current, several such banks of cells would have to be connected in parallel. Although the need for a multiplicity of cells appears awkward, it has already proved possible to power a full-size truck by this means. In that instance, the fuel used was methane, a relatively cheap derivative of liquid or solid hydrocarbon fuels. We may expect it to find numerous applications in the future. Fuel cells are already being used in space vehicles.

The fuel cell is a good example of the use of a new principle to convert a traditional energy source into use-

Right: The methanol-air fuel cell, mounted on a small vehicle and powering an electric drill, is believed to be the first commercially usable fuel cell. The methanol reacts with steam in a miniature chemical plant to produce hydrogen; this gas, with air, is fed to the battery of fuel cells in the foreground of the photo. Diagram above shows arrangement of the cells; the plates are of plastic (PVC) and, as enlarged section shows, are coated on the side farthest from the electrolyte with silver and a trace of platinum to form a catalyst.

Solar heating installation mounted on the roof of an apartment block in Israel. This provides hot water throughout year and space heating in winter.

Below: Basic layout of a conventional solar generator. Sun's rays are focused at A to heat fluid, which circulates through tube (B) and transfers its heat (at C) to the fluid in the large tank. This fluid vaporizes under pressure to drive a turbine (D), which turns the electric generator (E). At top left is a cooling tube where spent vapor condenses before returning to tank. Black bars represent rods that store heat, enabling the boiler to produce power, during only short intervals, when the sun is obscured by cloud.

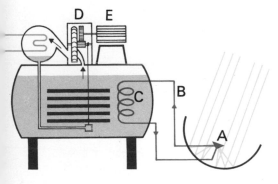

ful power. In this case, the sources are various chemical substances. What of the problems and possibilities of using other sources of energy? The one that seems most likely to make an early contribution to our requirements is solar energy. In India, for example, solar energy is beginning to replace animal dung, the traditional fuel used for domestic cooking. In a climate where continuous sunshine can be virtually guaranteed for long periods of the year, a concave mirror can be employed to focus the sun's rays onto a cooking stove. This is not only a big advance in hygiene; it could also prove a considerable help to the economy of a country like India. It has been estimated that India uses some three million tons of animal dung in domestic fires each year. If solar energy takes over the job, this dung could be used to fertilize fields and increase the yield of food crops.

The simple principle of focusing the sun's rays by mirrors can be extended and applied in a remarkable way. This technique, for instance, can create a very-high-temperature furnace for melting metal alloys. It is not easy to obtain a really high temperature for such furnaces by traditional methods. If large-enough mirrors are used in a solar furnace the only limit to the temperature is the maximum that the refractory material of the furnace can withstand. Furnaces of this type have been successfully developed in France.

Solar energy has also proved to be an ideal source of power for artificial satellites. One device employed for converting solar energy into useful power is the *solar cell*, or *solar battery*. This is somewhat like the *thermocouple*, which consists of two dissimilar metals joined together. When the junction of these metals in the thermocouple is heated, an electromotive force is produced. The heat is converted directly into electricity. In the solar cell, the junction is of two different kinds of semiconductors, elements that lie between metals and nonmetals. The cell is energized not by heat but by light.

Semiconductors are substances that permit little or no flow of electricity at low temperatures but increasingly large flows at higher temperatures. In this they are unlike ordinary metallic conductors, which behave in precisely the opposite way. The basic semiconductor employed in the solar cell is silicon in the form of a single crystal. An atom of silicon has four electrons in the outermost orbit. In a silicon crystal the atoms arrange themselves in the tetrahedral diamond shape. The orbiting electrons interact, and each of the four combines with an electron from a neighboring atom. This produces a very stable arrangement so that at low temperatures there are no free electrons. The crystal behaves as a non-conductor. If the temperature is raised, however, a few of the electrons may acquire enough energy to

This 35-foot wide reflector at Mont Louis in the French Pyrenees
is made up of 3,500 small mirrors, which concentrate sunlight onto
a small area. At the point of focus, temperatures of over
3,000°C. are obtained. The reflector rotates on movable tracks
so as to follow the sun.

escape from their orbits. If an electromotive force is now applied across the crystal, a current will flow due to the movement of these free electrons. The conductivity will depend on the temperature—the higher the temperature, the better the conductivity.

The properties of a semiconductor can be considerably modified by introducing a very small quantity of some impurity. But this works only if the atoms of the impurity have a different number of electrons in their outermost orbits. Phosphorus atoms have five such electrons. When they are introduced as an impurity into silicon, each atom of phosphorus provides one free electron. Such a material is called *N*-type. Similarly, the addition of boron, with three outer-orbiting electrons, produces a conducting material called *P*-type. When a piece of *N*-type material is joined to a piece of *P*-type and light is allowed to fall on the junction, an electromotive force is produced. It is not even necessary to produce separate pieces of material. Scientists have found a way of introducing the phosphorus impurity into one part of a silicon crystal itself. Communications satellites such as Telstar and Early Bird, as well as many other satellites, owe much of their success to these wonderful devices. And solar cells are also being used to supply power for telephones, lights, and various communication devices.

However, it must be remembered that the power-output from a single solar cell is small. For example, the satellite Ranger 3 required a power-output of between 155 and 310 watts. This called for the use of 8,680 solar cells. Solar cells are therefore only suitable for small satellites. The number required becomes impracticable if the power demand exceeds about 1 kilowatt. It has been suggested that larger space vehicles might make use of a solar turboelectric generator once such a satellite had been placed in orbit. A solar radiation collector in the form of a concave mirror would be erected. The satellite would then be oriented so that the mirror faced the sun. The concentrated solar radiation would then be used to power a mercury-vapor turbine.

Devices such as these, although developed specifically for satellites and space vehicles, represent a major step forward in technology. It is quite possible that the lessons learned may provide ways of using solar energy for more ordinary purposes in the not-too-distant future. If so, this would be one more example of what is called "spin-off" in the United States and "fall-out" in Great Britain. Both phrases refer to the economic application of scientific activities that originally seemed quite uneconomic and even impractical.

Already, in suitable climates, architects have designed and built houses to be heated by solar radiation. The

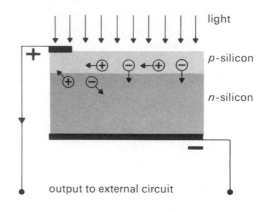

A silicon solar cell. It uses two different types of the semiconductor silicon. When light falls on the surface of the cell, an electric current flows around the external circuit.

Below: The Battelle solar engine converts solar energy directly into rotary motion. The regenerator piston, blackened on top so that it heats rapidly, is loose fitting. It is, in effect, a steel sponge whose sole purpose is to heat air trapped between the working piston and the dome. Hot air exerts pressure on the working piston, which drives the crankshaft and flywheel. As the air performs work, it cools and is then ready to take up more heat from the regenerator piston, whose reciprocating movement causes air to flow through it.

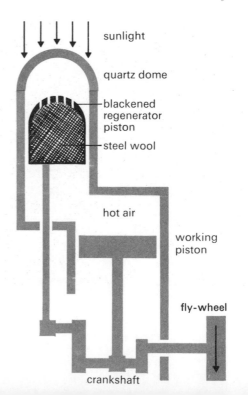

solar collector is built into the roof, which slopes to face the sun. It consists of a number of overlapping, blackened metal plates with spaces between them. The whole array is covered with glass to keep down re-radiation. Air is circulated between the plates to carry the heat away. The heated air then passes through a heat-store, a large container filled with gravel. During the day the gravel heats up. At night, cold air is passed through the hot gravel and then to the rooms where warmth is required. However, homes using this form of heating must also be provided with some other form as well. They must be equipped to cope with cold spells if there is a long period without sunshine. The initial cost of such an installation is therefore bound to be high, but the running cost will be much lower than for heating by conventional means.

For the foreseeable future, the direct use of solar radiation will probably be confined to relatively small-scale installations. But what prospects are there of completely new devices, using new sources of energy for large-scale power production? There appear to be two promising possibilities. The first is controlled atomic fusion. The second is magnetohydrodynamic generation which we shall deal with later in the chapter.

We saw in Chapter 1 that the sun's energy is produced by a fusion of hydrogen atoms into helium atoms. The resulting loss of mass reappears as energy. There are good prospects that this reaction can be reproduced artificially, and in a controlled way, on earth. We have a vast store of hydrogen in the oceans, enough to satisfy the world's power requirements for thousands, if not millions, of years.

The reaction that takes place in the sun is made possible by the extremely high temperatures—millions of degrees—that exist in the sun's interior. Now the highest temperature commonly reached on earth can be measured in mere thousands of degrees. An electric arc, for instance, has a temperature of about 5,400°F. If temperatures go much higher than this, most of the materials at our disposal melt and even vaporize. It is really necessary to use temperatures of millions of degrees for atomic fusion. If so, how can we conceivably obtain and control such temperatures?

To answer these questions we must first look more closely at the way in which hydrogen atoms can join together to form helium. In fact, it is possible to demonstrate such fusion in the laboratory at ordinary temperatures. Hydrogen may exist in the form of three isotopes (p. 82)—ordinary hydrogen (with only a proton in its nucleus), deuterium (with one proton and one neutron), and tritium (with one proton and two neutrons). Tritium, a fairly stable radioactive isotope, even-

Above: The Early Bird communications satellite is 28 inches in diameter and its instruments are powered by 6,000 solar cells. These cells and their batteries are shown red in the cut-away drawing below. The other equipment is for orienting the satellite and relaying radio signals.

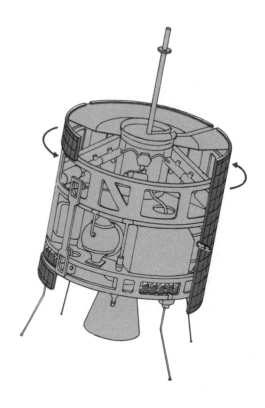

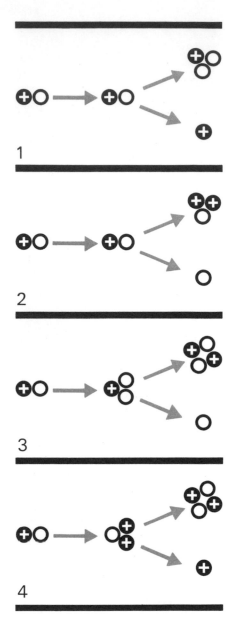

1

2

3

4

Nuclear fusion reactions that may possibly be exploited for power production. (1): Two deuterium atoms—each with one proton and one neutron—fuse to form a tritium nucleus (triton) and a proton, releasing energy in the process. Slightly less energy is released in (2), where two deuterons form helium 3 and a neutron. In (3), which releases four times more energy than (1), a deuteron combines with a triton to form helium 4 and a neutron. (4): A deuteron fuses with helium 3, producing helium 4 and a proton. This last reaction gives the largest energy yield.

tually decays to form an isotope of helium. This helium isotope, with an atomic weight of 3, has two protons and one neutron. Experiments have been made with the ionizing chamber described on p. 83. If deuterium atoms are used, then a stream of high-energy deuterium nuclei are produced. If these nuclei are then used to bombard other deuterium atoms, two possible reactions can take place. Two deuterium atoms may combine to produce tritium and a proton. Or they may produce helium 3 and a neutron. In both cases, there is a loss of mass and a corresponding release of energy. There is also another way in which helium can be produced from hydrogen in the laboratory. When tritium is bombarded with deuterium ions, helium 4 plus a neutron is produced. Again there is a loss of mass and a release of energy.

Unfortunately, in all these experiments the chances of an atomic collision occurring are very small indeed. Deuterium is a gas, not a solid, and its atoms are therefore spaced very, very far from each other. This means that great energy is required to accelerate all the deuterium ions, very few of which will score a direct hit. Indeed, the energy required is much greater than the total energy released by the few direct hits scored. However, it pays to remember the goal of the experiments. Scientists are trying to achieve the combination of two atoms of the same element. If they can find some way of making *all* the atoms possess very high velocities, then the chances of the atoms' uniting are greatly increased. There is no need to keep one group of atoms in a chamber and bombard them with other high-energy atoms. We can leave all of the atoms together and increase the velocities of the whole mass.

The obvious way to do this is to raise the temperature. When a gas is heated, the atoms move with higher velocities. The heat absorbed by the gas is converted into kinetic energy of the atoms. Now it is possible to calculate how the chances of fusion vary with temperature. It is found that they do indeed increase rapidly as the temperature is raised. But to obtain a net surplus of energy, the energy released by fusion must exceed that due to heat losses. It soon becomes apparent that extremely high temperatures are required to cause such a reaction to sustain itself. The temperatures must be so high that any material used for a container would vaporize immediately. Evidently, therefore, the hot gas must be kept away from the walls of the container. This simplifies the calculations, for if the material does not touch the walls, all heat losses must be by radiation. It turns out that a temperature in the region of one million degrees centigrade must somehow be attained.

The construction of the hydrogen bomb provided a

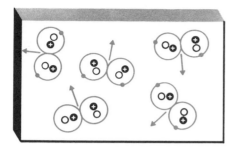

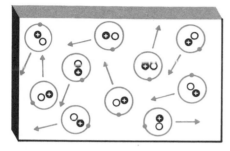

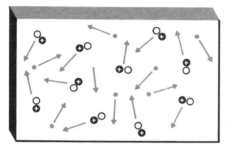

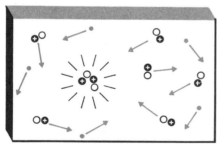

Diagrams illustrate stages in the heating of deuterium gas. Top shows gas at room temperature. At a temperature of 5,000°C. (second diagram), the molecules split to form deuterium atoms. When the temperature is raised to 100,000°C. (third), atoms are ionized. The electrons have escaped from the nucleus, forming a plasma of electrons and deuterons. At a temperature of 100,000,000°C. (fourth), some deuterons fuse, producing energy.

practical check on these calculations. It is possible to estimate fairly accurately what the initial temperature would be when a nuclear fission bomb is exploded. The temperature was reckoned to be of the magnitude required for fusion to take place. Accordingly, an ordinary uranium or plutonium bomb was surrounded by deuterium and exploded. The resulting release of energy was about a hundred times more than would have resulted from the uranium or plutonium alone. This demonstrated the accuracy of the calculations and, incidentally, released to the world a weapon of indescribable destructive power.

The hydrogen bomb proved that fusion could be made to take place on earth. But the problem of controlling this reaction and obtaining useful power from it has eluded scientists up to now. However, several very promising lines of research are now being actively pursued. Indeed, at one time it was thought that a British machine called "Zeta" had done the trick. Unfortunately, some snags occurred, and "Zeta" was subsequently abandoned. Yet it is probably only a matter of time before a solution is found. With the solution will come the certainty of cheap, abundant power for a virtually unlimited period.

The first problem that must be attacked is how to obtain the extremely high temperatures required. Obviously, no ordinary furnace arrangement could possibly approach such temperatures. It is well known, however, that an electric current passed through a wire causes it to heat up. Likewise if we pass a large enough current through the deuterium gas, we can raise its temperature to any value we choose. As the temperature rises, the velocity of the deuterium atoms increases. Collisions between nuclei, resulting in fusion and energy release, become more frequent. This energy-release itself then contributes to the rise in temperature. If the container in which the reaction takes place is surrounded by a water-jacket, the heat produced can be carried away by the water and converted into useful power. By surrounding the whole apparatus with a uranium sheath, we could also utilize the neutrons produced by the fusion process. The water-jacket itself would act as a moderator. As such, it would slow down the neutrons so that they could be captured by uranium nuclei (in the manner described in Chapter 4).

All this sounds fairly straightforward, but we have not yet examined the difficulty of keeping the hot gas away from the walls of the container. It turns out that this problem almost solves itself. The "almost," however, proves to be a serious obstacle. It was this, for instance, that prevented the British machine "Zeta" from being a success.

When an electric current is passed through a gas, the electricity produces another effect besides that of heating the gas. The gas tends to contract into the center of the container, thus automatically keeping the heated gas away from the walls. This is called the "pinch effect," and it is not confined solely to gases. In fact, the effect can be demonstrated in the laboratory by passing a heavy current, simultaneously and in the same direction, through two parallel wires. If the wires are held at their ends, the middles of the two wires will then be seen to move toward each other. The explanation is not a difficult one. When an electrical current flows along a wire, a magnetic field is produced. When two parallel wires each carry a current in the same direction, the two magnetic fields interact. This causes an attractive force to be set up between the wires and brings them closer together.

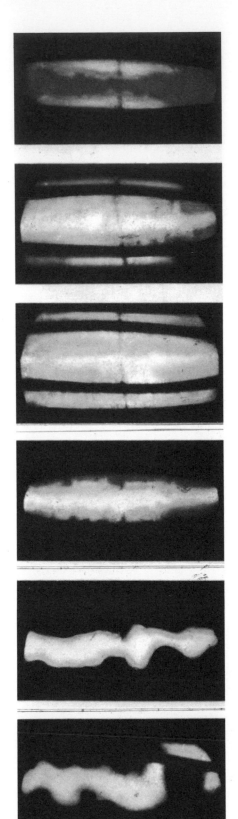

When the current is passed through a gas, the gas behaves as though it were a large number of parallel wires. The attractive forces compress the gas into a "tube," or "stream," within the walls of the vessel. It looked at first as if the pinch effect would provide a neat and elegant solution to the problem of keeping the hot gas away from the walls of the container. In actual practice, it was found that the stream of gas was unstable. Any very slight lack of uniformity, and the stream immediately jumped away from the center of the containing vessel. The gas then touched the wall and, because it was so hot, vaporized a hole in it. The discharge, in fact, behaved rather like a stroke of lightning, following a jagged path instead of a straight one. Experiments showed, however, that the pinch effect did take place. A stable discharge occurred, but only for a few microseconds. It was found that stability could be improved by subjecting the tube to an additional magnetic field. This magnetic field was produced by passing a current through a coil of wire wound around the tube. With such an arrangement, the length of time that elapsed before the stream became unstable was increased by a factor of three or four.

In more recent devices, the discharge container was made in the shape of a thick ring, or toroid. The idea here is to avoid the need for the electrodes used in the straight tube. In such a device, the current in the gas is "induced" with the help of a coil of wire wound around the outside of the toroid. When a current passes through this coil, a secondary current flows in the opposite direction in the deuterium gas in the toroid. (The principle used here is exactly the same as in the electrical transformer, where a current flowing in the primary coil induces a current in the secondary coil.) In addition to this coil around the outside of the toroid, a stabilizing

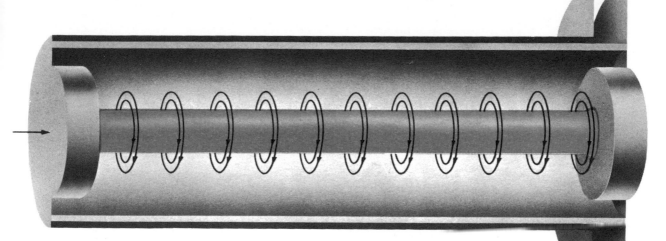

Above: The pinch effect occurs when a very large electric current is passed through a gas in a cylinder. The current produces circular magnetic lines of force that contract and pinch the plasma into a narrow column.

Right: Instabilities in the plasma column are quick to occur, within a millionth of a second or so. One type arises from a slight kink in the column (1), which grows rapidly. Another is a kind of sausage effect, due to a constriction (2). A more stabilized pinch is achieved by imposing a magnetic field on the plasma (long arrows in 3).

Left: Birth and death of a pinch. Top three photos show a pinched column forming (bright band). Lower photos show its disintegration as kink instabilities develop.

Below right: A doughnut-shaped pinch tube, made by threading a transformer coil through the ring containing the plasma. The British machine Zeta (below) employed such a device.

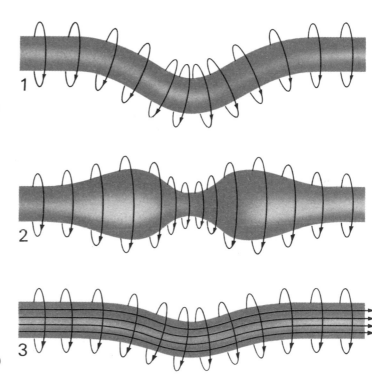

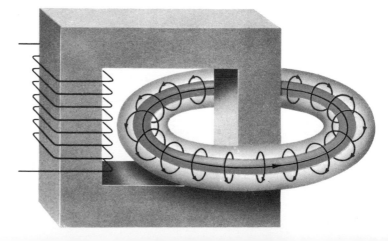

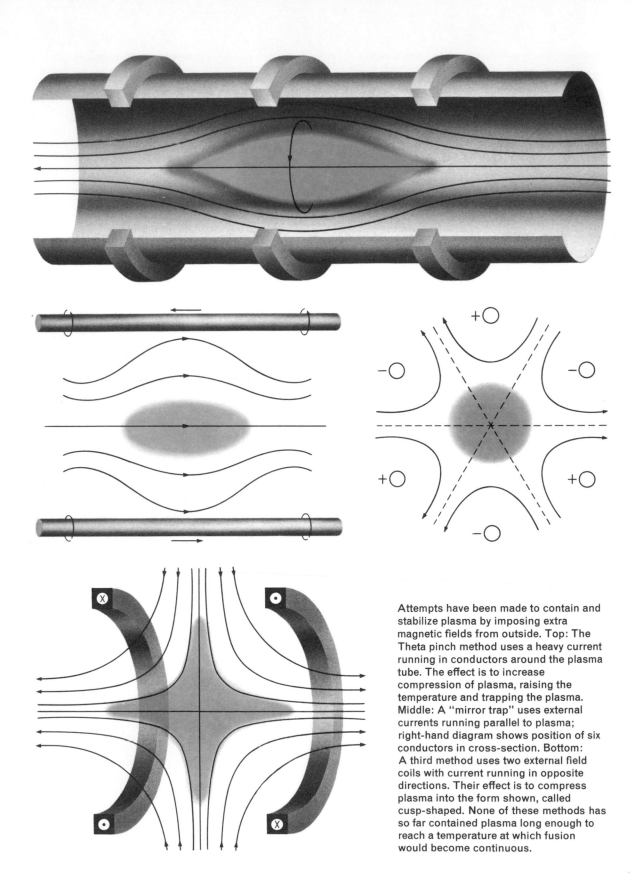

Attempts have been made to contain and stabilize plasma by imposing extra magnetic fields from outside. Top: The Theta pinch method uses a heavy current running in conductors around the plasma tube. The effect is to increase compression of plasma, raising the temperature and trapping the plasma. Middle: A "mirror trap" uses external currents running parallel to plasma; right-hand diagram shows position of six conductors in cross-section. Bottom: A third method uses two external field coils with current running in opposite directions. Their effect is to compress plasma into the form shown, called cusp-shaped. None of these methods has so far contained plasma long enough to reach a temperature at which fusion would become continuous.

coil is wound around the tube itself. Although experiments with such machines showed that the principle was sound, it was still impossible to achieve stability for more than a fraction of a second.

Controlled atomic fusion is still in the laboratory stage. Scientists are experimenting with a variety of different methods of achieving a stable high-temperature discharge through a gas. If they succeed, they must then incorporate the device into a complete power-producing system that will show a usable surplus of energy-output over energy-input. If and when they are realized, a major breakthrough in technology will have been made.

In the meantime, scientists and technologists are actively pursuing another line of research that could improve the efficiency of conventional power stations to a remarkable extent. This technique goes under the somewhat frightening name of magnetohydrodynamic generation—usually abbreviated to MHD. The principle of MHD is by no means new. But the high-temperature conditions under which it works present special problems. Until recently, materials were not nearly good enough even to allow an experimental start to be made. Like conventional electric generators, MHD relies on a basic fact: If a moving conductor cuts across a magnetic field, an electromotive force is produced in it. In MHD, a stream of ionized gas flows through a duct, across which is a magnetic field. Because the gas is ionized—i.e. contains free electrons—it acts as a conductor. An electromotive force is developed in it. If two electrodes are inserted in the wall of the duct, a current can be taken off from them.

Above: Model of the stellarator at Princeton. The figure-8 shape prevents certain drifts of the plasma.

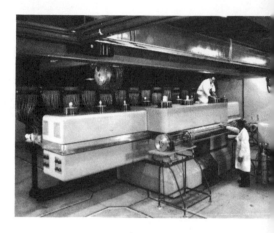

Above: Large thetatron assembly at the Culham Laboratory, Berkshire, England. The theta pinch is formed in the six-foot-long horizontal tube in foreground.

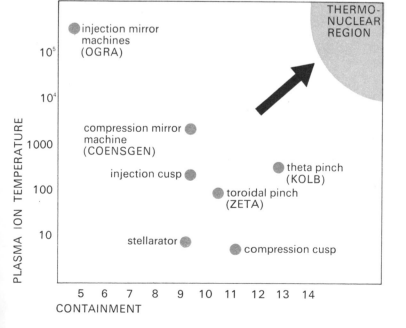

Diagram plots capabilities of these and other plasma containment devices on a graph of plasma temperature (converted to electron volts) and containment time (in powers of 10 sec/cc). It emphasizes that much remains to be done before controlled thermonuclear fusion is a reality.

231

Extracting electrical power in this way is accomplished at the expense of the heat content of the gas. The gas temperature falls. MHD is thus another method of converting heat energy directly into electrical power without the need for expensive and complicated machinery. It cuts out the mechanical middleman, just as do fuel cells, thermocouples, and solar cells. But unlike the latter devices, MHD holds out the prospect of really large-scale power generation.

The central problem it sets is to ionize the gas. Now a gas becomes ionized when its temperature is such that the kinetic energy of the atom is sufficient to free some of the electrons from their orbits. Indeed, if the temperature is high enough—many thousands of degrees—the gas becomes *plasma* and consists almost entirely of charged particles. At a most practical level, ionization starts to become noticeable at about 3,500°F. At temperatures in this vicinity, ionization can be increased sufficiently to produce some MHD effect by "seeding" the gas with a small percentage of some metal such as potassium or cesium. These metallic "seeds" are materials that readily ionize at about 3,000°F. Thus they substantially increase the concentration of free electrons in

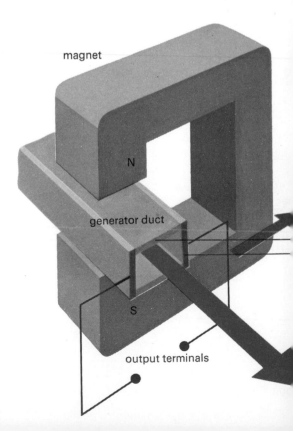

magnet

N

generator duct

S

output terminals

Above: Photograph of actual ionized gas discharge. Despite difficulties of controlling it in the search for fission energy, such a discharge can be used in another way at much lower temperatures—in magnetohydrodynamic generation (left). If a moving conductor cuts across a magnetic field, an electric current is induced in it. In MHD, the conductor is a stream of ionized gas flowing through a duct. Current is taken from opposite walls of duct (blue in diagram), which are separated by insulating walls (green).

rection of induced
ectric field

sulating wall
etal electrode

gh velocity
onducting gas

the gas. Already a small experimental machine has been made to work for several hours using this method.

One of the biggest difficulties about making such machines really serviceable is to find some material for the duct. The material must stand up to temperatures of over 3,000°F. for long periods at a stretch. Even the special materials used in furnaces break up after exposure to such temperatures for more than a few hours. The electrodes, on the other hand, do not seem to present such a difficult problem. Simple water-cooled copper electrodes have been used quite successfully.

There is no immediate prospect of MHD replacing existing methods of power production. What is hoped is that MHD will provide a sort of "topping" unit in conventional heat or nuclear power plants. The idea is to place the MHD duct between the steam boiler or nuclear reactor and the turbine. The temperature of the fluid entering the MHD duct will be higher than that for which the turbine is designed. Thus the overall efficiency of the plant will be substantially increased. MHD offers a possibility of stretching the thermal efficiency of new and existing power stations above the values now obtainable or visualized for the future.

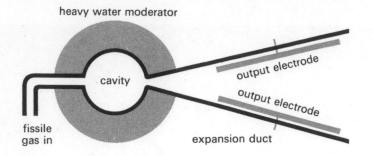

heavy water moderator

cavity

output electrode

output electrode

fissile gas in

expansion duct

Left: Project for linking MHD generation direct to a nuclear reactor. Nuclear fuel in the form of fissionable gases is fed into a cavity surrounded by a heavy water moderator. Fission takes place in cavity and hot ionized gases emerge at high velocity through expansion duct in which electrodes pick up current. (The magnetic field surrounding the electrodes is not shown.)

Over the past few years, the average overall efficiency of generating plants has increased by about one-half per cent per year, due to the steady improvement in design of new plant. In even a small nation such as the United Kingdom, this small improvement represents a saving in fuel costs of about fifteen million dollars a year. It is too early to say what improvement in efficiency would result from the large-scale application of MHD. Certainly it would bring about a very worthwhile saving in cost.

Another method of converting heat directly into power—although now only at the experimental stage—has already achieved promising results. This is called *thermionic generation.* This is based on the phenomenon of thermionic emission—the giving off of electrons by a hot metallic cathode. It uses the principle of the ordinary thermionic valve, as used in radio and television. The simplest valve, called a *diode,* contains two elements, a cathode and an anode. These elements are contained in an evacuated glass bulb. If the cathode is heated by passing a current through it, a small current

Diagram of a proposed MHD power-generating plant burning fossil fuel. The MHD is used as a sort of "topping" device. After the hot gases have been used to produce MHD power, they pass into a conventional steam-turbine plant. To achieve the necessary initial temperature, preheated oxygen-enriched air is used.

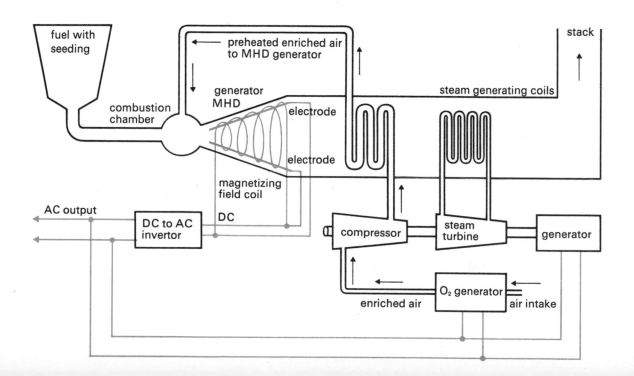

fuel with seeding

preheated enriched air to MHD generator

stack

generator MHD

electrode

steam generating coils

combustion chamber

electrode

magnetizing field coil

AC output

DC to AC invertor

DC

compressor

steam turbine

generator

O_2 generator

enriched air

air intake

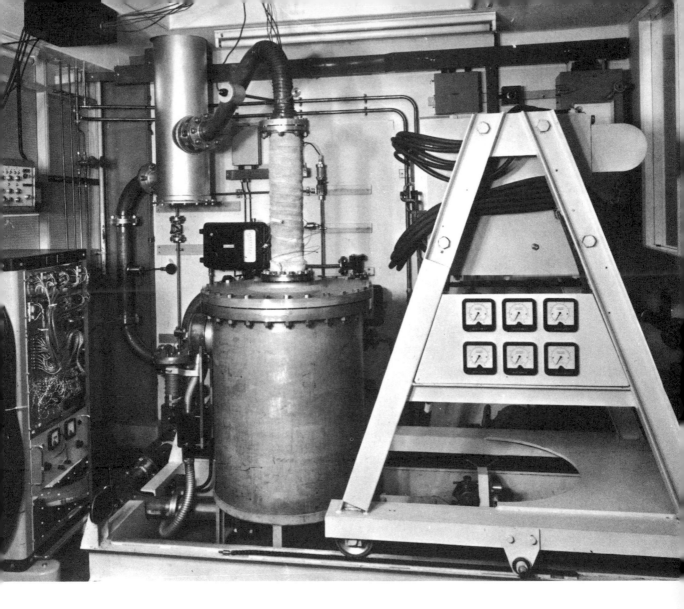

Experimental device at Harwell, England, for investigating MHD and the possibility of using a nuclear reactor to provide the necessary hot gases. In the set-up shown above, a reactor is not being used; instead a pebble-bed furnace (center) provides a stream of hot gas with which to energize the MHD apparatus at right.

will flow from the cathode to the anode. This occurs if they are connected externally, even though they are physically separated inside the valve. The reason for this is that, when the cathode is heated, some of the electrons on its surface gain sufficient energy to overcome the attraction of the nuclei and leave the surface. A few of these electrons succeed in reaching the anode, thus establishing a current flow. This process is rather like boiling off steam from water. The heat supplied to the water increases the energy of the water molecules. Eventually the attraction between the molecules is overcome, enabling some to leave the water surface in the form of steam.

Unfortunately, the thermal efficiency of the thermionic valve is very low—only a very small fraction of one per cent. Such a low efficiency would be quite unacceptable in a device primarily concerned with converting heat energy into power. There are, however, a number of ways by which the efficiency can be substantially improved.

The energy required to free an electron completely from the surface of the cathode is called the *work function*. This is usually measured in volts and is of the order of 2 to 4 volts for most materials. The electron striking the anode produces an electromotive force exactly opposite to that required at the cathode. For a net electromotive force to be produced, the work function for the anode must be less than that for the cathode. Thus one important factor in the design of a thermionic generator is that the material used for the cathode must have a high work function. The material of the anode must have a low work function.

The amount of energy converted depends upon the number of electrons that pass from the cathode to the anode. The higher the temperature of the cathode, the more electrons will be freed. If, however, the anode's temperature also goes up, the anode may also begin to emit electrons in a reverse direction. This tends to neutralize the effect of the hot cathode. For the best results, therefore, the cathode must be as hot as possible and the anode as cool as possible. Such a temperature difference is not easy to maintain because the anode cannot help receiving heat from the cathode by radiation. There is another factor that tends to reduce the number of electrons passing from the cathode to the anode. That factor is the mutual repulsion, or space charge, between the negatively charged electrons in the stream. This repulsion tends to drive some of the electrons back to the cathode.

The work function and ability to withstand high temperatures are properties of the materials selected for the cathode and anode. It is possible to obtain alloys for the

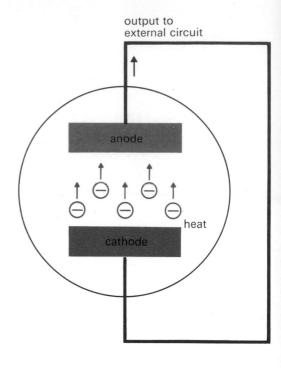

The principle of thermionic generation: When the cathode is heated, some electrons escape from its surface, much as water molecules leave boiling water in the form of steam. A few of the electrons reach the anode, so constituting an electric current.

A small thermionic generator in operation. The cell uses ionized cesium from the reservoir at the bottom; this gas neutralizes the mutual repulsion of the electrons in the stream, allowing a better electron flow between the cathode and the anode.

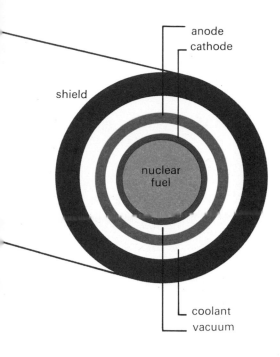

anode
cathode
shield
nuclear
fuel
coolant
vacuum

Diagram of a thermionic generator incorporating a nuclear fuel element. Between the cathode and the anode is a vacuum or low-pressure plasma. The first experimental devices of this type used a fuel of zirconium carbide and uranium carbide and operated at temperatures of about 3,500°F.

Below: A more sophisticated thermionic generator. In this case, the gas argon is used and is continuously circulated through a purifier to remove gaseous fission products. These would otherwise "poison" the reactor—that is, absorb an excessive number of electrons.

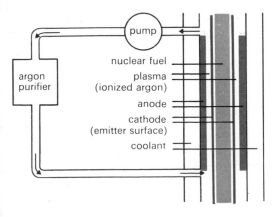

pump
nuclear fuel
plasma
(ionized argon)
anode
cathode
(emitter surface)
coolant
argon
purifier

cathode that can be used at temperatures up to 3,500°F. and that will give a work function of 2½ volts. For the anode, materials are available with a work function of about three-quarters of a volt. The problem of the space charge is the most serious one that has to be overcome.

One remedy is to place the cathode and anode very close together. Then the distance between them is such that the space charge effect is minimized. But a serious disadvantage of such an arrangement is that the high temperature of the cathode causes material to be evaporated from its surface. This material then builds up on the anode. This means that the work function of the anode gradually increases until it equals that of the cathode.

A more promising arrangement is to accelerate the electrons as they move from the cathode to the anode. This is done by introducing a third electrode connected to a high voltage source. The whole device is then surrounded with coils that produce a strong magnetic field. The combination of the third electrode and the strong magnetic field causes the electrons to move in a curved trajectory with accelerating velocities.

The third method that has been used is to neutralize the negative charges of the electrons. To accomplish this, positive ions are introduced into the space between the electrodes. This can be done by inserting suitable material such as cesium into the inter-electrode space.

In spite of these difficulties, thermionic generation offers a practical possibility of direct conversion of nuclear energy to electricity. Such a device would have the central rod of combined nuclear fuel and moderator contained in a can. The can itself would form the cathode. The anode would consist of a tube of suitable material separated by an evacuated space from the nuclear fuel rod. The whole arrangement would be contained in a nuclear shield. The coolant would pass through the ring-like space between the anode and the shield. An experimental set-up of this kind has actually been demonstrated at Los Alamos. It operated with a cathode temperature of 3,500°F. and gave an output of 90 watts. An efficiency of 10 per cent conversion of heat into electricity was achieved. This may appear to be too low to be of practical use. But we must remember that this branch of energy conversion is quite new—there are bound to be many refinements and improvements in the future. And, as with the MHD generator, it may well be that the extremely high temperature in the fission cell will be used first to produce electricity directly. The residual heat will then pass to a conventional heat exchanger.

So far in this chapter we have considered various possible ways in which heat or light energy can be converted directly into electrical energy. We have also considered the ways in which chemical energy can be converted directly into electricity. We now come to one of the most recent developments of all—a way of converting chemical energy directly into *mechanical* energy. And here, curiously enough, we come around full circle to where we started at the beginning of the book—with the action of man's muscles. Muscle fibers consist of interlocking protein molecules, which are made to shorten their length by chemical, or electrochemical, action. In the case of these new developments, we find something rather similar, not in living matter but in synthetic compounds. Thus, it seems quite fair to refer to these new substances as *artificial muscles*. The pioneer work has been done in this field by the late Professor Werner Kuhn in Basel.

This new development depends on recent advances in our understanding of the behavior of plastics. The so-called artificial muscles are, in fact, films of plastic that change their shape when exposed to certain chemical compounds. A good example of the kind of molecule that gives active contraction is polyacrylic acid, an enormous molecule with about a thousand acid units all strung together like beads on a necklace. If we dissolve this polymer in water, the individual molecule chains lie about in the shape of a loosely coiled sphere. That is to say, instead of a long string we have a bundle. But if we add an alkali like sodium hydroxide to a solution of this acid in water, a very distinct change takes place. Negatively charged hydroxyl (OH–) ions (see p. 220) become attached to some of the acid links in the chain. These ions repel each other, and the effect of that is to straighten out the chain of the molecule. The molecule thus becomes much longer and thinner than it was originally. But if we now replace the alkali by an acid, the hydroxyl charges disappear and the coil of the molecule will regain its original shape. That means that the molecule will become as much as 50 per cent shorter. This is what happens with individual molecules and, of course, these happenings would occur on such a small scale that we could not even see them. In practice, we prepare a film of this polyacrylic acid by dissolving it in polyvinyl alcohol and then spreading the solution on a plexiglas plate. When the solvent has dried out, it leaves behind it a film of the polyacrylic acid which, when lightly cooked for a short period, produces a network of the two polymers. After it has been cooked, the film is no longer soluble but it does swell if immersed in water. The interaction of water and film is fairly complicated, but we do not need to go into the details. The main thing to remember is that the water trapped in the film serves as a vehicle for the application of acid or alkali.

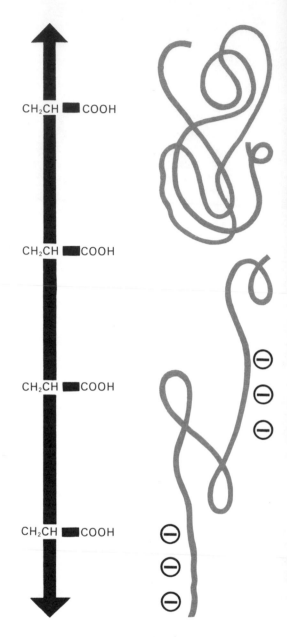

A molecule of polyacrylic acid is made up of about a thousand acid units strung somewhat like beads on a necklace (left). Its "normal" shape is in the form of a loose coil (top right). Under the influence of an alkali—such as sodium hydroxide— some of the acid groups are neutralized. This results in negatively-charged ions' being introduced into the necklace. Since the negative charges tend to repel one another, they force the acid groups apart, thus stretching the molecules (lower right).

It may seem surprising, but we can regard a sheet of such film as a two-stroke engine powered by two contrary fuels. One fuel is an alkali, which makes the film stretch, and the other an acid, which makes it contract. In order to demonstrate the process, we first make the film expand by treating it with alkali. Then we hang a weight on it and treat it with acid, and the result is that the film contracts sharply and lifts the weight up an appreciable distance. This may seem a very primitive experiment, but the fact remains that, by the use of chemicals, *direct mechanical* work has been done. And there is also no reason why this machine should not go on working indefinitely if it is exposed to acid and alkali alternately It might seem that this is no more than a laboratory experiment. But Dr. Aharon Katchalsky, in Israel, has recently demonstrated an engine, based on this principle, which converts chemical energy into *rotary motion.* He reports that this engine had an efficiency of 65 per cent—nearly half as much again as the efficiency of the best diesel engine.

In the course of this chapter, one curious fact has emerged in connection with new approaches to energy conversion: Good prospects seem to lie in the direction of using large numbers of small power units that, taken together, will produce a large amount of power. And here, too, in this artificial-muscle engine there is a possibility of using hundreds or even thousands of films. Each film would contain millions of polymer chains; linked together, they would produce power on a massive scale.

The example that we selected in order to explain the process makes use of acid and alkali as contrary fuels. The working model used lithium bromide and water. But what about cheaper fuels? Two fuels are necessary, as we have seen; the decisive condition is that the two fuels should have different chemical potentials. Surprisingly, there is a considerable energy difference between sea water and fresh water, both freely available fluids. This is logical, because considerable energy is needed to extract salt from sea water to make fresh water, whether by distillation or by freezing. Dr. Hans Kuhn, following up the work of Professor Werner Kuhn at Basel, has shown that films of pure cross-linked polyvinyl alcohol form a gel. This jellylike material expands in a dilute solution of salt in water and contracts when the salt concentration is increased. Thus it seems possible that we shall one day be able to extract untold quantities of power from the alternating application to films of salt and fresh water.

The forward-looking plans and experiments we have discussed in this chapter are a clear reminder that the technology of energy and power is a vital and basic part

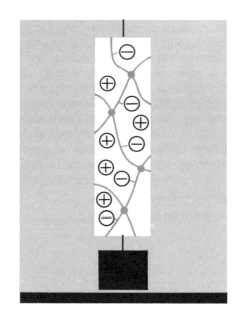

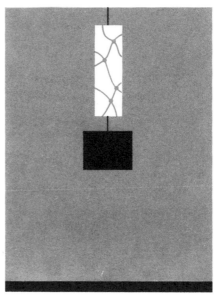

A simple engine, making use of a foil containing polyacrylic acid. Top: When the foil is immersed in sodium hydroxide solution, it stretches. We then connect a weight to the foil. Bottom: If the sodium hydroxide solution is replaced by a solution of hydrochloric acid, the foil returns to its original shape, thus lifting the weight. By substituting alkali again, the foil regains its stretched state. All these changes have been brought about entirely by chemical action.

The Laws of Thermodynamics

Thermodynamics is the branch of physics upon which the theory and development of heat engines is based. It is concerned with heat and work, and the properties of the fluids that are used in heat engines. As a science, thermodynamics is based upon a few very fundamental concepts. The results are obtained by a chain of reasoning, often long and involved, using these concepts as a starting point. This appendix will give a short introduction to the subject and a fuller exposition of some of the arguments briefly mentioned in the text. As a starting point, we must first define some of the terms used.

Heat

We have come to associate heat with the vibrations of the molecules in a body. We thus think of heat as a form of kinetic energy due to these vibrations. In thermodynamics we are not concerned with individual molecules. Indeed, it can be argued that the laws of thermodynamics would still be true if matter did not exist in molecular form. Our definition of heat is "that which passes from a hot body to a cooler one when they are placed in contact."

Temperature

The above definition of heat has brought in the concept of "hotter" and "cooler," so that we are at once confronted with ideas of temperature. To compare the temperatures of two bodies we need some device that produces a measurable reaction to hotness or coldness. Various effects can be used, such as thermal expansion, electrical resistance of a wire, the voltage produced by heating the junction of two dissimilar metals, and many others. The simplest thermometer is the mercury-in-glass thermometer. It consists of a glass bulb, containing mercury, to which is attached a glass tube of very small bore. The hotter the bulb, the higher the mercury will stand in the tube. We can tell which of two bodies is the hotter by observing which one causes the mercury to reach the higher point. We can assign numbers to the temperature of various bodies by introducing arbitrary standards of temperature. These standards are nowadays accepted as the melting point of ice and the boiling point of water. A thermometer is calibrated by placing it in turn in melting ice and boiling water and marking the level of the mercury in each case. In the Centigrade, or Celsius, system, the lower mark is called zero and the higher 100 degrees; the distance between the marks is divided into 100 divisions. In the Fahrenheit system, the two marks are called 32 and 212 degrees; the distance between is divided into 180 divisions.

The setting-up of a scale of temperature can thus be seen to be of a very arbitrary nature. Indeed, the scale set up by Gabriel Fahrenheit was originally based upon two quite different fixed points. He chose as his zero the lowest temperature he could obtain. This was done by a mixture of ice and salt. His higher fixed point was the temperature of the human body, which he called 100. He must have had a slight fever at the time he performed his experiment, however, as the normal temperature of the body is now taken as 98.6°F.

Closed System

A closed system is any collection of matter physically separated from its surroundings. Such a system may be subjected to changes of volume, pressure, and temperature; heat may be transferred to or from it. The gas enclosed by the piston of a reciprocating internal-combustion engine, for example, constitutes a closed system.

Open System

In an open system, matter flows continuously through some device, such as a turbine or duct. It is not, as in a closed system, confined and physically separated from its surroundings.

Work

In thermodynamics, we are interested in work done on or by a system. The best test of work transfer is to decide whether a weight *could* be raised or lowered.

Fluid

The term *fluid* means anything that can flow, and includes both liquids and gases.

Thermodynamic State and Properties

The thermodynamic state of a system is described by the values of the *properties* of the system. Temperature, pressure, and specific volume, for example, are properties; if we know the values of these properties, we have described the state of the system. Fixing the values of two properties determines the state of a system, and hence the values of all other properties. For example, if we have a container of one cubic foot, filled with air at 15 lbf/in², we cannot change the pressure without also altering the temperature. Thus, fixing the specific volume and pressure also fixes the temperature.

Process

A process is an operation that changes the state of a system. A process is usually qualified as to the manner in which it is carried out, such as constant volume, constant pressure, constant temperature (isothermal), or no heat transfer (adiabatic).

There is one important characteristic by which a property may be recognized. The state of a system is changed from state A to state B by a variety of processes or combinations of processes. The values of all properties will change by a definite amount between these two states, whatever the process used. This is not true of heat and work, so these are not properties and cannot be used to define the state of a system.

Reversibility

A process between states A and B is said to be reversible if, after returning from state B to state A, no change can be detected in either the system *or its surroundings*. This implies, for instance, that there must be no friction. Consider a quantity of gas enclosed by a

cylinder and piston. If the gas is allowed to expand, the piston moves and can be made to do work by raising a weight. If friction is present, more work will be necessary to compress the gas back to its original state. The weight would need to fall by a greater distance than it rose during the expansion process. Thus, a change would have taken place in the surroundings. Friction may either be mechanical in nature, or caused by intermolecular turbulence due to rapid motion of the gas in the cylinder. All processes in nature are irreversible to some degree; the concept of reversibility is an ideal with which to compare actual processes. Irreversibility may be caused by phenomena other than friction. Any heat transfer process is irreversible, as is the flow of electricity along a resistive conductor.

The First Law of Thermodynamics (see Fig. 2) Imagine a quantity of fluid contained in a cylinder fitted with a piston (Fig. 1). Suppose, also, that a method is available for measuring the heat supplied to or rejected from the fluid, and for measuring the work done by or on the fluid. By a combination of heat and work transfer, we can vary the state of the fluid, which according to our earlier definitions constitutes a closed system. We can represent the states of the system by plotting a point on a pressure-volume graph. Suppose that the initial state of the system is represented by point 1. We change the state—measuring values of pressure and volume, and heat and work transfer—until the pressure and volume are as at point 2. If we plot all intermediate values of pressure and volume, we can represent the

Fig. 1

Fig. 2

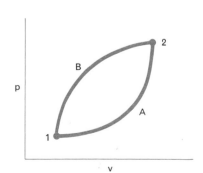

process by which the state has been changed by the curve A. Suppose that the net heat transfer to the system was Q_A and the net work done W_A.

Now let us return the system to state 1 and repeat the experiment, this time by a process represented by curve B. In this case, the heat transfer will be a different amount Q_B, and the work done will be W_B. The First Law of Thermodynamics states that $Q_A - W_A = Q_B - W_B$. By whatever process the change of state is effected, the difference between the heat and the work will always be the same.

It follows from what was said earlier that the quantity $Q - W$ must be a property, as the change in its value is independent of the process and depends only on the state of the system. The name *internal energy*, denoted by u, is given to this property. We may therefore write an equation that is the mathematical representation of the First Law:

$$Q - W = u_2 - u_1$$

On page 114, in examining the energy changes that take place in fluid passing through an engine, we introduced the idea of "heat energy," to which the symbol u was given. The above analysis gives a much more fundamental meaning to this concept—internal energy, a property whose value is dependent upon the state of a system. It also follows that if the state of a system is defined by, let us say, the pressure and temperature, the internal energy will have a unique value corresponding to that state.

Let us return to our experiment and suppose that, after process A, the state of the system is returned from 2 to 1 by reversing process B. This would constitute a *cycle*—that is, a combination of processes at the end of which the system returns to its original state. In the reversed process 2, the heat transfer would have the same numerical value, but with a negative sign (that is, $-Q_B$) and the work done would be $-W_B$. For the cycle, the net heat transfer would be $Q_A - Q_B$, and the work done $W_A - W_B$. Since the system returns to its initial state, there is no change in the internal energy, so the First Law gives:

$$Q_A - Q_B - (W_A - W_B) = 0, \text{ or}$$
$$Q_A - Q_B = W_A - W_B$$

In this equation, care must be taken to use the same units for measuring heat and work. If Q is measured in Btu and W in ft.lbf, we must multiply Q or divide W by J (the mechanical equivalent of heat, using the value 778 ft. lbf Btu).

The above equation applies to all heat engines, which by their nature are cyclic in character. Expressed in words, the equation becomes: "Net work done by a heat engine equals heat supplied minus heat rejected."

In the analysis of the heat engine (pp. 113-114) we found that applying the First Law to an open system always resulted in the term u being associated with a pv term. This came about because of the work required at inlet and exit from the engine. For the sake of convenience, the sum of the terms u and pv was given the name *enthalpy*, h. Since all the quantities u, p, and v are properties, it follows that h is also a property. Like u, h has a unique value at a particular state defined by the temperature and pressure. For steam, sets of tables are available in which the values of u and h are given for various combinations of pressure and temperature.

The Second Law of Thermodynamics (see Fig. 3) The First Law was discussed with the aid of an experiment in which a fluid was taken through a process and the heat and work transfers were measured. There are many ways of stating the Second Law, of varying degrees of difficulty. Here we shall consider an experiment in which the state of a fluid is changed from state 1 to state 2 by a *reversible* process. Let us imagine

Fig. 3

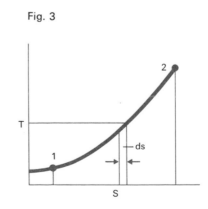

that this process is carried out by a series of small steps, and that the heat transferred during each step is measured, as is the mean temperature at each step. For each step, the heat transferred is divided by the mean temperature, and all these quotients are added together for the whole process. The Second Law states that the sum of all these quantities is the same no matter what reversible process is used to change the state of the system from 1 to 2.

If we express this in the notation of the calculus, we can signify by dQ the heat transferred during a typical step where the mean temperature was T. The quotient of heat transferred divided by temperature is then $\dfrac{dQ}{T}$,

and the sum of all these quotients for the whole process is $\displaystyle\int_1^2 \dfrac{dQ}{T}$. The Second Law states that $\displaystyle\int_1^2 \dfrac{dQ}{T}$ is independent of the process, provided the process is reversible. So here we have another quantity whose change between two states is independent of the process, and is therefore a property. This property has been given the name *entropy*, denoted by the symbol s. We can now write an equation for the change in entropy between these two states:

$$s_2 - s_1 = \int_1^2 \frac{dQ}{T}$$

Note that the measurement of dQ and T must be during a reversible process.

For each small step of the process, the change of entropy is given by $ds = \dfrac{dQ}{T}$, which

may be rewritten $T\,ds = dQ$. This equation enables us to make practical use of entropy. Suppose we plot a graph of entropy against temperature for this reversible process, and at temperature T consider a small change in entropy ds. The area of the strip of height T and width ds is $T\,ds$, which is equal to dQ. The area under the whole curve between points 1 and 2 is thus $\int T\,ds$, which equals $\int dQ$. The area under the curve on a $T - s$ graph for a reversible process therefore gives the heat transferred.

Now consider a cyclic process (see Fig. 4). Area ABCDE represents heat supplied, and area ABFDE heat rejected. The First Law tells us that, for a cyclic process, heat supplied minus heat rejected equals work done. The area enclosed by the cycle on the $T - s$ graph BCDF therefore equals work done. In this cycle, the maximum temperature is T_1 and minimum T_2. To obtain maximum work and hence maximum efficiency, for an engine working between these two temperatures the irregular area BCDF ought to be straightened up into a rectangle, MNOP (that is, all the heat must be supplied at T_1 and rejected at T_2). The efficiency of such an engine would be

$$\frac{\text{area MNOP}}{\text{area AMNE}} = \frac{T_1 - T_2}{T_1},$$

an expression that was used in the text without rigorous proof.

A more usual statement of the Second Law is that it is impossible to raise heat from a low temperature to a high temperature without doing work. The truth of this statement is made clearer from an examination of the diagram.

In the text, reference was made to the use of the enthalpy-entropy chart for steam. A reversible adiabatic process was said to be also one in which the entropy remained constant. This follows from the equation $T\,ds = dQ$ for a reversible process. If such a process is also adiabatic, $dQ = 0$ and therefore $T\,ds = 0$. T is not zero, therefore ds must be zero. Thus, entropy remains constant in a reversible adiabatic process.

Fig. 4

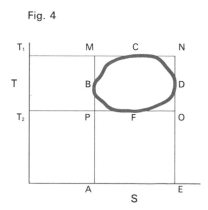

Index

Entries in *italics* refer to captions.
Where two or more pages are linked
together (e.g. 36-7), both text and
captions are implied.

Credits

ILLUSTRATION CREDITS
Key to picture position:
(T) top, (C) center, (B) bottom, and
combinations; for example (TL) top left,
(CR) center right

Eighteenth century water wheel
Francis turbine